Building Your Own

DOCK

CRE**A**TIVE
HOMEOWNER®

Building Your Own Dock
Vice President-Content:: Christopher Reggio
Editor: Anthony Regolino
Copy Editor: Katie Ocasio
Designers: Christopher Morrison, Mary Ann Kahn
Illustrator: Seth D. Merriam
Indexer: Jay Kreider

ISBN 978-1-58011-819-4

Library of Congress Cataloging-in-Publication Data

Names: Merriam, Sam, author.
Title: Building your own dock / Sam Merriam.
Description: Mount Joy, PA : Creative Homeowner, [2019] | Includes
    bibliographical references and index.
Identifiers: LCCN 2019000699 (print) | LCCN 2019001237 (ebook) | ISBN
    9781607656531 | ISBN 9781580118194 (softcover : alk. paper)
Subjects: LCSH: Docks--Design and construction--Amateurs' manuals.
Classification: LCC TC355 (ebook) | LCC TC355 .M47 2019 (print) | DDC
    627/.31--dc23
LC record available at https://lccn.loc.gov/2019000699

We are always looking for talented authors. To submit an idea, please send a brief inquiry to
acquisitions@foxchapelpublishing.com.

Printed in Singapore

Current Printing (last digit)
10 9 8 7 6 5 4 3 2 1

Creative Homeowner®, *www.creativehomeowner.com*, is an imprint of New Design Originals Corporation and distributed exclusively in North America by Fox Chapel Publishing Company, Inc., 800-457-9112, 903 Square Street, Mount Joy, PA 17552, and in the United Kingdom by Grantham Book Service, Trent Road, Grantham, Lincolnshire, NG31 7XQ.

Building Your Own
DOCK

DESIGN, BUILD, AND MAINTAIN FLOATING AND STATIONARY DOCKS

SAM MERRIAM

CONTENTS

Minutes before the sun sets on the shores of Frye Island, Maine, do-it-yourselfers pause for a thumbs-up, having completed their first dock installation.

PREFACE

More Than Just a Tie-up for the Boat

Do you spend more hours on the dock than offshore in your boat? Reoccurring engine failure or the exorbitant cost of fuel could be the cause for some. For others, it's enough to simply be on the water for its allure, where the dock is convenient and sometimes has a living space. After spending enough time on the dock, eventually you'll walk away with a "dock tale" or two and realize the added value that comes with a dock. It is more than just a tie-up for the boat. As a lifelong dock builder, I've come to know many who live out all they can on the dock. It's their favorite destination and the center stage for making memories with family. Perhaps you can recount a favorite dock tale of your own.

A Dock Tale

It is with one of my favorite dock tales that I'd like to dedicate this book to my father and mother, Fremont and Norma Merriam. Their little cottage on Mousam Lake in Maine gave me and all my siblings childhood vacation experiences that remain treasured to this day.

The cottage was so small, my mother had to cleverly manage—like playing a game of Tetris—to fit her brood of five (at the time) all inside for the night. My father, who could have built an extra bedroom or two, decided it was more urgent to build a dock. His logic went like this: "You kids have bedrooms at home. We're here for the lake, so a dock is what we need at the cottage, not bedrooms." When completed, he had more than a dock, he had what appeared to be an airstrip floating on barrels. Since our corner of the lake was always calm, devoid of wind, he moored the deep end with chain and anchors, while the shore end, under its own weight, simply nested into the sandy beach. This held the dock with his runabout tethered alongside.

A dock of its size could not be ignored, especially by a pack of kids, many of whom came together from cottages nearby. They ruled the neighborhood all day from the woods to the water including the

large dock that would become center stage for many stories. One morning, my brother, Tom, who was always fascinated with the contents of *National Geographic* magazine, became inspired particularly by its features covering the adventures of the world-renown SCUBA diver, Jacque Cousteau. With a mask, snorkel, and a buddy, Tom set out off the dock to uncover the lake's sunken secrets. Minutes later, they exploded with elation on the surface about ten meters beyond Dad's dock. Could it be the wreckage of an alien spacecraft or gold bullion? Now that would have been something! But, more like you'd expect, they found a lost and forgotten anchor.

To Tom and his buddy, this was a very good find, one to be proud of, especially after figuring out how to retrieve it. With all the young and curious spectators crowding onto the dock, Tom saw his opportunity. He swam down with a long rope and slipped its end through the anchor's eyelet. Returning to the dock, Tom enlisted everyone to grab onto the rope like a tug-of-war team and commence pulling. The next scene became very intense. Everyone who had been a spectator was now in on it, hands locked onto the rope, bodies leaning and knuckles turning white. Though the team was impressive and determined, the anchor's hold was proving to be unconquerable. With the team's last ounce of spirit and strength, one final pull surprisingly made the difference. Hand over hand with the rope, tugging the anchor to the dock, brought victory closer and restored the team's spirit with every pull.

About that time, my father arrived at the cottage and thought he should investigate all the hoopla coming from the beach. From his perspective, it appeared they had an alligator on the other end of that rope and clearly they did not know what they were doing. Suddenly, the team hears my Dad's alarming shout from the shore. All heads turned back to see that the dock had been dislodged from the beach and that instead of pulling the anchor to the dock, they were pulling the dock to the anchor. My father did not know then that ten years later he would

be in the dock business, designing and building nice docks for others. You can bet, he never once again anchored the shore end with just its own weight.

The family fun at Mousam Lake inspired my mother and father to eventually find a home where they could live on the lake year-round—one that had bedrooms. Eventually, their dream came true in the Sebago Lakes region of Maine. My father, a self-employed building contractor with an engineering background, discovered a lack of dock builders or good dock-building methods near his new home. With his design talent and ingenuity, he developed a dock system for himself that would become the prototype for a new business venture in docks. There, he continued to design and manufacture his own line of specialty dock hardware, making it available to do-it-yourselfers and other contractors.

In a region that was lacking much-needed specialized knowledge and proper materials for docks, I credit my mother and father for building a business that would fill the void, set the standards, and propagate the knowledge. Today, the designs and methods established during their years in business can still be seen, relied on by a newer and much larger generation of dock builders. Thanks to my Creator above and my mother and father who founded the business, bringing me in at a young age, I dedicate this book to them, Fremont and Norma Merriam.

Back to the story, the situation, though looking grim, improved tremendously once enough rope had been pulled in so that the floating dock was now drifting over the anchor. Standing directly over the anchor, Tom and his buddy were able to lift straight up on the anchor to break its grip from the bottom. What they realized was that the rope's original angle upon tugging pulled the anchor deeper into the mud, only making it harder to release. Adding ten more kids to pull would not have helped. Instead, by standing right over the anchor with the line straight up, Tom and his buddy were able to manage it alone. Understanding this principal comes in handy when mooring a boat or a floating dock.

INTRODUCTION FROM THE DOCK PRO

For the dock owner, user, "do-it-yourself" mender, and builder, a unique set of challenges at the shore must be faced with specialized knowledge and skill. Although self-learning through first-hand experience and tip exchanges between neighbors will always have high value, sometimes it would be nice to hear from a career dock builder, aka a "dock pro," someone devoted to his calling, studious to the challenges you're facing, and with the fervor to find remedies that bring resolve. In the chapters ahead, you will find the dock pro's tips, based on decades of proven methods for simple things like installing a tie-up cleat, improving dock stability, and ways for protecting your boat while docked. You will also find complete details for planning and building various kinds of docks perfect for the "do-it-yourselfer" (DIYer), who wants to "hit a homerun." If you have a dock or you're about to build one, a windfall of special information is just ahead for you to take full advantage.

Exploring this book, you'll learn about docks that stand fixed on legs, permanent methods where winter ice isn't a problem, and removable methods for climates with severe winter ice. You'll also learn about docks that float and different ways to attach or anchor them in place. Along with showing how to build these docks, the dock pro will help you first evaluate an environment and how the dock will be used so that you choose the right kind of dock. Importantly, the dock pro's project plans are made with sensitivity to the limitations of the DIYer and has scaled them to convenient sizes. Even if you're hiring someone to build a dock or provide

a pre-manufactured dock, this book will equip you with the dock pro's knowledge to decipher if you'll get the desired value from the product before purchasing.

For the many docks that have not yet fallen to disrepair, the dock pro can help you stay ahead of maintenance before repair turns into replacement. You'll find tips for breathing new life to your dock. Whether you need to apply wood preservative, bracing to prevent unwanted instability or repairs to the decking and frame, see what the dock pro has to say; the advice makes this book worth its weight in gold.

If maintenance and repair isn't your thing and better left to hired help, you can expect this book to inspire and get you thinking about how to make the most of your dock whether you build it yourself or get someone to help. While a dock is key for access at the shore and getting the full value of your waterfront, the dock pro recognizes for some, it's a destination. Of all the places you could spend your available hours of leisure, dream about how the dock will be an extension of your outdoor living space, a place for making lifelong memories with family and friends. To help with that, explore the various floor plans that invite leisure time opportunities utilizing either fixed or floating docks while seeing yourself in the plans. Begin with your dream and let the dock pro help with making it real.

Who Is This "Dock Pro"?

Imagine a hardware store that is all about dock building, stocked up on chain, cleats, flotation, galvanized bolts, and an array of marine-grade gear that you wouldn't find at the usual hardware store. It's Saturday morning and you're beginning a DIY dock project at the lake, after stopping at this supply store first to see what they offer that will help. Once inside, you find experienced, trained helpers who are ready with all the tips and guidance to put you at ease. It might sound too ideal to be real, given how specialized your task is, but this describes a unique business that my father, Fremont Merriam, started in 1979. Greetings . . . I'm Sam Merriam, aka the "dock pro," and it has been my pleasure to have worked many years in a family business where I've helped countless DIYers like you make improvements to an existing dock or build a new dock from start to finish. Located in the beautiful state of Maine, where bodies of water and shoreline are abundant, it's no wonder how someone could sustain a business like this.

Now, after decades of experience and acquired specialized knowledge from the business, my tips and guidance for DIYers, which were available only in my store, are now here in this book. If you have an existing dock, and looking for ways to improve, embellish, or problem solve, make this book your user guide for invaluable tips and ideas. For your new dock building project, start with my guidance on relevant topics along with instructions and plans for some of the most popular DIY dock building methods. The added knowledge base you'll gain here will add significantly to your confidence level before and as you build, saving you time and costly futile efforts.

Growing up in Maine, I was never far from water. With the profuse amounts of precipitation New England is known for, I've advocated at times that Maine should change its name to Raine. Seriously though, all that moisture is responsible for the privilege I've experienced, both playing and working in water. A vast array of water environments such as lakes, rivers, tidal inlets, and coastline has been my world since a youngster. If it has a paddle, oars,

"Weekenders" at the lake camp carry a section of dock to be installed on the shore.

power, or sail, I have used it. Chances were fair that my future occupation would have something to do with water. In Maine, the variety of water environments present a large demand for docks across varying degrees of challenges. With that, there is the demand for people who know how to make docks for a specific environment and application. While I was in middle school, my father was self-employed as a building contractor within the lakes region of southern Maine. He started offering docks as a sideline that over a ten-year period became his sole business. During those years, his dock business offered reliable summer work for me. Naturally, it was from my father where I learned the trade and the business, though I had other plans while in college. I thought my calling might be TV journalism or becoming an ad executive, but there seemed to be a gravitational pull on me to come back to the water. After college, I made my decision: I was going to grow the dock business with my father.

My father was a talented structural designer. Before his building contractor career, he designed bleachers and stadium seating at Hussey Seating

More than just being a dock, a ready-to-be-furnished outdoor family living space is made on the water for good times and memories.

Not your everyday hardware store, this place bustles at winter's end with do-it-yourselfers who find specialty components and guidance on all sorts of dock projects.

Company for nearly 20 years. His background revealed itself in the dock business after an investment into metal fabrication equipment whereby he made specialty hardware components for wooden docks. Most of the components were his own design and made to facilitate the mobility of wooden docks to go in and out of the water. To folks who are south of New England, it seems absurd that one installs a dock only to remove it from the water in the same year. In the north, that's what you do; winter ice requires it, especially on larger water bodies. The northern ice is powerful and can destroy the most rugged docks. Working with the northern climate in Maine played a big part in defining his business that he named Great Northern Docks. His specialty dock hardware components proved very effective in making a sturdy wooden dock that could be annually installed and removed relatively easily. While in business to provide complete dock systems to turnkey customers, his parts raised the eyebrows of DIYers and contractors who wanted to build their own docks. In time, he saw his business evolve into

the supply house and information resource center for dock building.

Since my father retired some time ago, I've been online with the business serving DIYers far from my home. Naturally, this has inspired me to become familiar with dock techniques used throughout North America and Europe. Not to my surprise, for example, the way docks are done in Ontario is slightly different from the way docks are done in Florida. The insight gained from my travels, coupled with decades of experience in Maine, has equipped me with knowledge that will help any DIYer anywhere. So that you'll be equipped with that same knowledge, I've written this book for you, capturing the fundamentals you'll need to successfully utilize, improve upon, or build your own dock from scratch.

Boundaries for Building a New Dock

Some jobs should be left to the experts, of course, but when it comes to dock building, there are a vast number of opportunities just right for the DIYer. Regardless of your motivation, be it budget constraints, a shortage of locally skilled dock builders, or, simply, that you like to build, this book was written with you in mind, the DIY dock builder who probably doesn't own a commercial barge, crane, and pile driver.

No worries. . . . You'll find I've set the boundary where the scale of the project can be done using common carpentry tools and the materials can

Above the treetops at my store, water is near in every direction.

be hand carried or lifted into place without heavy equipment. Most of the dock designs that I've included are comprised of portable, standard-size sections of dock, each serving as a building block to make up whatever configuration you desire.

So that you're not on a wild goose chase, I've limited the material requirements to what you would expect is on hand at your local building supply along with specialty dock components that, if not found at a local retailer, can be easily found online. Where codes and conditions require heavy pilings to be driven, I recommend that you hire that part out to a qualified marine contractor, just as you would likely hire a concrete foundation contractor for the house you plan to build. Once your marine contractor has left you with pre-installed heavy pilings, follow my step-by-step instructions to build your heavy dock or pier upon them.

In upcoming chapters, I've presented **four classifications** of docks that you can build using wood:
- fixed,
- floating,
- fixed to floating,
- rolling portable.

With each one, I'll provide a summary of the benefits and a description of the types of

With the help of specialty dock components, DIYers connect two sections of floating dock together.

environments where they are suited for use. I've included a special chapter about the nature of tidal waters and rivers with some important advisories to consider for docks in these places. I will also help you complete a site survey where you will learn my approach to decisions such as choosing the best location for a dock on the property, choosing the best classification or type of dock, the size limits, and distance the dock should extend out. Along with it constituting your mapped-out plan, the site survey exercise will help to separate your good ideas from bad ones, cement the good ideas into actions, and thwart a bad decision from coming to fruition. Finally, this guidebook would not be complete without tips for installing your dock into the water, where the dock will be a splash. Each classification of dock has its own details for setup that follows its construction details. Begin with the Special Safety Measures (right column) before you take to the shore with your project.

Even after you've completed your project with the help from this book, much of the information covered will not become obsolete, making this book a relevant resource for many years to come. For as long as you and your family have anything to do with docks, keep this book handy for future reference.

Special Safety Measures

From start to finish, operating safely is the most important objective through the process for any project. I always encourage people to follow the safety precautions that come with any of the equipment you'll be using. From my years of working on docks, hearing about or bearing witness to human failures, I want to share with you some precautions specific to working on or around the water.

- When it's strength you lack, someone should "have your back." Objects too heavy for you deserve patience and additional help.
- Even the best swimmer should wear a life vest when working where the water's deep. Have you ever tread water with work boots on? I hope you'll never have to.
- Seatbelts saves lives; safety glasses saves eyes. Eye injuries are caused by the "darndest" things—the thing you weren't expecting.
- Sandals are shoddy shoes for doing dock work. Covering your bases means covering your feet.
- Know where you're stepping. On the golf course, try for a hole in one. On the jobsite, don't be the one in the hole.

Most of the dock methods featured in this book are comprised of portable, standard-size sections.

- Good gloves means glad hands. Be prepared—you may not know entirely what your hands will get into.
- On the pond or pool, the fool holds a corded tool. Stick with cordless tools when near or over water.
- When there is lightning about, it's time to clear out. I know the job is important to you, but so is your life.
- Overhead and under feet, no power line is safe to meet. Be aware of all electrical lines near your work. Sometimes it's easy to assume there is none near the water—you should never assume.
- If it's windy and choppy, the dock work is sloppy. Choose your time of day wisely. The work goes much better when conditions are calm.
- Onlookers are obstacles. We can't blame them for wanting to watch, just keep them at a safe distance.
- Critters count. Always treat wildlife and pets with respect. Their safety is important too.
- Buddies are the best. Working alone leaves no one to help if you get into trouble.
- Is your equipment right or will it bite? Make sure your tools are all in good working order and safe to use.
- Secure the scene. Leaving your jobsite on the fly, considers not the passerby. Defuse all traps before you go, moor what matters the wind could blow. For the short time you're away could make or break someone's day.

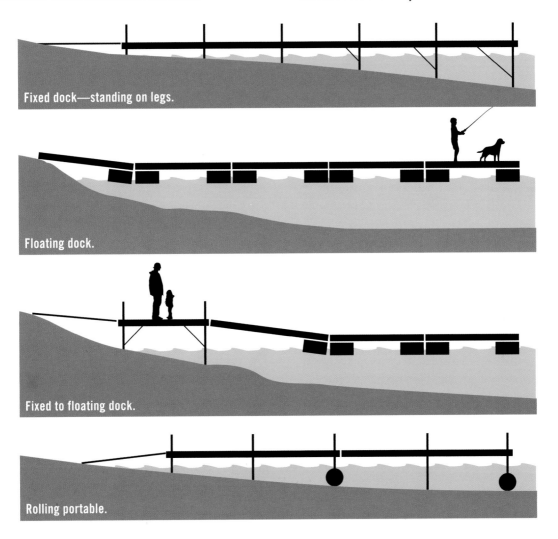

Fixed dock—standing on legs.

Floating dock.

Fixed to floating dock.

Rolling portable.

CHAPTER 1:
PERMITTING

Seek permission before starting any kind of dock project. You need to know what you can do legally before the dream gets too far ahead of reality. Oftentimes, in rural country, folks feel removed from their government and seem surprised or dismayed when I broach the subject with them. I recommend going online to your local town, city council, municipality, or county website to the building and or environmental code section to learn about dock permit requirements. Most often, standard codes begin at the top levels of government. In Canada, that would be the Ministry of Natural Resources and Forestry. In the United States, it would be the U.S. Army Corps of Engineers along with the department within a state or county government, with a title such as Natural Resources or Environmental Protection. Codes are often handed down from top levels of government to local levels. Local levels of government may have the authority allowed by upper levels to add more stringent codes within their jurisdiction than what is administered from above. By beginning at the local council level with your inquiry, I expect you'll find guidance on what is required. Depending on the location, I've experienced a broad range of possibilities, such as no permit required at all to acquiring multiple permits from different agencies. If your project is in a location so rural and far removed from the jurisdiction of any kind of local government, then likely there is a commission or department at the province or state level where you should inquire that manages unorganized territory. If you find there is absolutely no regulation for your waterfront, the best policy is self-regulation. A dock that is environmentally safe, non-offensive, and doesn't reasonably compromise someone else's enjoyment may keep unwanted over-regulation out.

Sometimes, talking with a neighbor who has a dock and has the experience to advise can save you some time, but it's not uncommon, especially in rural areas, to hear the neighbor say, "You don't need a permit; I never bothered to get one." That may be what you want to hear, but I recommend prudence and responsibility by checking with the local authority to be safe.

I hear this a lot too, "I'd rather beg for forgiveness than ask for permission." This assumes that there is a good chance that if you build whatever you want, you can have it, and the authority probably won't notice. In the unlikely event they discover you don't have a permit, then you'll talk your way out of trouble, cooperatively pay the fine, and pay for the permit to keep what you have built. Otherwise, if you ask for permission up front, you'll be cut back to something less than what you want. At that point, you're on the authority's "radar," and building what you want won't be as easy to sneak in. The potential trouble here is that if what you built isn't up to code, and code enforcement comes calling, they could require you to make changes, and in addition to paying fines, you'll have to take everything down. I'm not trying to play bad cop here. I just want to point out, for your sake, that there may be rules to play by, and I encourage everyone to follow them. After all, though in some cases the rules don't seem fair, they are there for everyone's protection and the preservation of the environment that we enjoy.

If you're feeling anxious about the thoughts of a permit application, don't be discouraged too quickly. Quite often, the requirements are simple and can

be handled entirely through your local government council. If there are not instructions, an official should be able to guide you with completing the application. If required, they should direct you to any other agency or organization for additional permits. For extra environmentally sensitive areas or urban areas, I would expect more than one permit, each from a different agency, would be required.

Once you've established that one or more permits are required, you'll want to become familiar with the specific rules for constructing the dock. Some of the rules originate to ensure the dock is safe for people, such as specifying dimensional lumber sizes to use, the distance between supports, where railing is required, marking for visibility at night, or specifics that prevent it from becoming a navigational hazard. Your code may require pilings that are heavier than practical for a DIYer to install. In that case,

you'll look for a marine contractor to do that part. In many cases, ironically, I've seen no rules that reflect a concern for the safety of people, but only the impact on the environment. Environmental rules control things like the size of the dock, its "footprint," "shading" (which is the blockage of light that can lead to erosion and adversely affect the ecosystem), visual pollution, specific materials that could cause harm to the environment, and anchoring standards to prevent its destruction that could result in littering debris. The plans, materials, and methods of construction that are provided in this book may or may not be permitted in the jurisdiction where your project is going to be built. The rules you'll need to comply with in building your dock will dictate what methods and designs you'll be able to choose. My advice is to apply what you can from this book that does meet compliance with your local code. In some cases, a simple alteration of dimensions within the structure or its overall size may be all that is needed. Once you know the rules and what will be allowed, bring that knowledge together with what it is you want to build. Adjust your plan until it complies so that you can arrive at the specific dock you want the permit(s) for.

When filling out the application(s), include specifically what it asks for. If it wants any drawings attached with dimensions or photos of the site, be sure to meet the criteria of the instructions. If it doesn't say it has to be a professional drawing, then provide a simple sketch. Do not give more drawings and photos or details than what it asks for. If it doesn't ask for drawings and photographs, don't provide them.

Too much information can cause confusion for the official who reviews it, resulting in questions and misunderstandings that will stall the approval. For example, accessories such as a ladder or bench should go on the drawing and labeled if asked. Otherwise, don't show them. Also, stick to the language that the application uses. When writing a description, for example, avoid referring to the dock as a "deck." Though some portion of it may seem like it should be called a "deck," it is a *dock* you're applying for. Ridiculous as it sounds, the reaction from the official could be, "We permit docks over the water, not decks." Based on your findings, after your inquiry as to what's required, you may be pleasantly surprised at how simple it is. If that isn't the case and there is more red tape than what you are willing to get wrapped up in, then I would consider hiring an engineering firm experienced with the process. They know their way around the red tape and are efficient at getting the approval you need.

If your project involves the replacement of an old dock that has exceeded its life expectancy, there may be characteristics of it that wouldn't be allowed under the modern code. An example of this could be its size if today's code for a new dock

would allow something smaller than what was there. Depending on the ordinance or zoning, there may be a "grandfather clause" that would enable you to replace it as it was originally built. Be sure to save all evidence of whatever the characteristic is that you want to transfer to the new dock. Maybe you should have the official come out to inspect it. Take plenty of pictures and retrieve any old photos you have of the old dock structures for your files should you wish at any time to make a case for restoring or copying desirable characteristics from the dock you're replacing.

Finally, when making your inquiry to all agencies that you'll require a permit from, find out what the time frame is before you get an answer. Depending on the number of agencies involved, it could be a day or two. It could be a month or even more sometimes. I've known cases that took up to two years. Hopefully that's not your situation. Anticipating that a wait is possible, submit your applications early enough so that your approvals come before it is time to build. Once the permit is in your hand, you'll rest easier than your neighbor who didn't get one.

CHAPTER 2:
FASTENATION

While in high school, I worked part time at a hardware store, and ever since, believed that all young people should experience that, even for a short time. You get to learn about all the things that will come in handy when you own a home later in life. Of all the departments in that store, none were more important than fasteners. Becoming familiar with fasteners is only the beginning. It takes time and experience to apply that familiarity and years of observation to prove what the best fastener is for the job. Since fasteners are quintessential for so many dock-related projects, the topic deserves its placement near the front of this book. The purpose of this chapter is to give you my fastener experience with dock building, conveyed to you firsthand so that you may avoid common

mistakes and get an edge that will facilitate your project and leave you with the desired result.

Since our structure is in an aquatic environment which happens to be corrosive, let's consider alloys and coatings for a moment. The usual shiny plain steel, electro-galvanized fasteners you find at the hardware store will begin to rust in a short time, especially around salt water. For the time it takes to build your project, it is worth spending extra money for better corrosion resistance so you're not re-doing it in a few years. Around fresh water, electro-galvanized screws with a resin coating, offered in a choice of colors, perform well on decking and framing. Buying coated screws can be a "pig in a poke," not knowing the quality of the coating. To qualify what you're buying, begin with the specifications offered on the product's label. It should boldly say that it is suitable for marine environments, otherwise, keep shopping. If your project will be exposed to salt water, make sure the product states specifically that it has been tested for salt water. If you can correspond with the company, ask how rigorous their testing is. An adequate test by my standards would be a continuous six month to a year period. If rapid corrosion will occur in a salt environment, they would see early stages of it within that time. Also make sure that the manufacturer recommends their product for the type of chemically treated lumber you may be using.

The alternative to resin-coated screws would be hot-dip galvanized nails or stainless nails and screws. To reduce damage by electrolysis in salt water, I would go with grade 316 stainless if your budget will allow it. I realize that it could be cost prohibitive, especially when you look at upgrading

Electro-Plated Zinc

Hot-Dip Galvanized

Stainless Steel

bolts to stainless. In that case, for salt water, I would attach zinc bars, as used on marine outdrives, under the dock frame to retard corrosion on hot-dip galvanized fasteners. In fresh water, hot-dip galvanized fasteners perform excellent above the waterline. Below the waterline, from my experience, the galvanization will be gone in a few years. Once the galvanizing is gone, the plain steel in fresh water could hold out for many years but there is no telling exactly how long. For anything that you're building that will be underwater, lean toward stainless.

If you plan to use a nailing gun, you'll likely speed up the assembly time significantly. I recommend using a 3-inch (7.62-centimeter) hot-dip box nail that is ring-shanked or with a spiral. Be sure to blunt the tips to prevent splitting at the end of a board.

If nailing red cedar or redwood, you can expect the galvanized nail heads to turn brown from an interaction between the zinc fastener and tanning oils in the wood. It never bothered me but it might bother some people.

Though the nails hold very well, one complaint I hear about is the nail heads creeping up over time. This is more of a problem with floating docks than fixed. Wood floating docks can torque or twist from end to end as waves roll through, a little or a lot, depending on how well they were made. Prolonged torquing can cause nails to work up through their holes. The shrink and swell cycle of the boards may also contribute to this. Either you cope with the problem, appreciating the other attributes to nails, or use screws instead. Just be aware that if torquing is the culprit, it will work on the screws too. They either creep out like a nail will or fatigue and snap at the heads. You should use a heavy-enough wire, like a #10, and work on reducing the torque in the dock.

As a framing fastener, structural screws install very nicely with a variable-speed cordless impact wrench. These are available by several manufacturers in various lengths, coatings, and head types. If you haven't used these before, don't be surprised at

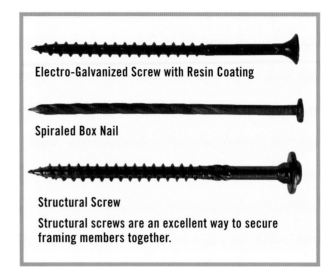

Electro-Galvanized Screw with Resin Coating

Spiraled Box Nail

Structural Screw
Structural screws are an excellent way to secure framing members together.

how easily an 8-inch (20.32-centimeter) screw will install. As with any fastener, make sure that the manufacturer rates the product you're looking at for the treated wood you're using and your environment.

When considering your choice of head types available, whether for decking or framing, Phillips drives work well when going into cedar. If you're going into a harder material, such as treated wood, either use a square or star drive. Structural screws are available in a hex drive that I've never stripped out, but I prefer the heads that are round or flat with a star drive as they are more hull friendly if brushed by a boat. If you experience trouble with the bits breaking, try a higher quality brand made with a harder steel. On deck screws, fluted tips are worth getting to reduce the chance of splitting the end of a board. If using conventional tips, pre-drill the ends of all deck boards since decking should be cut flush with the frame on a dock.

For mounting specialty dock hardware, joining posts with a frame, or cap boards, I recommend through bolting. Do not rely on lag bolts where through bolts can be used.

If possible, use all carriage bolts, keeping the heads to the exposed surfaces as they are hull- and skin-friendly while the hex nuts will be turned in. If the hex nut and the threaded end of a bolt must be on a surface that could be exposed to a hull or

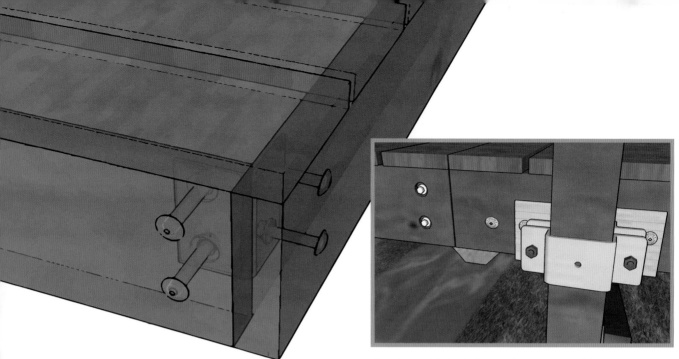

Dock hardware should be through-bolted.

Countersunk holes help to reduce contact with an abrasive bolt.

skin, countersink an area so that the nut and bolt set within.

Around fresh water you should use hot-dip galvanized screws. In salt environments, I prefer stainless if it's in the budget. I have a word of caution when using stainless bolts and nuts. They have a strong propensity to "gall" or seize together. Sometimes they seize before the nut is tight against the surface you're fastening to. Once this happens, applying torque to the wrench will likely snap the bolt. Before putting stainless bolts and nuts together, inspect the threads for grit or imperfections. Then hand-tighten before applying torque with a hand wrench. Tightening at a slow speed prevents heat that can cause galling. An alternative to this would be to use brass or aluminum nuts on stainless bolts.

When drilling for bolts, match the hole size with the bolt diameter. Sometimes a slightly bigger hole is preferred so that the bolt fits into the hole with ease. That may be okay, but if it is on a component that will experience motion, such as a hinge for a floating dock, I recommend keeping a tight fit. Locking nuts, such as a nyloc, would be great if you could find them for galvanized bolts. Otherwise,

locking washers are the "go to" but I recommend liquid thread lock and or double nutting. They add another level of protection to secure parts that experience motion, vibration, and wear. RTV silicone applied to the threads will also dampen vibration and help prevent bolts and nuts from working apart. Upon tightening bolts to wood, be sure to include flat washers where a hex head bolt or nut tightens directly against a wood surface.

If you're planning to use eye-bolts for hinging dock sections or holding significant loads, be sure to use load-rated, shouldered, forged eye-bolts. Eye-bolts that have been formed into shape with a rod may not do the job. Make sure you know its capacity and that it is fit for the job you're subjecting it to.

Pipe leg dock hardware, made for holding the weight of dock sections and additional loads, use a setscrew to hold the weight onto the pipe. Sometimes a standard-grade three-bolt is used where the setscrew threads into the part. A better setscrew is one that is made for biting into the pipe. It is case-hardened and has a concave or cup-shaped tip. A ½ inch (1.27 centimeter)–diameter setscrew of this type has a holding capacity of 500

1. A locking nut resists loosening due to vibration and shrinking of material.
2. A locking washer keeps tension on the nut to help prevent loosening.
3. Use flat washers where hexagonal nuts tighten against wood. Use them under hexagonal bolt heads that are in contact with wood.
4. For fixed docks that stand on pipe legs, the setscrew with "a cup point," used with pipe leg hardware, cuts into the pipe for the best hold and adjustability.
5. Forged eye-bolt with shoulder.
6. Liquid thread lock is an alternative to a locking nut.
7. In a pinch, without locking nuts or liquid thread lock, apply a second nut onto the bolt to resist loosening.

pounds (226.80 kilograms). When tightening, as the setscrew begins to press the pipe against the socket, only a quarter turn more to the right is needed to hold it securely.

Finally, when you think about all the projects you've worked on, building a new dock or rehabilitating an old one will possibly require a greater investment in fasteners than many of the other projects did. This is partly because bolts are a staple in holding the structure together along with your need for corrosion resistance. I'm not going to sugarcoat this. Fasteners are expensive, so before you run out to five different hardware stores and clean out their bins of the sizes you need, use the big shopping list to your advantage. Especially when

it comes to stainless fasteners, give your favorite hometown hardware store manager some time with your list. Let him or her see what they can do. If they bring it in special for you, theoretically, they don't need to make nearly the full markup since it doesn't consume overhead sitting on their shelves. It will skip the shelves and go right to you.

Another place to try is a fastener company. Fasteners is what they do, often importing or dealing direct with a mill without a middleman. There may not be one in your town, but even if it is an hour's drive away, the savings will be worth going there. I have no doubt that if you plan this right and shop smart, you can save big. This will be most helpful if stainless is really what you need.

CHAPTER 3:
DOCKS IN SECTIONS

The Building Blocks to Any Plan

Depending on your experience around the waterfront with docks, you may already be familiar with the idea of building wooden docks in sections versus "stick building" them in place, plank by plank. Except for the chapter that shows you how to build a permanent dock on heavy driven pilings, the DIY methods in this book feature the use of sections throughout. Thinking about your finished dock being comprised of sections—like building blocks—will facilitate the planning, construction, and installation of any DIY wooden dock. Having moved plenty of docks myself, often with no more than one other person to help, I understand the importance of sectionalizing the dock into manageable segments. This is never truer than for folks in the north where docks, subject to winter ice damage, must be removed in the fall and then re-installed in the spring.

For others, where docks may be left in place through the winter, they will appreciate how building in sections allows most of the carpentry work to be done over safe, dry land or preferably in a

Designed, built, and installed in sections, think of each one as the basic building block to your plan.

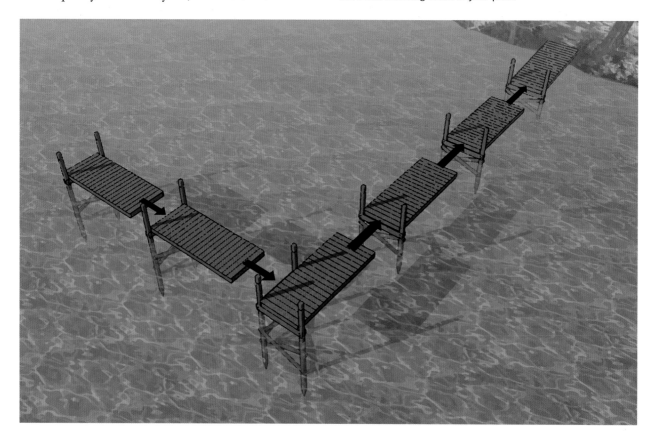

comfortable shop environment with a flat floor that has all the tools handy. Whether you're in the north or south, you'll appreciate the techniques found in this chapter to lessen your load while erecting your dock and maintaining a sturdy end-result that will provide years of service.

In this chapter, you'll see a couple ways you can choose from to build your dock sections. For each choice, I'll also include plans to build common sizes that can be mixed and matched to create your desired footprint. You can apply the dock section plans shown here to most of the leg support methods featured in this book. The section designs, as shown in this chapter, may be used for fixed or floating docks. If you will be building a floating dock, be sure to visit Dock Sections That Float (page 130) for special details you'll want to learn about.

Keep it Manageable—I won't deny that a dock with some weight to it is a good thing. You'll appreciate weight when the dock gets glanced by the boat. However, keeping your dock to the scale of a DIY project that doesn't demand lots of hands on deck or heavy equipment to erect requires your

cognizance to the heft of your finished product and your safe capacity to handle it. Therefore, it is important to avoid overbuilding, ending up with sections that are too heavy for maneuvering. For most DIYers, I recommend building a dock that you'll look forward to assembling, not something to dread. Even if you expect plenty of help from friends and family or you plan to hire help to install it for you, make it something they would want to help with. Don't build the dock that no one wants any part of.

Framing Material—Lumber for a wooden dock section merely calls for framing and decking. Keeping within the scale that is ideal for a DIYer who wants the sections to be lightweight and manageable, you can go as light as a nominal 2x6 (38 by 140 millimeters) stringer size for framing on most residential applications. Compare that to your knowledge of deck building where usually a minimum of 2x8 (38 by 184 millimeters) is recommended, and you might think I'm off my rocker for going that light. Your application could indeed demand larger stringers. For example,

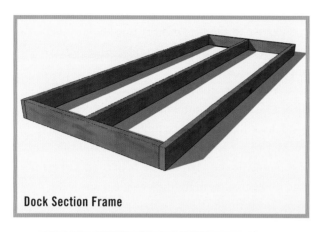

Dock Section Frame

you might be carting commercial fishing gear, supporting vehicular traffic, or gathering the Dolphins' line-backers on it for a group photo. In that case, put the plans on steroids by increasing the stringer size. Just bear in mind, more time and strategy for maneuvering heavier sections will be needed, but it can be done. However, for most residential applications, if your loads are under 40 pounds per square feet, (190 N/m²), the modest stringer size 2x6 (38 by 140 millimeters)—combined with keeping the section size to a modest limit—will yield a more than sufficiently sturdy structure whereby a team of two can comfortably manage. In warmer climates where winter ice is not a concern and doesn't require docks to be annually removed, I would consider stepping up the stringer to a nominal 2x8 (38 by 184 millimeters), given that the sections will be handled only one time.

Pressure-treated (PT) yellow pine and Douglas fir is a favorite framing material for many deck and dock builders. While known for its resistance to rot and infestation from insects, PT is readily available at a reasonable cost. For many years, the PT industry infused arsenic as a preservative into wood, until enough concern was raised over the proper disposal of PT waste to influence change. The industry voluntarily switched to an arsenic-free treatment, resulting in a ban on arsenic-treated wood across the U.S., Canada, and Europe. News of the ban has left some consumers unclear as to the current legal status and availability of PT. Though it is on the market without the arsenic and approved by the EPA, NRC, and EU, check with your local code office to make sure its use for docks is compliant. A couple alternatives to PT that have a natural resistance to rot are cedar and redwood. These materials may cost more than PT, but they will be considerably lighter, making less work during the installation. A few other choices for framing include untreated Douglas fir, hemlock, and spruce.

Decking Material—The decking on your dock sections is the most visible feature and has the largest surface area of all the material going into the project. You'll be asking a lot from the decking you choose as it gets full sun, rain, and, of course, traffic from people, pets, and waterfowl. Regardless, if every other feature of the dock is looking great but the decking is not, then the dock, overall, looks in poor condition. In other words, a dock's condition is often judged by its deck's appearance. When shopping for what fits your vision, it's important to understand the nature of all the deck choices available, how they will look and feel over time, and how much care they will require. The standard deck board readily available is a nominal 1x6 (19 by 140 millimeters), and can be found at almost any lumberyard. PT decking remains a popular choice for its expected longevity, low cost, and availability while cedar, whether it be Western red or Eastern white, is also available and much lighter than PT decking. Plenty

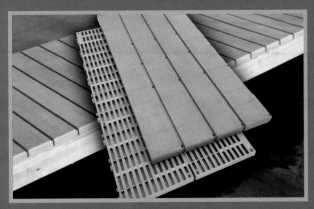

Pre-molded deck panels.

Western red cedar decking.

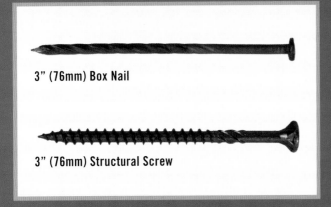

3" (76mm) Box Nail

3" (76mm) Structural Screw

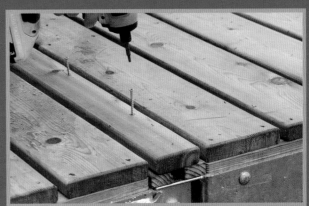

Fastening down the decking.

of synthetic deck boards can be found today at your local home center or lumberyard, such as PVC and composite. These will add considerable weight over the others I've mentioned thus far, but they may be your answer to reduced maintenance. For a low-maintenance option that is lighter, you may consider pre-molded deck panels, made specially for dock sections, that simply screw down to the frame. These, being a specialty item, if not found at your local lumberyard, can be ordered online.

Fasteners—When assembling the frame, I prefer using a nailing gun that shoots 3-inch (9-gauge) box nails. They should be ring-shanked or screw-like, and available with a glue coating that cements them into the wood upon entry. Try backing one of these out with a claw—you'll likely break the head

off before it gives. If you prefer screws over nails, and you have a cordless impact wrench, use a 4-inch (100-millimeter) coated structural screw with a hex- or star-driven head. Though more expensive than nails, they will bind a butt joint together with a bite like no other.

When applying deck boards, such as PT or cedar to the frame, the same 3-inch (9 gauge) box nails that are good for the frame will also work on the decking. Prevent splitting at the end of a board by blunting the nail, or better yet pre-drilling, and drive with a hammer. If you prefer screws over nails, use a coated 3-inch (9 gauge) deck screw. Don't mistake galvanized drywall screws for deck screws. For synthetic decking, such as PVC and composite, follow the manufacturer's specifications for screws

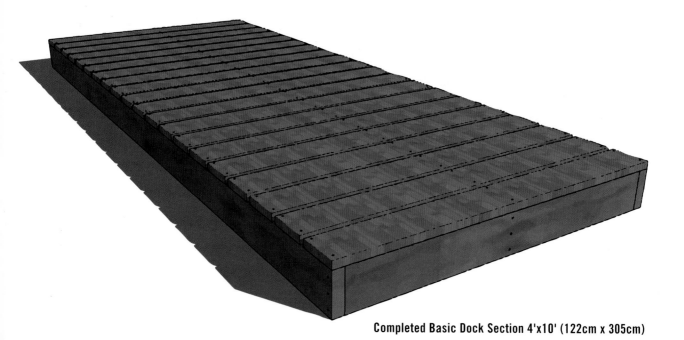

Completed Basic Dock Section 4'x10' (122cm x 305cm)

and method of installing so as not to nullify their warranty.

Stainless steel nails and screws will cost two or more times that of regular steel, and your supplier, be it a hardware store or home center, is not likely to have the variety in stainless that they have in coated steel. Other than a matter of preference, stainless might be a good choice if your dock will be over salt water. See if the manufacturer of the coated screws recommends their products' use in salt environments. If you can't find it in writing, you might want to give stainless serious consideration.

The Basic Dock Section

Plain and simple, this dock section is framed using nominal 2x6 (38- by 140-millimeter) stringers and 1x6 (19- by 140-millimeter) decking. With its timbers spaced about 2 feet (60.96 centimeters) apart, the capacity is sufficient for 40 pounds per square foot (1,900 N/m²). If made completely with PT wood, a 4-foot-wide by 10-foot-long (1.22- by 3.05-meter) section as shown here has a weight of about 200 pounds (90.8 kilograms). Use cedar decking on the PT frame and the weight drops

to about 170 pounds (77.18 kilograms). Increase the frame to 2x8 (38 x 184 millimeters); with cedar decking it would weigh about 210 pounds (95.24 kilograms).

Frame Assembly

When building any dock section, lay out your cut framing members on a flat surface like a concrete floor or elevate them on sawhorses. Nail or screw the butt-joints together as shown in the plan. To prevent splitting at the end of a board while using structural screws, you may want to pre-drill. To reduce the chance of splitting the end of a board while using nails, blunt the tips of the nails. Once the frame is fastened together, check for squareness using your tape measure diagonally across opposite corners. Adjust while continually checking with the tape measure until the two measurements match.

Apply Decking

On a porch or deck, it is common to overhang the deck boards beyond the outside edge of the frame by a couple inches (a few centimeters). The nails or screws nearest the end of a deck board are less likely to split the board if back a few inches

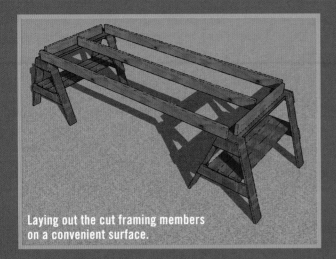

Laying out the cut framing members on a convenient surface.

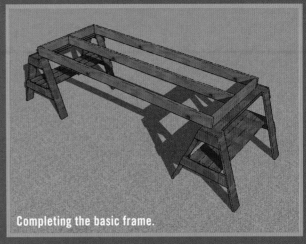

Completing the basic frame.

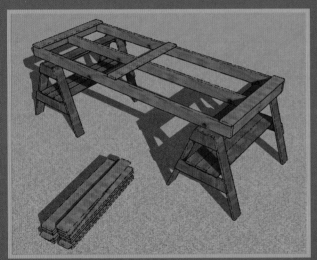

Apply decking.

Tip:

To hold the frame's squareness, begin with fastening down one deck board, flush with each end of the frame. Place additional deck boards on the frame and find the appropriate spacing between each one (no greater than ½" [13mm]). Begin nailing or screwing down deck boards near the center of the frame before working toward each end.

Pre-drill for nails or screws at the end of each deck board to prevent splitting.

Easing the edge with a router or sander removes the sharp edge and prevents splintering.

(several centimeters). Though seemingly helpful, this technique should not be used on docks, especially where boats could be moored alongside. Not only does it add edges, extended toward the boat that could gouge the boat's finish, it provides an unwanted lip for the boat to catch from the underside of the decking. You can probably imagine some of the consequences when that happens. Deck boards should be cut flush to the outside face of the frame to provide a blunt surface. If you're concerned about splitting the end of a deck board having the fasteners close to the end of the boards, then pre-drill in those spots. Blunting the nails will also help prevent splitting.

When using wooden deck boards like PT or cedar, face the crown up when possible. Half of

the time it seems the better side of a board is opposite to the crown. In that case, put the better side up.

On a 10-foot (3.05-meter) long dock section, the typical deck board that will vary slightly in width, when spaced evenly apart, will usually leave about a ½-inch (13-millimeter) gap between each board. The first and last deck board on the section should be flush with the end of the section. On your table saw, you can make wooden strip spacers to help position the boards at an even distance apart. Varying widths of the boards will likely require some improvising on the space for the last three of four. To prevent tripping, gaps between boards should not be greater than ½ inch (13 millimeters). If using new PT decking, which is usually very swollen with moisture when fresh from the lumberyard, prepare your material in advance, allowing time to dry and shrink closer to its finish size.

Once the decking is nailed or screwed down to the frame, the dock section will not skew under normal handling. For wooden decking such as cedar or PT, I recommend easing the top edge on all the ends of the deck boards, using a ⅜-inch (1-centimeter) radius bit on a router. A palm sander also does a nice job to ease the edges and smooth over the rough ends of deck boards.

Removable Decking

Consider making your decking into panels that lay and fasten on top of your dock section's frame. That way, you can reduce the weight significantly when it is time to move the dock section to and from the water. You'll also find the removable decking handy while working under your dock by moving panels back or out so that everything is reachable from the top side. Another key advantage to this is if you're on a body of water that could rise significantly from unexpected profuse rain events. In this situation, the deck panels can be taken up quickly, leaving little surface area for the rising water with waves to lift and pound against.

For lightweight portability, consider making your decking into removable panels.

In the north, where docks are annually removed and stored on the shore for winter, wood decking will last much longer if laid flat, supported evenly into dry storage, such as a shed, garage, or under a camp. Leaving wood stacked under the damp evergreens to wick water into its cells, buried under feet of melting snow, or drawing moisture from damp ground will likely reduce the years you could get out of it. Finally, if you plan to re-treat your decking with a wood preservative, applying stains and clear coats should never be done over the water. Docks in the north that get removed after summer can be treated as they get stored on the ground. Otherwise, panels can be removed while the dock is installed and taken to dry ground before applying your preservative.

Removable decking does compromise torsional strength and some of the rigidity you get from permanent decking. You'll also need to think about the placement of some accessories that utilize permanent decking for proper and safe attachment, such as a tie-off cleat or ladder rails that bolt through the deck. Nevertheless, its benefits are rewarding enough to earn serious consideration by DIYers, and a willingness to work around its inherent compromises. You could opt to build it with removable decking, and if not satisfied after some experience, screw it down permanently. I have had it on my dock for years and couldn't be more satisfied. In places where I have a cleat or ladder, my decking is screwed in permanently. I then panelize where I can to get the advantage where possible. Typically, my panels are all the same size on all my sections, but where I need permanent boards, my panels on that section are smaller in size. At the end of this chapter you'll find the plans that I built my sections from. Alter them as you see fit to suit your personal needs for the attachment of permanent deck accessories.

Hollow PVC decking.

Solid synthetic decking made to resemble wood.

Synthetic Decking

For a low-maintenance option, when talking about synthetic deck boards made by process of extrusion or pultrusion, you could mean one of seemingly endless companies, brand names, and products. Just when I think I've seen them all, another one appears on the market. If you're serious about this option over wood decking, naturally there is the convenience factor when going with a product carried by your local lumberyards. When you search beyond your backyard, the options open up and may prove overwhelming to determine which is the best product to use for docks. You'll find a vast choice of compounds, shapes, sizes, colors, and surface patterns, each with unique characteristics. Though character differences distinguish them, subtle or extreme, a common trait is greater weight than that of the usual PT wood or cedar decking. The added weight won't matter as much

for permanent installations that are a one-time move; otherwise, think twice before putting this material down on dock sections that are meant to be portable. When you read the specifications on a given product, you'll often find that the spacing of timbers in your framing will need to be at 16 inches (40.64 centimeters) apart, not 24 inches (60.96 centimeters), and should each be of a 2x8 (38 by 184 millimeter) minimum. Hollow composite decking will alleviate some of the weight, but it can be heavy and more suitable for permanent docks that won't be handled annually (such as portable docks in the north). I have known people to panelize the heavy composite as described above with varying degrees of success. Many synthetics may warp if not fastened permanently down to the frame, so beware

Synthetic pre-panelized decking.

of that potential before panelizing. Comparable to most of the solid synthetic boards on the market, hollow PVC decking that has a material much like vinyl gutter, but more durable, is likely a better choice for portable dock sections. To minimize the overall dock section's weight, I recommend shopping for the hollow PVC decking by the specifications. Look for brands rated to span 24 inches (61 centimeters) and with the least weight.

Pre-Panelized Decking

If maintenance-free panelized decking is important to you, consider buying a synthetic deck panel that is already made. Don't be surprised if you cannot find this sort of thing on the shelf in a local store, but search "deck panel for docks" online, and I'd expect you'll find different types and companies that will ship directly to you. One popular choice that I have used many times has an anti-skid, perforated surface that stays cool under the sun and allows dirt that tracks onto the dock to pass through before ending up in the boat. The perforated surface can also save a dock on a body of water that is likely to flood at times, allowing the tips of the waves to break through instead of pounding along the underside. It fastens down easily with screws and is much

lighter than many other synthetic choices. If you would rather have a solid surface or the simulation of wood, there are premade panels without the perforation, some with a resin base, others made from aluminum. If keeping the weight down is one of your objectives, I recommend shopping by the specifications. Determine the weight per square foot (per square meter) of the panel when comparing one to another. Also, the more it will span between supports, the fewer framing members you'll need, keeping the weight in lumber down as well.

Smart Sizes

There is economy in making dock sections longer over shorter ones when deciding how to best make up the footprint. There will be fewer sections to handle, fewer legs or pilings to install, and less hardware needed. But, remember, the longer you make them the heavier they'll be, potentially weighing more than what you want to lift. Since many DIYers work alone or with no more than one other person, keep in mind the fact that size sections for your project shouldn't be larger than what you can handle. To follow, I've included plans for some popular sizes that many DIYers work with. For light, residential-grade docks, the sizes featured ahead can be built with 2-inch by 6-inch (38- by 140-millmeter) stringers and 1-inch by 6-inch (19- by 140-millimeter) decking. Choose a lightweight decking, like cedar, and opt for a plan that minimizes the framing to a 24-inch (61-centimeter) span. Also, consider making removable deck panels as shown earlier if you really want to lighten it up.

Summing It Up

In the upcoming chapters, you'll see how I think of docks as comprised of sections: at the planning stage (where I visualize the footprint coming together in sections), the building stage, and the installation stage. Regardless of the classification (fixed, floating, fixed to floating, and rolling), you'll see how sections will be used in this book for all types.

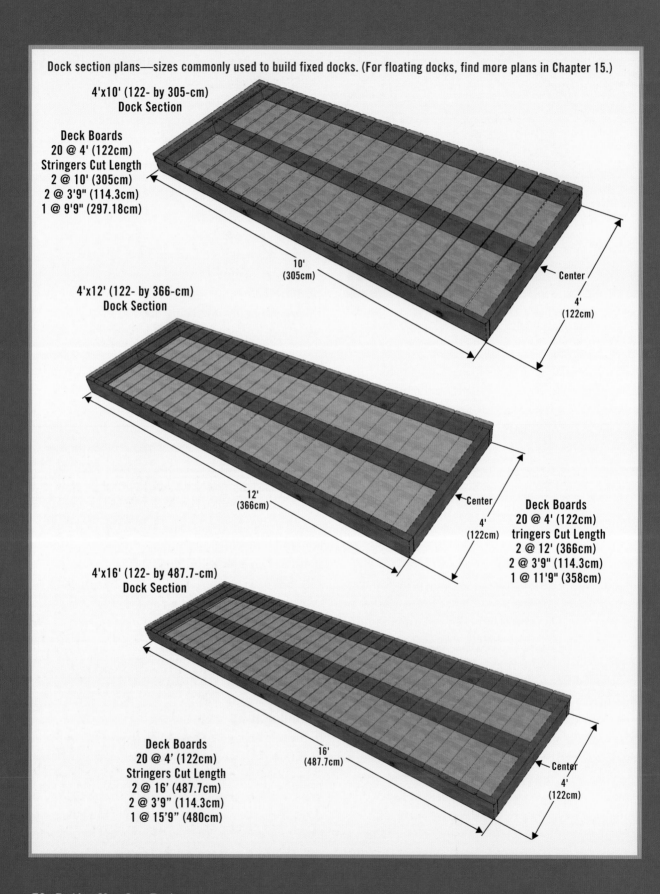

Dock section plans—sizes commonly used to build fixed docks. (For floating docks, find more plans in Chapter 15.)

4'x10' (122- by 305-cm) Dock Section

Deck Boards
20 @ 4' (122cm)
Stringers Cut Length
2 @ 10' (305cm)
2 @ 3'9" (114.3cm)
1 @ 9'9" (297.18cm)

10'
(305cm)

Center

4'
(122cm)

4'x12' (122- by 366-cm) Dock Section

12'
(366cm)

Center

4'
(122cm)

Deck Boards
20 @ 4' (122cm)
tringers Cut Length
2 @ 12' (366cm)
2 @ 3'9" (114.3cm)
1 @ 11'9" (358cm)

4'x16' (122- by 487.7-cm) Dock Section

Deck Boards
20 @ 4' (122cm)
Stringers Cut Length
2 @ 16' (487.7cm)
2 @ 3'9" (114.3cm)
1 @ 15'9" (480cm)

16'
(487.7cm)

Center

4'
(122cm)

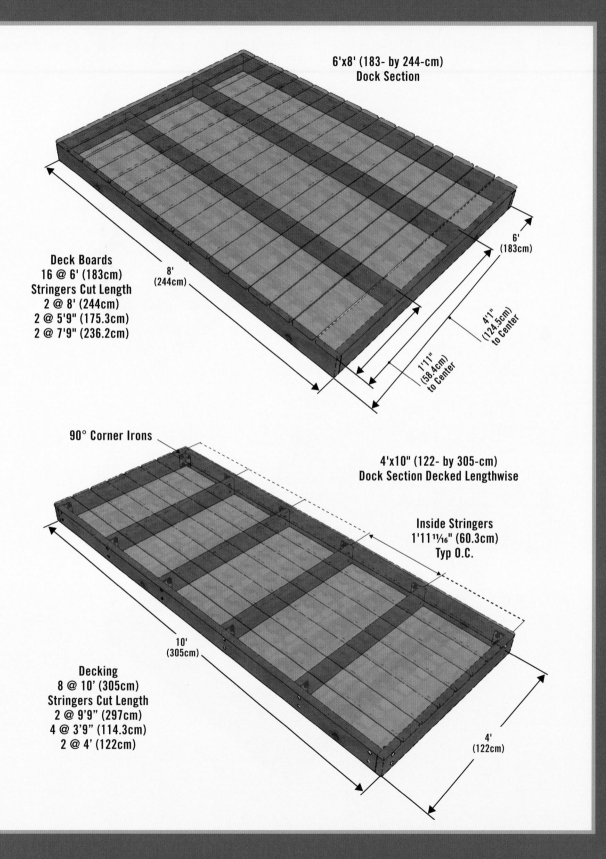

**6'x8' (183- by 244-cm)
Dock Section**

**6'
(183cm)**

**Deck Boards
16 @ 6' (183cm)
Stringers Cut Length
2 @ 8' (244cm)
2 @ 5'9" (175.3cm)
2 @ 7'9" (236.2cm)**

**8'
(244cm)**

**4'1"
(124.5cm)
to Center**

**1'11"
(58.4cm)
to Center**

90° Corner Irons

**4'x10" (122- by 305-cm)
Dock Section Decked Lengthwise**

**Inside Stringers
1'11 11/16" (60.3cm)
Typ O.C.**

**10'
(305cm)**

**Decking
8 @ 10' (305cm)
Stringers Cut Length
2 @ 9'9" (297cm)
4 @ 3'9" (114.3cm)
2 @ 4' (122cm)**

**4'
(122cm)**

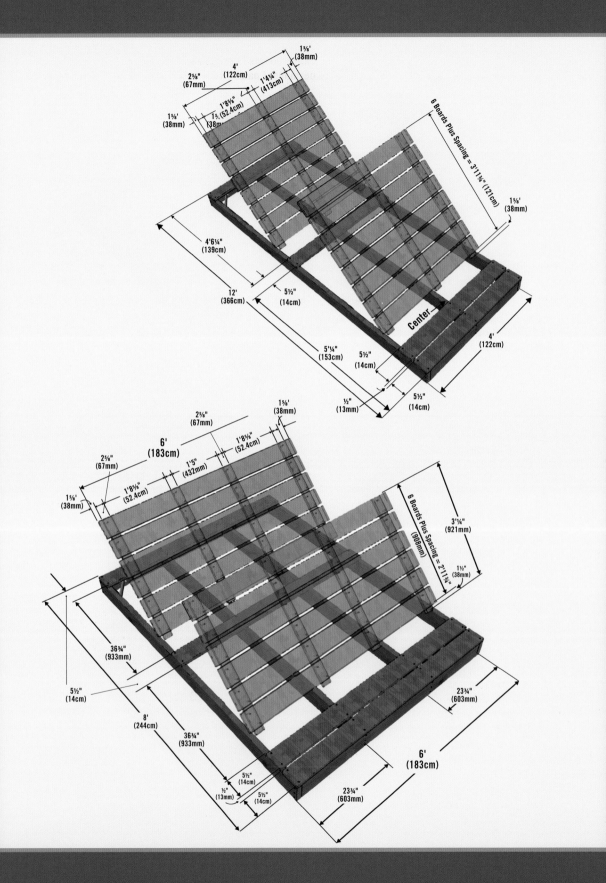

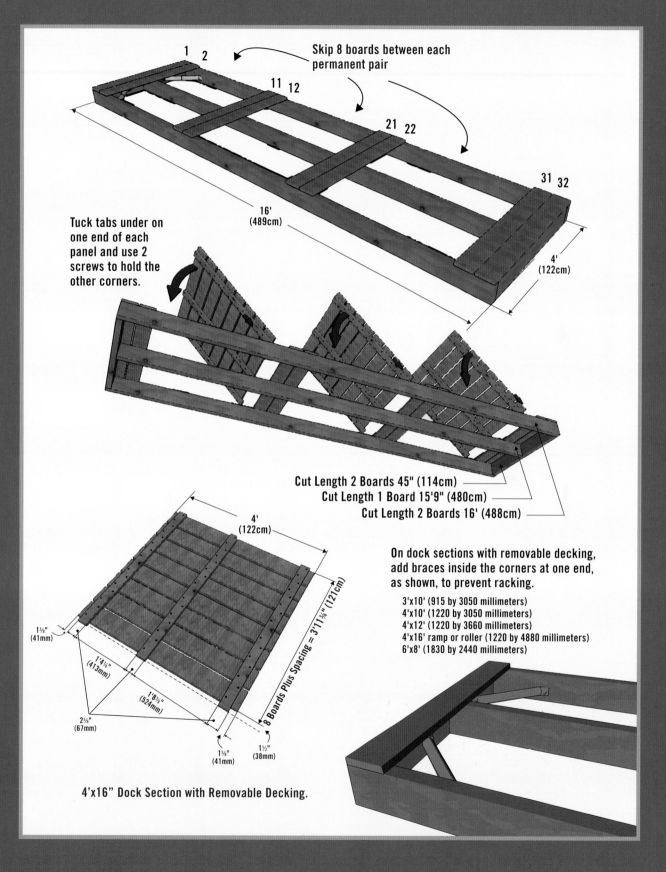

Skip 8 boards between each permanent pair

1 2

11 12

21 22

31 32

16'
(489cm)

4'
(122cm)

Tuck tabs under on one end of each panel and use 2 screws to hold the other corners.

Cut Length 2 Boards 45" (114cm)
Cut Length 1 Board 15'9" (480cm)
Cut Length 2 Boards 16' (488cm)

On dock sections with removable decking, add braces inside the corners at one end, as shown, to prevent racking.

3'x10' (915 by 3050 millimeters)
4'x10' (1220 by 3050 millimeters)
4'x12' (1220 by 3660 millimeters)
4'x16' ramp or roller (1220 by 4880 millimeters)
6'x8' (1830 by 2440 millimeters)

4'
(122cm)

1⅝"
(41mm)

1'4¾"
(413mm)

1'8⅝"
(524mm)

2⅝"
(67mm)

1⅝"
(41mm)

1½"
(38mm)

8 Boards Plus Spacing = 3'11¾" (121cm)

4'x16" Dock Section with Removable Decking.

CHAPTER 4:
FIXED DOCKS

The Benefits and Best Conditions

Standing on legs like an oversized table, the fixed dock provides sturdy and stable access from ship to shore. Fixed means that it is not meant to move or to float on the water; the fixed dock remains stationary. A fixed dock may be a permanent structure or one that is made portable in severely cold climates, removed before winter ice takes effect. Its legs, using standard wooden posts from a lumber store or galvanized steel pipe, are usually set into the riverbed, lake bed, or seabed for dependable boat anchorage. For lighter service applications, depending on the environment, there are options that simply stand the fixed dock's legs on feet or skids. Following my description of suitable environments for fixed docks, I will provide you, in detail, four of the best proven DIY methods for building them that won't break your wallet or your back.

For seven years, I lived on Long Lake in Naples, Maine, where my fixed dock faced north with several miles of open water between it and Mt. Washington. Some days, it was a peaceful paradise. On other days, wind swept down from the nearby mountain to deliver an onslaught of waves. Relentless were the rollers, 2 to 3 feet (60.96 to 91.44 centimeters) high with whitecaps that would crest and crash over the rocky shore. Intrepidly, however, the fixed dock stood firmly on its legs in the middle of it all. At the right height, it provided the most solid and dependable walking surface, regardless of the ominous turbulence below. When a wave rises under a fixed dock—provided the decking is above the largest wave—there is practically no surface area significant for the wave to lift against,

A well-built fixed dock stands firm and ready to receive its vessels.

Pounding white-capped waves roll relentlessly under a fixed dock that remains unmoved and unscathed at its safe height above the water.

leaving the dock and it occupants unscathed. On fair days, the lake buzzed with boats zipping around and cutting up the water. Nevertheless, with all the chop, anyone could sit out there and read or sunbathe without getting jostled. Properly built, the fixed dock should not shake or sway when walked on. There should be minimal motion if it experiences a normal bump by a boat. For anyone physically challenged or with poor balance, the fixed dock (in the right environment) is what I would recommend. For the best results, consider the following conditions.

The Body of Water

A fixed dock could be put into water that is either calm or choppy, but it works best where the water level doesn't fluctuate greatly. Near my home in Maine, where northern climates require most docks

to be portable and to be removed before winter ice sets in. Not far away is Sebago Lake, where fixed docks are most popular because of the chop from wind and heavy boat traffic. Floating docks often don't stand up well on that lake unless they are on a protected shoreline. As with the dock I had on Long Lake, fixed docks on Sebago aren't affected by waves provided they are at a safe height above the maximum wave. The challenge there is that the water drops several feet (meters) from the mean water level between July and August, leaving folks to jump down from the dock into the boat by September. Another challenge they face is a propensity for the water level on Sebago to rise significantly from spring rains after the dock has been set for the season. This is a potential disaster for the portable dock should waves pound against its underside. My advice to anyone on a lake like

Sebago has been to hold off on installing their portable fixed dock until spring rains have passed. As for the water level dropping, I recommend an adjustable fixed dock that can be lowered on its legs later in the summer.

Rivers that swell suddenly and drastically or bodies of water fed by those rivers are not usually a good place for a DIY fixed dock, nor are tidal waters in latitudes where daily levels fluctuate more than a couple feet (about 10 decimeters). In either of these situations, the DIY fixed dock will provide access over the shallows until it can transition to a floating dock in deeper water. This dock describes what I've classified as "fixed to floating," which I will help you with in this book.

Exposure to Waves and Current

This exposure should not be greater than what makes practical sense. When considering the scale of a fixed dock suitable for a DIYer to build and install, be sure it matches the scale of the exposure. I've known DIYers to install a dock where the body of water was so big that the amount of wind and the size waves proved to be a mismatch for the dock. If you're unfamiliar with the body of water, I recommend looking around the neighborhood. On a large body that has a ravaged shoreline where you don't see any docks, heed the warning sign. If there are other fixed docks nearby that have the same exposure, chances are your dock should look similar in scale to those. Look at the ones that seem to be weathering well and the ones that aren't, taking note of what appears to be working well from what doesn't. Ask the neighbors about the history of weather, including winds, floods, and droughts, to give yourself a better idea of what your dock will be up against. If it is a sandy beach that gets pounded by wind and waves, expect lots of sand to move around the legs. The same thing can happen where there is a sweeping current. The legs of the fixed dock in these environments will need to be set deep enough into the bed to prevent undermining.

A sandy lake bed makes a firm base for a fixed dock.

An "L" or "T" platform at the end of a fixed dock adds convenient usable space while adding stability in deep water.

The Bottom

The floor of the seabed, lake bed, or riverbed where the fixed dock will stand should be firm and made of sand, gravel, clay, or stabilized rock. Putting a fixed dock on loose rock such as cobble or submerged rock piles could cause shifting under the legs, requiring seemingly constant adjustments to keep level. Extremely soft ground, such as detritus and silt (where you'd sink to your shins), will also prove challenging to keep a fixed dock level upon if there isn't some harder material, such as gravel or clay, beneath the muck.

In this case, the legs need to extend through the soft matter until seated in something firm below. In northern climates where docks need to be removed, I wouldn't use a fixed dock if solid ground couldn't be found less than 6 inches (1.52 decimeters) beneath the muck. Even with mud pads or feet to support the legs, the portable dock will be a bear to remove in the fall after it has had a whole summer to hunker itself down. A floating dock would be my preference in that situation.

Depth Range

The depth range for a fixed dock installed by a DIYer shouldn't exceed much more than six feet or two meters. Installations kept within this range will be much easier for you to manage and will feel more stable than if you go deeper. If you must go deeper, then I would recommend the dock to be at least six feet or two meters wide. If permittable, an "L" or "T" shape dock providing a platform off to the side at the deep end will add stability. If you're looking for enough depth at the end of a dock for swimmers to dive into, you'll need no less than nine feet or three meters. I recommend discouraging any diving from the dock.

Your Assessment

If the fixed dock sounds like a good fit for you and your environment, step into the next chapter to learn how you can complete a thorough survey where you plan to put the dock. Now that you know the main criteria required, your site survey will verify specifics about the location that you'll need to know before moving forward with a fixed dock.

CHAPTER 5:
COMPLETING THE SITE SURVEY FOR A FIXED DOCK

Now that we've considered the best conditions for a fixed dock, let's see if one will be a good fit for your waterfront. When I visit a shorefront to measure for a fixed dock, I am sometimes unfamiliar with the body of water, so I will start with these questions.

- Where should the dock begin at the shore?
- Where will I set the first set of dock legs?
- Is the water level somewhat stable here?
- What is the exposure here to waves and current?
- What direction does the predominant wind come from and is it formidable?
- Is the ground firm and stable?
- Will it be in an acceptable depth range?

Perhaps you've had plenty of time to become familiar with the waterfront where you'll be installing a dock; in that case, you're ahead of the game. Almost half the time, when I meet with people about building a dock, they are unfamiliar with the nature of their shoreline, perhaps they just bought the property, so a little detective work is in order.

Choosing a suitable location: Quite often there is clearly one place the dock can go off a property, be it a narrow lot, code-restricted area, or proximity to adequate depths. Otherwise, if your waterfront gives you options, here are some things I would consider. Begin with a comfortable elevation off the water. If possible, avoid having to build stairs or an extra-long ramp that will require needless climbing when there is a lower approach nearby that could be used instead. See that the location provides the right depth for your boat and activities while being free of obstacles. If there is a barrier with a leeward side from wind and storms, take full advantage of it. For privacy's sake, keep a comfortable distance from the neighbor's dock. The huge pine tree at the water's edge could offer shade for the dock if that's your thing, but keep in mind that it could also rain sap and soot. A dock at the side of a swimming hole is preferred over a dock that is in the swimming hole. The same can be said for the scenic view; it is better to keep the dock on the side rather in it. I guess that depends on what you'd rather look at, the dock and boat or the water and mountains behind them. Having it where you can see it without spoiling the vista would be ideal. Finally, make sure you include your significant other on this one. It's much easier to move an idea than the real thing.

Establish the location of dock legs nearest to the shore: Their location will set the course for placement of all the other dock legs. Most of the DIY docks in this book are comprised of standard-size sections that become building blocks adjoining to one another. Each section typically gets two legs at its farthest end. It may be your preference to place the first set of legs above the shoreline to support the shore end of the dock section or place them out into the water at a distance so that the shore end of the first section rests on dry land.

Right: A family cooperates to survey offshore for the desired length and depth of their dream dock.

So often, the path, bank, or seawall leading to the dock is at a different elevation from where the dock is to be set. Therefore, I prefer to use my first section as a ramp from the shore that spans across and slants toward my second section. In this scenario, the first section will get no legs at all since pitching it would cause them to be off plumb. The two legs that were assigned to the first section get bumped over to the second section. The second section can free-stand now on four legs like a table and is bridged to shore with the first section.

If you use the standard sections shown in this book, they are typically 10 feet (3050 millimeters) in length. Using the first section for a ramp, determine the length needed to slant safely, while spanning between the desired resting point on the shore and the second section. Though I like to stick with 10-foot (3050-millimeter) long standard sections

as often as possible, you may need to make them longer if starting from a high elevation. The shore end of the second section is where your first set of legs will stand. Flag the spot where the ramp rests on the shore while making note of the length it needs to be.

Check for fluctuating water levels: I would first establish what the stability of the water level is like. If the dock gets only seasonal use, concern yourself mainly with what the fluctuation is doing during the months it will be in use. Look for a fluctuation not to exceed a range of about 2 feet (6 decimeters). Fluctuations greater than this would better suited for a fixed dock that can be adjusted during the season or maybe a floating dock. Facts about the water level are often revealed close by, just by observing other docks in the area. If there are other fixed docks, make note of the distance they are set

Determine where the first set of legs should stand.

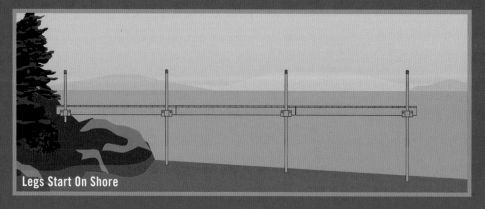

Legs Start On Shore

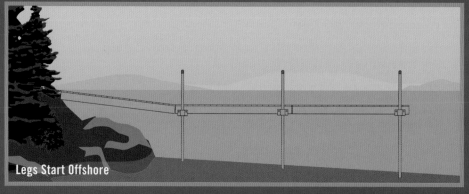

Legs Start Offshore

off the water. Seeing more fixed docks than floating is an indication that the water level is stable. You'll also notice water stains, like a dirty ring in a bathtub, upon rocks, boulders, and seawalls along the shore. If there are no references like that to observe, check for a debris line further up the bank away from the water's edge. You'll see where the high water pushed twigs, rogue weeds, and other litter. Ask a neighbor or two who has experience with the body of water about how great and how frequent the level deviates from the mean level. It would be helpful to know typically month by month what the level does and if you should be aware of any sizable event such as a "twenty-year flood." If there isn't a neighbor to supply this information, then a local marina operator should know. If your body of water has a dam, the ones commissioned with its management can tell you.

Predicting exposure to waves and current: Boat chop and large waves driven by prolonged winds can damage a fixed dock if the dock isn't set at the proper height. The surface area under the decking is enough for a large wave to push against from below and lift the dock, dislodging the legs from the lake bed or seabed. While at the site, I look at the reach to the farthest shore opposite from me. If it is close to 1 mile (1.61 kilometers) or more, the chop from the wind could become severe. The longer the reach, the larger the waves could get. Find out what the maximum wave height could reach. Once you know, plan on setting the dock so that large waves will pass underneath, clearing the underside. For example, if the highest wave measures vertically no more than 3 feet (915 millimeters) from crest to trough, the dock will need to set no less than 1½ feet (460 millimeters) off the water when it is flat and calm.

The first dock section may stand off the shore while another section is used as a ramp to bridge the gap.

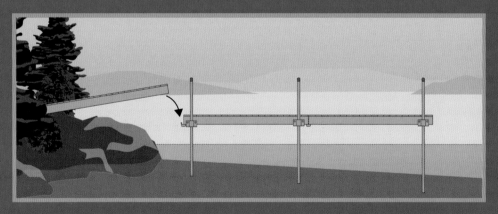

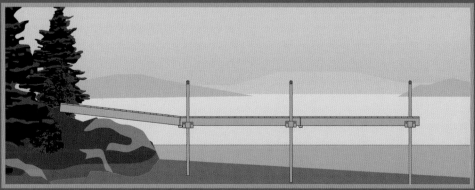

Fixed docks should be set at a height so that the largest waves present will not pound and lift the dock from its position.

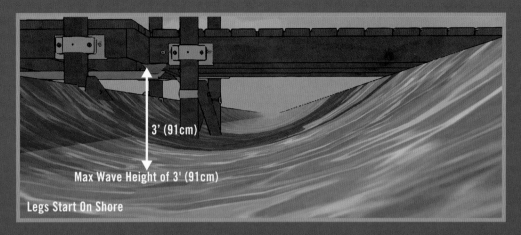

3' (91cm)

Max Wave Height of 3' (91cm)

Legs Start On Shore

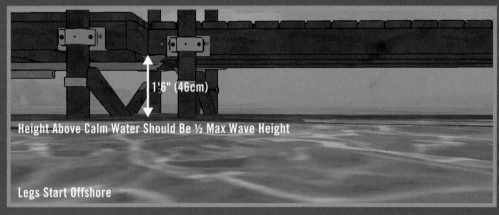

1'6" (46cm)

Height Above Calm Water Should Be ½ Max Wave Height

Legs Start Offshore

If your shoreline happens to be a sandy beach that, at times, gets pounded by wind-driven crashing waves, recognize that the sand will likely wash in and out from the shore. A fixed dock set only on feet or skids will likely be undermined and not remain level. River currents and outgoing tides on coastal waters will also sweep sand away from the dock. Plan on setting the legs deep enough into the lake bed, seabed, or riverbed to prevent effects from wave and current erosion.

Direction of wind: If there is a significant reach to the opposite shore, even a "narrow window" between islands or other barriers, there could be enough wind from that direction to consider when planning where a boat will be moored at the dock. During your site survey, make a note as to the direction any significant wind can come from. This is useful information when floor-planning the dock so you can be cognizant of where the protective leeward side is.

Checking the ground and water depths: For a fixed dock, you'll need to verify that the lake bed, seabed, or riverbed is stable enough so that the legs can stand firmly. In "one fell swoop," while checking for this, you can measure the depths along the path of the dock where you expect the legs to stand. Legs will be present at the end of every section, so it will help you to know the length of dock sections you plan to use. Their length will be the unit of measure used to pace across the water with and guide where to measure the depths. During your survey over the water, you can also determine the total dock length required to reach the desirable capacity for boats and all activities you have in mind. Once this information is collected, it can then be mapped out on paper to use in your planning process and to arrive at your material requirements. Unless you're willing to wade out there or you're replacing an old dock that is still present and safe to walk on, I would use a human-powered canoe or dinghy for this part. Additionally, have ready the following implements.

- A lifejacket.
- A flexible tape-measure to extend from shore out over the water, good for the overall length of the dock. I carry a 100-footer (30 meters) with me.
- A rigid tape-measure, for checking the depths, one that you don't mind getting wet. Even better, use a length of 1½-inch (3.81-centimeter) PVC pipe, marked and numbered every 6 inches (15.24 centimeters) if you expect to be in deeper

than 5 feet (1.52 meters). For shallow water, less than 5 feet (1.52 meters), you could mark the oar or canoe paddle the same way provided the marks won't bother you later.
- Have a pencil, notepad, and graph paper ready.
- A friend to assist will come in handy.

For this exercise, choose an occasion when the water is calm and there is good visibility. Again, I recommend a small boat for this, such as a canoe, and the operator to be skilled with its handling. Take the measuring implements into the boat with you, leaving the hooked end of the flexible tape measure to be held firmly by your helper on the shore. He or she should hold it at the spot where the dock will meet land, such as where the ramp rests on the bank. Have your helper take the pencil and notepad so your hands are free to handle the boat while measuring. You can then call out the information for your helper to jot down.

Before getting too far offshore, agree with your helper on a landmark that is on the opposite

Consider the direction of predominant winds that your waterfront is exposed to. Boats usually weather the wind better when kept on the dock's leeward side.

shore, in line with the direction you want your dock to go. With that, your helper can visually line up your position with it and verbally guide you to keep your measurements on course. While holding the flexible tape measure taut between you and your helper, begin moving away from the shore, stopping where the first legs will stand or at the end of what would be the first section. Then measure the depth while checking for bottom stability and call out the information to your helper. Be sure to clarify the distance out and its respective depth.

As you move out, jab at the bottom with your paddle or PVC pipe to check for firmness. A firm bottom may have a small layer of muck over the top; that won't matter. If there is deep muck on the bottom, such that you could sink into it, up to your shins, then that may be a game changer for the classification of dock you'll choose. Nevertheless, proceed with your site survey as you'll need to know the details of your submerged waterfront before choosing any option. You should also make note of any significant obstacles as you move along, such as stumps and boulders. Have your helper write down what it is, its distance under the water's surface, and its distance from the shore with any other references as to its location. Use a GPS device or app for this if you have one. If visibility into the water is poor, use your paddle or PVC pipe to sweep around and find obstacles that are not visible. If an immovable obstacle will impede the installation or intended use of the dock, you may consider setting over

from it in another spot and repeating the survey there.

Continue to drift away, toward the location of the next set of legs. Once over the spot, hold the tape measure taut and get the next depth measurement while checking for firmness. Repeat this procedure for each additional dock section that may be in your plan. For docks that extend over to the side, such as an "L" or "T" shape, set over to check that the depths there are no different than what you measured along the main portion. Keep in mind that most power boats need a minimum of 3 feet (91.44 centimeters) in depth for the stern end. If there is potential for severe chop, then more distance out for greater depth may be required to prevent the pitching boat at the dock from hitting the bottom.

Drawing Up the Plan

Finally, after you've exited the water, go for a clean sheet of graph paper. From a bird's eye view, plot out your water depth to scale on the graph paper, beginning at the shore and then moving out. Draw in the dock, section by section, and the legs adjacent to their respective depth measurements. Add in any obstacles or landmarks that may be important to you. Indicate anything to help with erecting the dock, such as the height off the water you want it set at, the landmark on the opposite shore you're aiming it toward, and a landmark on the shore near where the dock should start. At this point you have the basics down. Add more details if you'd like. Show where the ladder or the bench is supposed to go

A marked paddle for measuring depths is a great tool for probing the bottom while checking for hardness and for obstacles that need to be included in your plan. For depths greater than the length of your paddle, consider a marked length of PVC pipe.

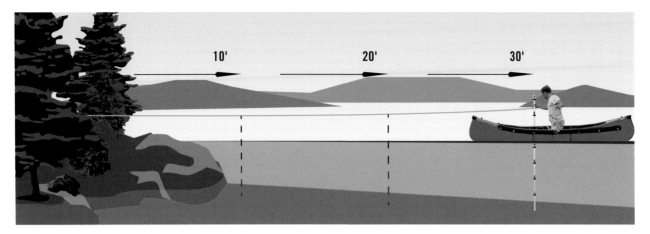

From shore, measure out where you want the dock to begin in increments equal to the dock sections' length that you've considered for your plan. At each increment, record the depth needed to determine the length of each dock leg. Check the bottom's hardness and see that your plan doesn't take you into depths greater than what is practical to manage.

and where each boat gets moored to the dock.

This is your plan. However, if you will be using this survey drawing for a permit application, keep the one with all the extra details for yourself. Make a separate drawing that only includes the details asked for within the application instructions.

If your site survey findings are not suitable for a fixed dock, the information you gained from this exercise will most certainly assist with the planning of any other classification. If you do have the right conditions for a fixed dock, the next few chapters describe a host of different support methods for fixed docks in sections, each with its own chapter that details a different support technique. Look and learn about them to find the method that best suits your environment, your wallet, and the purpose you have in mind for a dock.

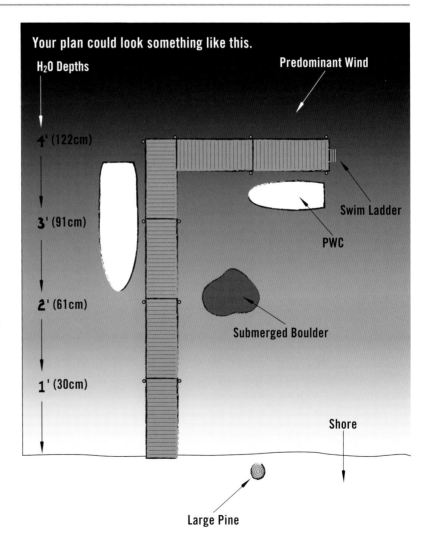

Your plan could look something like this.

H₂O Depths

Predominant Wind

4' (122cm)

3' (91cm)

2' (61cm)

1' (30cm)

Swim Ladder

PWC

Submerged Boulder

Shore

Large Pine

CHAPTER 6:
SKID DOCK

For shallow waters that remain at a somewhat constant level, here is a simple and economical structure that may be all you need. The skid dock depends on a firm lake bed and your carefully measured water depths taken where each leg will stand. That is so the posts can be pre-bolted directly to the frame pre-setting the dock at the intended height before it is brought to the water. For climates that require docks to be annually removed before the season ends, consider using the dock section plan with removable decking to lighten the load. The skid dock when underway will maneuver much easier without all the weight of the decking on top. After the sections are in position, the weight of the deck panels back in place will be a welcome contribution to holding the dock's position.

Prepare a Level Plan

On this dock, use 4x4 (76- by 76-millimeter) posts, bolted to the end of a dock section. The post can either be on the outside of the frame or, for a clean outer face, with a small modification to the deck plan, they can be on the inside.

Of course, with the legs bolted to the frame, there is no adjustability aside from shimming under a post with a patio block or digging out under a post. I do not recommend shimming or raising with cinder blocks as they are too light and are apt to kick out from underneath the posts. Often the depth on the left side of the dock is very close to that on the right, a bottom characteristic that is preferred for this dock. If your depths happen to be very different between the adjacent posts, then you would be better to go with another method.

Ideal for shallow and calm waters, lightweight sections of dock are slid into position using skids attached to the legs.

On smooth, firm ground, a section of skid dock can be pushed or pulled along with ease.

Preparing the Dock Sections

After your dock sections are built and ready for the posts, place the first dock section on a couple sawhorses with each end cantilevering beyond the horses.

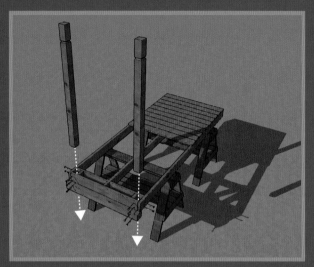

A slight modification to the dock section's frame provides a socket to insert post legs through before securely fastening in place.

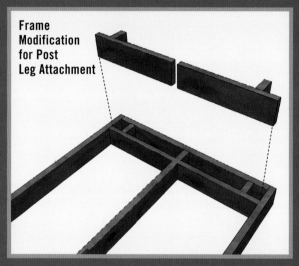

Frame Modification for Post Leg Attachment

Fasten all blocking in place with structural screws.

If your dock sections were made with removable decking, most of the work, right up to the installation into the water, will go easier with the deck panels removed. *Before using any fasteners in the upcoming instructions, be cognizant of all outside surfaces on the dock that will be in contact with flesh, boats, and other objects. Keep the threaded end of all bolts turned toward the inside or underside of the dock. Favor carriage-head bolts where possible, keeping the rounded heads toward the outside exposed surfaces. Never be satisfied with an exposed thread to a bolt, a sharp edge, or pointed object protruding out that could ruin someone's day.*

The first dock section usually gets four posts attached, one near each corner. Prepare each post respective to its assigned location by cutting to a length that will give your dock the desired height off the water. Add to that the height of the dock section and whatever amount you want above the decking. This will be the total length of your post.

Mark a line on the post where it should meet the bottom edge of the dock section. While maintaining squareness with the dock section, clamp the post in place and fasten with carriage bolts through the frame. Repeat this procedure for the other three posts on the first dock section.

Apply cross bracing on the adjacent posts at the outbound end and side (longitude bracing) to prevent the frame from racking. Fasten braces to the posts with galvanized carriage bolts, ⅜ inches by 5½ inches (10 by 140 millimeters). Where side braces meet the frame, fasten with galvanized carriage bolts, ⅜ inches by 4 inches (10 by 100 millimeters).

On the outbound and inbound posts, mount a ledger block up tight against the bottom of the frame that extends forward enough for the adjoining dock section to rest on. Fasten the ledger block to each post using two carriage bolts ⅜ inches by 6 inches (10 by 155 millimeters), nuts, and washers.

Make the skids for the bottom of your outbound end posts. Of course, there are many ways you could do this. The first objective is to resemble skis, curved up at both ends so that they glide over the ground and lake bed as the dock section is pushed or pulled into position. They should be kept to a short length for steerability and secured to the post firmly so that they don't snap off. One simple way to meet these objectives is with two 12-inch (280-millimeter) pieces of 2x6 (38 by 140 millimeters). I would radius each end so it resembles a short Popsicle stick. Turned in a longitudinal direction with the dock's length, attach two skids, flush and centered with the bottom of each post so that the post is sandwiched between them. Use three marine-grade structural screws, 4 inches (100 millimeters) in size, to fasten into the side of the post.

If continuing straight out, the second dock section only gets two posts and two ledger blocks at the outbound end. Before you prepare additional dock sections with posts and bracing, consider skipping down to the installation instructions (next page) and install the first dock section into the water. That way you'll get to see first-hand if you will be satisfied with its height before working on more dock sections. If satisfied with the results, continue the same procedure from the first dock section for attaching posts on additional dock sections.

One dock section should be used as a ramp to span between the shore and the next dock section. Post attachment is not required for the ramp.

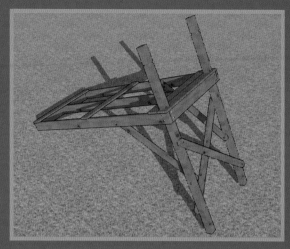

Cross bracing between the posts and to the frame adds rigidity while mobilizing the sections, and adds stability while the dock is in use.

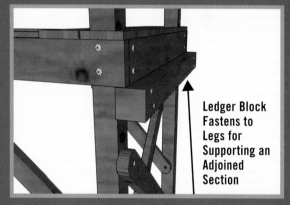

Ledger Block Fastens to Legs for Supporting an Adjoined Section

Fasten a ledger block to the legs as shown to support an adjoining section.

Wooded Skids

Applying wooden skids that look like Popsicle sticks will help the skids slide over the ground. Fasten to the post with structural screws. Otherwise, a single carriage bolt passing through the skid and its post will help the skid stay firm to the ground's changing slope.

Installation of the Skid Dock

Referring to your site survey and plan, maneuver the first dock section into position so that the posts closest to the shore are standing in the intended location.

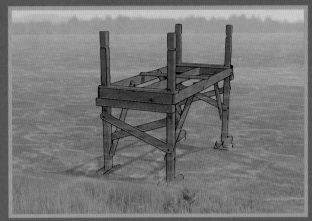

Install the first dock section, freestanding on four legs, just offshore. See that you are satisfied with its height off the water before bolting posts to additional dock sections.

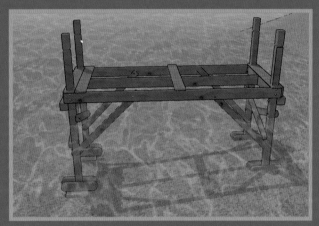

Side view of the first dock section moved into position.

If you pre-set the dock section to the appropriate height on the posts, you should see the right amount of clearance between the surface of the water and underside of the dock. And, if your depth measurements taken during the site survey were accurate, the dock section should be standing close to level. With your level on the decking, make the expected minor adjustment by shimming under the posts or digging out. Patio blocks or flagstone work well as a shim. If it

After the first dock section is positioned, use another dock section as a ramp that will bridge to shore.

Secure adjoining sections to each other by installing two carriage bolts through the headers where the sections meet.

The first section and ramp to shore should all be in place before adding more sections.

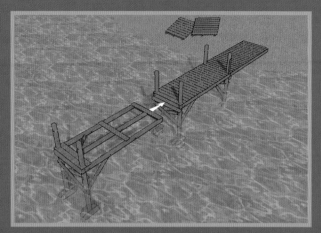

Additional sections, each with two legs at the outbound end, continue the dock straight out.

looks more like cinder blocks are needed, reposition the posts so that no more than a couple of low-profile patio blocks are needed.

Once you are satisfied with the first dock section's installation, bring the ramp section to the shore and place one end onto the ledger blocks. With a cordless drill and ⅜-inch (10-millimeter) bit, bore two holes through the adjoined headers within reach from each side so that center bolts, ⅜ inches by 4 inches (10 by 100 millimeters) with nuts and washers, can pass through and secure the ramp to the first dock section. After the center bolts are fastened, secure the deck panels onto the dock and ramp frame.

Seat the ramp into the landscape so that it is firmly positioned and shim unsupported corners if needed.

If continuing straight out, bring the second dock section to the shore and maneuver it until its inbound end is lined up with the outbound end of the first dock section. Install center bolts, as before, to secure the two dock sections together. Make the minor-level adjustments that may be needed, just as you did with the first dock section. Copy the installation procedure for additional dock sections.

As a means of anchoring your skid dock in place and providing a more solid structure for boats to glance off, lay sand bags over the tops of the skids. I recommend two per leg. Along with keeping the dock in place, they will help keep waves from washing sand out from under the skids.

A swim ladder at the narrow end will make a nice addition to a space that is too small for a boat. Bumpers on posts and along the sides to finish it off will make this one the "darndest" desirable dock on the block.

Completed skid dock.

CHAPTER 7:
PERMANENT POST DOCK

The permanent post dock is the most basic and trusted method for building a sturdy wooden fixed dock. It uses a series of large "H"-like structures formed with two posts deeply planted into the bottom and joined with a cap board above the waterline. Dock sections or stick building in place with stringers with decking will span from cap board to cap board and tie it all together. By permanent, I'm referring to an installation that is not portable and not made to be easily taken down as is often required in climates effected by severe ice. If you happen to be in a climate where ice wreaks havoc on docks, this may not be your method of choice, but rather some of the other options featured in this book.

Simple as it sounds, the task of setting posts ranges from duck soup to daunting, depending on the scale of your project. If your environment, the

A lighter-weight, manageable post is often sturdy enough to support a permanent dock.

size boat to be moored, or the local code demands posts to be over 4 inches (10 centimeters) in diameter and in more than 4 feet (1.22 meters) of depth, then consider that project to be on the daunting end for a DIYer. It would likely be best to hire a qualified contractor for installing the pilings. In salt water where wood-boring marine invertebrates are present, fat, round treated pilings are preferred since they have an outer layer of sap wood impregnated with preservative that will protect the heartwood. If your criterion doesn't require such heavy construction, let's look at the lighter version first to see if that will work for you. Given the ideal conditions, the lighter options will save you from unnecessarily over-thinking, over-building, and over-working.

The Light Version

If your dock doesn't need to stand in depths greater than 4 feet (1.22 meters) and environmental conditions or codes allow you to use 4x4 (76- by 76-millimeter) posts, then make it easy on yourself with these simple methods. For best results, the lake bed, seabed, or riverbed should not be rocky or extremely mucky. Be sure it's mostly sand or gravel, or has minimal muck with a sand or gravel base beneath it. A clay bed may or may not be ideal depending on its thickness or density. Try setting one post into the bed in question using either of the methods described (see pages 56-57) as a test before investing completely in the idea. If the bed is too hard for setting wood posts, consider one of the other fixed dock options featured in this book.

Planning for Posts

Wood Posts for the Legs—4x4 (76- by 76-millimeter) and 4x6 (76- by 140-millimeter) posts are commonly available in various lengths at many lumberyards. If treated yellow pine or Douglas fir with preservatives is your preference, recognize that what is on hand may only be suitable for ground contact, not water immersion. For decades, copper chromium arsenate (CCA) pressure-treated wood has been used for posts and pilings in water immersion. In fresh water, 0.60 pounds per cubic foot (pcf) (94.25 N/m3.), and in salt water, 2.5 pcf (393 N/m3.) have been the standard treatments. In 2003, the industry for wood preservatives discontinued the use of CCA out of concern for improper disposal habits. Though pressure-treated lumber is still on the shelves at your everyday lumberyard, it is treated with a different recipe. For marine applications, CCA-treated lumber has been available through specialty lumber suppliers, at least until the industry replaces it or until regulators prohibit it from marine applications when an alternative is available. If you use the treated posts that are readily available, first make sure they are code compliant, and that it is okay to put any treated wood at all directly into the water. Secondly, beware they may require your attention to replace sooner than that of the old CCA-treated wood. Ask your lumber supplier about polymer-treated posts, with a thick and durable plastic outer wall that encapsulates the wood, sealing it from the elements.

Driving the Post—Driving the post into the bed can be facilitated with a steel point that fastens to the bottom of your 4x4 (76- by

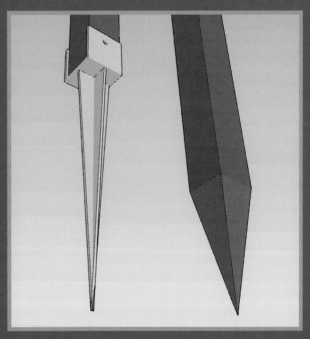

Driving posts into a lake bed, riverbed, or seabed is facilitated with a metal point attached to the bottom end. Otherwise, the post may be shaped to a point at one end by making angled cuts with a reciprocating saw.

76-millimeter) or 4x6 (76- by 140-millimeter) post. You may have seen something similar to this, for installing a rural mailbox post. It's essentially the same part, but with heavier gauge steel and hot-dip galvanized. You can buy them online from various suppliers.

For the driving tool, find a rental center that carries either a hydraulic post driver or gas-powered post driver. Find one that has a cup made to fit over the wood post so that the driver can be steadied onto the post.

If the bed is made of soft sand, you may get away with using a 10-pound (4.5-kilogram) sledgehammer to manually drive the post. Use a steel driving cap to protect the top of the post while hammering.

Gas-Powered Post Driver

Manual Post Driving with Sledgehammer and Steel Driving Cap

Your local tool rental center may have a gas-powered driver with an adapter that will fit your post size. Otherwise, you may choose to drive posts with a sledgehammer. A steel driving cap that fits over the top end of the post protects the wood from the hammer's blow.

Drive your post until the point is completely buried. Continue to drive if the wood post will seat itself into the bed as well until "refusal." During the post's descent, pause the driving periodically and check with a level both ways to see that it is plumb. Correct its position before resuming.

Turning the Post—Instead of driving into the bed, it can be done with a similar part as the point but with a ground screw. Like the point, it also fastens to the bottom end of the post. Just down from the top of the post, or where it will be in reach, bore a ⅝-inch (16-millimeter) hole through the side of the post. Then insert a 24-inch (60-centimeter) piece of rod ½ inch (12 millimeters) in diameter as a handle to hand-turn or screw the post into the bed. Turn the post in like a corkscrew until the wood post is seated into the bed. During the post's descent, pause periodically while turning and check with a level both ways to see that it is plumb. Correct its position before resuming.

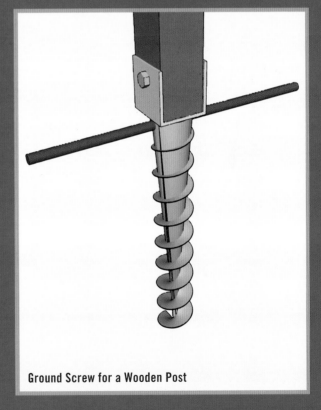

Ground Screw for a Wooden Post

Some soil conditions may be right for turning instead of driving the posts into a lake bed, riverbed, or seabed. A metal ground screw fastens to the bottom end of the post and is hand turned with a rod that slides through the top end of the screw.

Placement and Length of Posts—During your site survey, described in Completing a Site Survey for a Fixed Dock (page 40), you mapped out the location and respective depth for each post. Remember, it is important to establish the location of the dock legs or posts nearest to the shore as they will set the course for the others. Provided the water is calm, move the first dock section into position per your plan. If it is over water, let it float there temporarily as a guide to place the posts and verify the depths on your site survey.

Beginning with the legs nearest the shore, let's determine the length required by adding up the following dimensions. I will provide example measurements to help with this exercise.

• Depth at the mean water level, where the post will stand; for example, 1 foot (30 centimteters)
• Height of dock section off the water so that maximum wave height will clear underneath: 1.5 feet (45 centimeters)
• Height of post to extend up the side of the dock and above its deck surface: 3 feet (90 centimeters)
• Add extra length in case the posts seat deeper than expected: 1 foot (30 centimeters)

When all added up, the cut length for the posts nearest to the shore is 6.5 feet (195 centimeters).

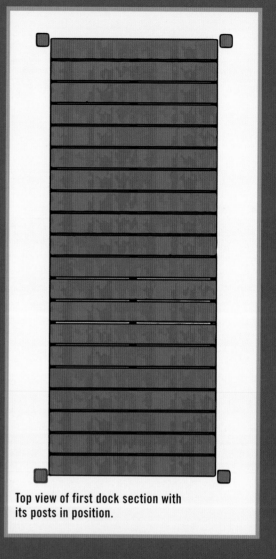

Top view of first dock section with its posts in position.

With the first dock section remaining in position, let it guide your placement and setting the first pair of posts into the bed. Keep them as close to the sides of the dock section as possible. Once they are firmly in their place, provide a temporary stop low to the water, centered on the inside surface of each post. The stops can be a long nail that is tacked in about an inch (a couple of centimeters) for the dock section to temporarily bear against while positioning the next pair of posts.

The next pair of posts at the outbound end of the dock section will likely be in deeper water. Simply add the difference in depth to the length that the previous posts were cut at to get the cut length for the next posts. For example, if the depth for the next pair of posts is 1½ feet (45 centimeters), add ½ feet (15 centimeters) to the previous cut length of 6½ feet (195 centimeters), totaling to a cut length of 7 feet (210 centimeters). With the first dock section in position, held against the stops on the first posts, set the next pair of posts the same way you set the first pair. The center of the post should be lined up with the very end of the dock section. Once the posts are set, move the dock section out of the way.

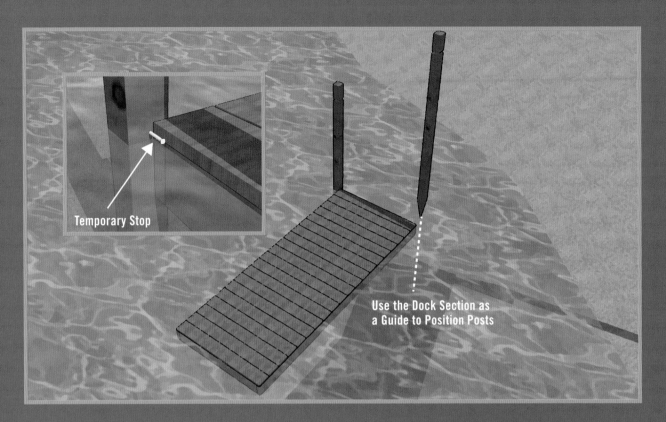

Temporary Stop

Use the Dock Section as a Guide to Position Posts

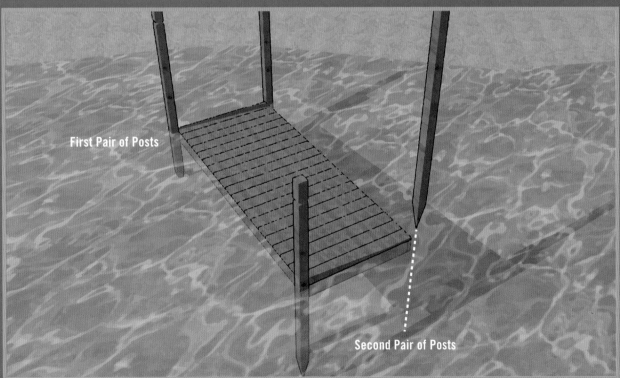

First Pair of Posts

Second Pair of Posts

Float the dock section to its desired location and use as a guide to position the posts. A protruding nail, halfway into the width of the post, provides a temporary stop for the dock section to bear against while positioning the second pair of posts.

Mount the Cap Boards—At the first pair of posts, make a mark on the posts as a reference for placing the top edge of the cap board. Place it above the maximum expected wave height. Using the example above, it would be 1½ feet (45 centimeters) above the calm water.

Next, get a horizontal measurement across the breadth of adjacent posts.

With 2x6 (38- by 140-millimeter) or 2x8 (38- by 184-millimeter) framing material, cut the cap boards to length. You'll need two for every pair of posts. Use one cap board on each side so that the posts will be sandwiched between.

Line the top edge up with the marks on the posts and temporarily clamp in place. See that they are level with both top edges. Drill and bolt the two cap boards to the posts with ⅜-inch by 7-inch (9.53- by 177.80-millimeter) galvanized carriage bolts, nuts, and flat washers, two per post. Repeat these steps to mount the cap boards on the next pair of posts.

While the next cap boards are clamped in place (but not bolted), check with a level to make sure they are even with the first pair. Gently tap with a hammer until the next cap boards match the height above the water as the first. Bolt in place just like the first pair.

Mount the Dock Section—Place the dock section up onto the cap boards between the posts. At the second pair of posts, position the dock section so that the very end comes to the center of the second pair of posts. Fasten the dock section in place with 6-inch (150-millimeter) structural screws, passing through the frame at a steep slant into the cap board.

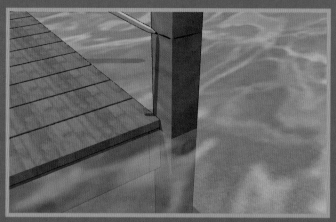

A mark is placed on the post, designating the dock's desired height off the water. The mark should be transferred, at the same height, to all other posts.

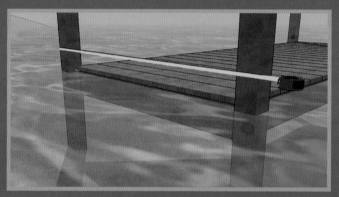

The breadth measurement across adjacent posts will be your cap board length.

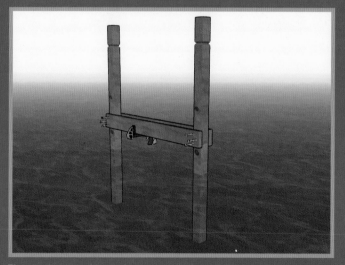

The mark on each post is your guide for positioning the cap boards before fastening. Clamps hold the cap boards in place while you drill and bolt them onto the posts.

Place the dock section upon the cap boards.

Fasten the dock section to the cap boards.

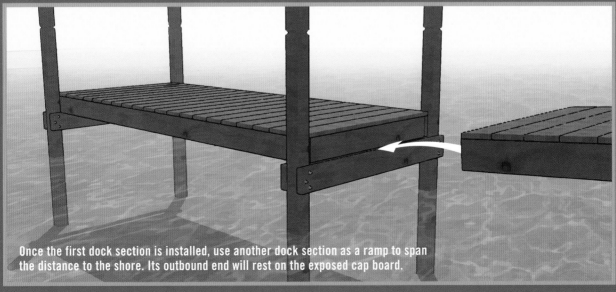

Once the first dock section is installed, use another dock section as a ramp to span the distance to the shore. Its outbound end will rest on the exposed cap board.

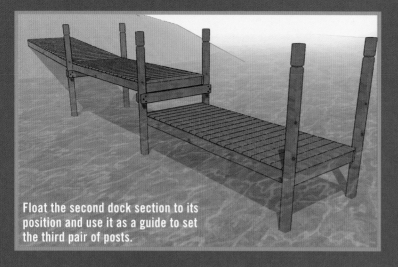

Float the second dock section to its position and use it as a guide to set the third pair of posts.

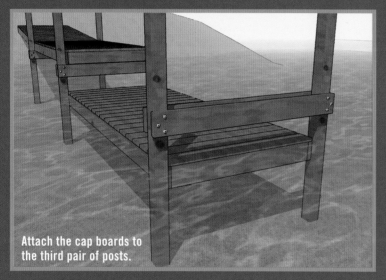

Attach the cap boards to the third pair of posts.

Place the second dock section upon its cap boards.

Adjoining Additional Dock Sections

—The second dock section can be used as your guide to locate its posts just as you did with the first dock section. Provided the water is calm, place it ahead of the first dock section with one end between and centered with the second set of posts. So that it holds its position, tack on some temporary stops as you did on the first posts to float the second dock section against, just long enough to get the third pair of posts started.

Once the posts are firmly set, attach the cap boards as before.

Float the dock section out from between the posts and place one end on the open half of the second cap board and the other end on the third cap board, snugging it up tight and flush with the first dock section. Fasten the second dock section in place as you did the first one.

Apply Cross Bracing

—As your dock goes out into deeper water with longer posts, you may find that it shakes or shimmies when walked on. If this motion is significant, it likely will only get worse over time and should be nipped in the bud sooner than later. It isn't necessary to cross brace over the entire post height, but brace about two-thirds of the height if possible. Using 2x4s (38 by 92 millimeters), cut the desired length of your braces and cut the sharp corner off the ends to 45 degrees.

Pre-drill ⅜-inch (10-millimeter) holes for fastening, 2 inches (5 centimeters) in from each end, and install using ⅜-inch by 3-inch (10- by 80-millimeter) galvanized lag bolts with a flat washer under the hex heads. I don't blame you for not wanting to go underwater for the lower end of the brace. If you don't want to turn the lags in with a ratchet wrench underwater, an air impact wrench off a compressor will work to wind them in fast. Your tools should get an immediate and thorough drying afterward if you go that way. A better way is to anticipate what legs will need braces, make the braces in advance, and have the lower end already attached when the post is being set. With a single fastener holding it on (⅜-inch by 6-inch (10- by 160-millimeter) carriage bolt with nut and washer) the brace will swing over to the opposite leg after the legs are set. Keep the braces swung inward toward the opposite post before attaching the cap boards. Ideally, the opposite end of the brace will land on the opposite post above water where attachment is more accessible. Keep in mind that bracing will only be effective if the fastening is tight. Oversized holes and wobbly bolts won't do much good; all of it needs to be tight and feel solid. Following my chapters that describe fixed docks (page 36), I have included a chapter that focuses on the principles of bracing that you'll find helpful (page 102).

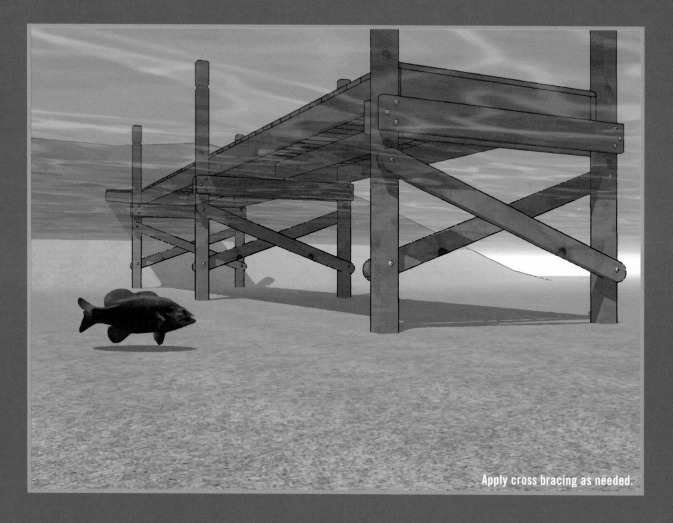

Apply cross bracing as needed.

Custom Configurations—Arrange your post dock to whatever plan you've created. Right-angled turns can be made to form "L" shape, "T" shape, and "U" shape docks.

Sample permanent post dock configurations are shown here.

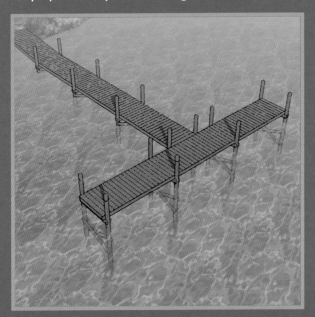

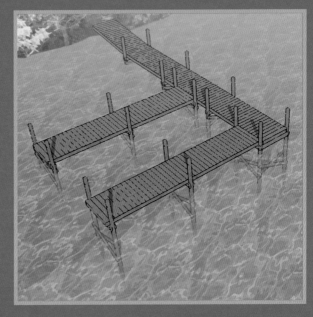

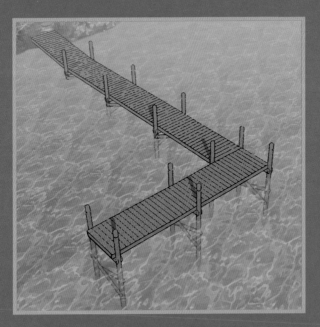

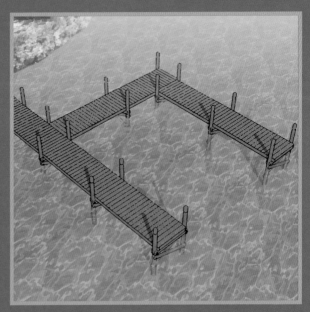

The light version of a permanent post dock provides an amazingly sturdy solution with relatively low cost and effort for the DIYer who doesn't need to go in deep with a heavy weight structure. If this lightweight version just isn't going to "cut the mustard," then peer ahead into what DIYers can do to build a heavy permanent post dock.

The Heavy Version

I certainly won't underestimate your ambition, ingenuity, and gusto to take on the daunting version of a heavy piling or post and timber permanent dock. DIYers can fill a tall order with enough patience and willingness to work for it. But I'm going to assert my opinion right here. The setting of heavy square posts or round pilings (6 inches by 6 inches [140 by 140 millimeters] or greater) into a lake, river, or seabed, should be done by a reputable marine contractor. When I think about what it will take for a DIYer to set the pilings properly, my visibility to what is potentially saved becomes blurred. Likened to building your own house, unless you happen to be a foundation contractor, it would be best if you take up the project after an expert does the concrete work. Therefore, I recommend DIYers for heavy docks take up their projects after the heavy posts or pilings are set by an expert.

Though it is not impossible for DIYers to make it happen, whose brave methods can be seen watching home videos online, let me provide a bit of insight

When your application, environment, or building code requires a heavier permanent dock, hiring a commercial pile driver is a good way to install the dock's foundation for you to build upon.

Heavy pilings are set by a marine contractor with a barge and pile driver before the DIYer takes over.

A minimum distance of six feet (two meters) into the lake bed, riverbed, or seabed is common for proper setting of large pilings. The equipment for this isn't likely to be found at your local tool rental center.

as to what they are getting into. The heavy weight of a wood piling can mislead us to expect it will cooperate under water, and that gravity will assist its descent into the bed. But instead, the post's buoyancy will cause it to resist when pushed down toward the bottom. A fatter piling with more weight would seem to aid in holding it down, but that will be offset by more buoyancy because it's more wood. As you go out deeper, the challenge intensifies with more water surrounding the post. If fighting buoyancy isn't enough, imagine the post in 6 feet (approx. 2 meters) of water depth, for instance, that must be plowed down into the bed, possibly 6 to 8 feet (2 to 2.5 meters).

The total length of the post to be handled will be about 20 feet (6 meters) in length (for the minimum proper amount to be driven into the bed) and around 200 pounds (90 kilograms). To set a post like this, DIYers have been known to make a budget barge from an old pontoon boat and mounting a low-cost jib crane on the front. While the jib crane holds the post or piling upright, the DIYer uses either a water pump to jet the post in or a hydraulic post driver powered by a portable generator to drive the post in. By the time the DIYer purchases the pilings, rounds up a crew of friends and not-so-ideal equipment, and factors the safety risks and learning curve, all in hopes to get the desired outcome . . . the option of hiring the expert starts looking pretty good.

The contractor who can set your posts or pilings will be obligated to follow the terms of your permit(s). Posts or pilings will be installed in pairs with 10 feet (3 meters) between each pair. If up to me, I would recommend round pilings over square posts. When square posts are driven as pairs, there may be difficulty keeping the flat planes parallel with each other, an important detail when you're ready to install the cap boards. With round pilings, there are no flat planes to worry about. The round piling also has its sap wood layer surrounding the heartwood, whereas the

Where permitted on lakes that drain, large posts may be set into holes and backfilled with cement.

6x6 (140- by 140-millimeter) square post has had much of the sapwood planed off at the mill. In salt water applications, the sap wood adds an important protective treated layer that resists marine boring organisms. When the contractor is done setting your pilings, you can take it from there.

Pilings in Concrete

Quite different from water jetting or pile driving into the bed, there are some lakes in the southeast U.S. where DIYers dug holes into the lake bed to set heavy wooden square posts or round pilings. They would then backfill each one with cement. These were lakes where the water would drain low during the fall and winter. If your body of water has such an opportune time when the water is absent, a DIYer could more easily manage the setting of heavy posts or pilings. This method, of course, must be code compliant before worth considering.

I once helped a friend install a wooden dock in South Carolina on a lake with a dam that routinely opened in the fall to drain the water level down about 6 feet (1.8 meters). My friend's permit allowed him to use a post hole digger where what would have been just over my head in water depth became bare ground. He poured cement into the holes where he stood up some very tall and heavy 6x6 (140- by 140-millimeter) square posts, forming what would become a concrete foot that surrounded the post. Temporary braces to the ground were used to hold the posts steady while the concrete set up.

Afterward, the cap boards were installed, standing on a step ladder if necessary.

The weight of the concrete stuck to the piling kept the piling down when the lake returned to its normal water level. The weight of a dock section when placed on top of the cap board also helped to hold everything down. Pouring concrete into the lake bed is restricted in many places so be sure to verify its compliance with the local codes before committing to it.

Building on the Pilings

For the DIYer who has opted to hire the expert who sets the posts or pilings, let's move forward to see how you would build the dock from that point. Begin with what to expect after the pile driver leaves the site. Even a reputable marine contractor with the best equipment may not get the pilings in perfect alignment to your expectations. No matter what any of us put our hands on in this life, we often meet obstacles that must be reckoned with, a reoccurring story for pile driving contractors who look at the seabed as a "pig in a poke." The contractor (if familiar with the bottom conditions in your neighborhood) may be able to tell you in advance what to expect. When finished setting, if the pilings are out of alignment here and there by 1 to 3 inches (2.54 to 7.62 centimeters), they may not lend themselves to being outfitted with dock sections that were made to pre-determined lengths and widths.

Mounting Cap Boards

Cap boards are the crossbeams that span across adjacent pilings that your stringers will rest upon. For heavy permanent post docks, use a nominal 4x8 (76- by 184-millimeter) timber cut to a length that spans across the face of both opposing pilings. Sometimes you'll see only one cap board bolted on one side, but I recommend two cap boards with bolts passing through everything at each end, sandwiching it all together.

The top of the cap board should be above the maximum wave height so that prolonged damaging waves will clear under the stringers. By measuring off the calm water, make a mark on the piling where the bottom of the cap board will meet. Transfer the mark onto the opposite side of the piling and to both sides of the adjacent piling.

So that you'll have something to rest the cap board on the pilings while bolting, nail a temporary block, such as a 2x4 (38- by 92-millimeter) that is 8 to 12 inches (184 to 305 millimeters) long, in a vertical direction with the top end even with the mark. Apply three more to the other marks.

Place the cap boards onto the blocks evenly while applying clamps near the middle of the span to hold them in place. Using a ½-inch (13-millimeter) extension drill bit, bore two holes through each end of the cap boards so that carriage bolts will pass through everything, the cap boards and piling, clamping it all together.

Counterbore about 1 inch (25 millimeters) into the end of the hole where the nut and washer fasten so that with the proper length bolt, its threads will be less likely to snag a ship or swimmer.

Cap boards and cross bracing on the pilings.

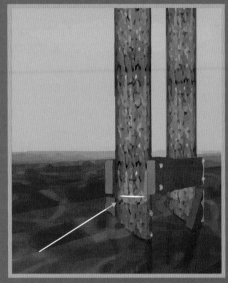

Mark piling above the maximum wave height, indicating the base of the cap boards' position.

Temporary blocks are nailed onto the pilings and flush to the marks. They provide a ledge to rest the cap board before fastening.

Clamp cap boards together for bolting to pilings.

Counterbore fastener holes so that the ends of the bolt will nest into the wood, preventing abrasion.

Adding stringers on top of the cap boards.

Bridge Cap Boards with Stringers

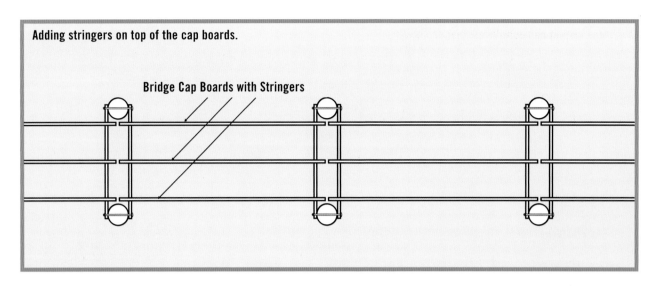

Insert Headers at End of Stringers

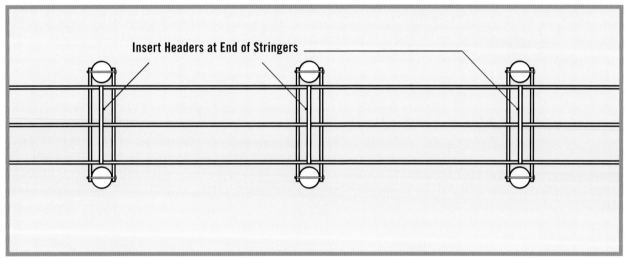

Apply Decking

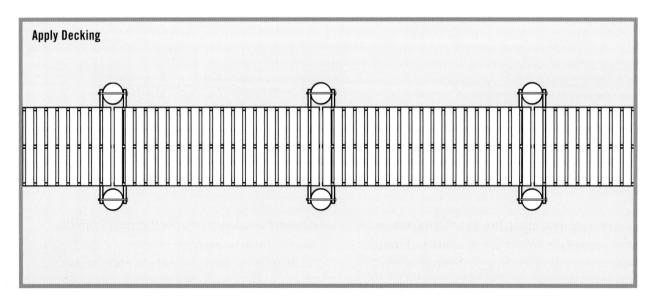

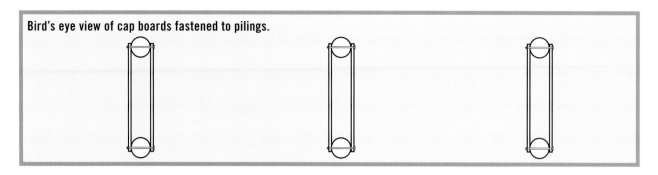

Bird's eye view of cap boards fastened to pilings.

To minimize carpentry work over the water, pre-built sections of dock may be brought out to the pilings and installed upon the cap boards.

It would be best to hold off on pre-building sections until after the posts or pilings are set. Since this is a heavy permanent dock, you may find it easier to stick-build the dock in place, plank by plank versus maneuvering sections out onto the pilings. This will also be a more forgiving proposition if the pilings end up set irregularly. You can then custom fit the frame to the spacing available.

Adding Stringers

With each pair of pilings spaced 8 or 10 feet (2.4 or 3 meters) apart, use heavy stringers such as nominal 4x8s (76 by 184 millimeters) to span from cap board to cap board. If you plan to use wood decking such as pressure-treated yellow pine,

the stringers can be up to 2 feet (61 centimeters) apart. A 4-foot (1.22-meter) wide dock would need one stringer in the middle and one on each side. If you plan to use a plastic deck product, such as composites and the like, expect to place them no less than 16 inches (41 centimeters) apart. In that case, with so many stringers required, you may want them on the outside of the frame to be 4x8s (76 by 184 millimeters) and the intermediate ones on the inside to be 2x8s (38 by 184 millimeters). Always follow the deck manufacturer's specifications for stringer spacing. Cut the outside stringers to a length that will extend from the center of one piling to the center of the next. The intermediate stringers should be shorter at each end, enough so that a header can be fitted flush between the outside members while butting to the intermediate one(s). I recommend using 8-inch (200-millimeter) marine-grade structural screws to fasten the framing together.

Add the Decking

Cut decking to a length that matches the width of the frame so that it is flush along the side. Overhanging the decking, as done on house decks and porches, may help prevent splitting while fastening, but will provide an edge for a boat's gunwale to snag, causing damage to the boat and dock. If you're concerned about fasteners potentially splitting the ends of deck boards, pre-drill along the ends for the nails or screws in those spots.

Pre-panelized decking, made from a resin base, is available from a variety of manufacturers in standard lengths and widths. For a maintenance-free, clean, and professional appearance, these panels go down

Close-up of a perforated deck panel.

Perforated pre-panelized decking allows storm waves to break up through its surface and prevent damage.

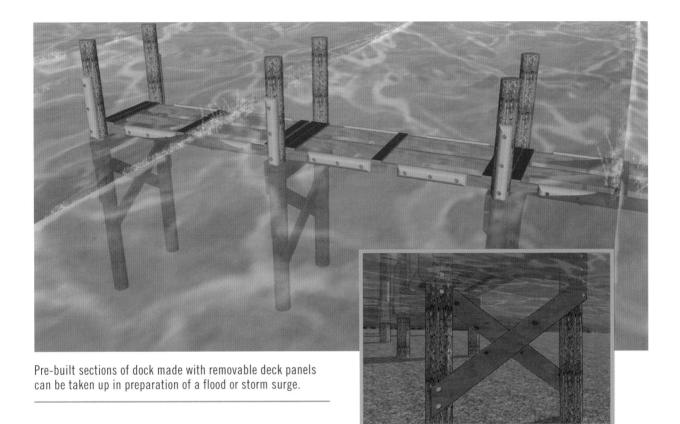

Pre-built sections of dock made with removable deck panels can be taken up in preparation of a flood or storm surge.

Add cross bracing as needed.

fast with screws and do not require cutting or trimming provided your frame dimensions were made to the product's specifications. Many of them are perforated and intended for docks regularly subjected to floods and damaging waves.

In Chapter 3, which features dock sections, I described a method of building and benefits of removable deck panels that set onto the frame. Just as the perforated pre-panelized decking prevents storm damage from flooding, so does removable decking. In the event of an impending flood from something like a hurricane storm surge on tidal waters, the decking made into ideal-sized panels for portability can be taken out and stored high away from the dock. The remaining skeletal frame with less surface area will more likely end up unscathed from large pounding waves.

Braces Below the Cap Boards

Finally, if there is any shaking about the dock when walking upon it, apply bracing where desired.

For portions of dock in water over four feet (12 centimeters) deep, the chances increase that bracing will be desired. Using 2x4s (38 x 92 millimeters) or 2x6s (38 x 140 millimeters) as a cross brace on adjacent pilings work remarkably well. The trick is to attach the end that is underwater. Some DIYers attach a cross brace just under the cap boards that only extends a short distance underwater to its opposite end where it is easy to reach. The further down your able to attach it on the leg, the more effective it will be. You can learn more about bracing ahead in Chapter 10: Stabilizing a Fixed Dock (page 102).

I won't deny that building your own permanent heavy-duty fixed dock will require an elevated level of ambition, tenacity, strength, and agility over the lighter options. But like any daunting challenge, abide by safe standards and pace yourself by thinking each step through. Your patience will pay off.

CHAPTER 8:
POST AND BRACKET DOCK

A DIYer's go-to leg support for light-duty fixed docks is often the 4x4 (76- by 76-millimeter) post. Available at local lumberyards, durable, and nice looking at a relatively low cost are reasons enough that many DIYers won't consider another choice. Already, in this book, I've given it a fair amount of attention, first in Chapter 6, with its application to the portable skid dock, and then, in Chapter 7, to the lightweight permanent fixed dock. Here, once again, the 4x4 (76- by 76-millimeter) post is in the spotlight, this time with special brackets that will help you change the dock's height and re-level if needed. Before starting your project, consider the possibility that you may want or need to change the height of your dock from where you originally set it. You may also experience a leg or two settling into the bed, a common occurrence with light-duty fixed

Ease of height adjustment and leveling is made possible by a special bracket made to clamp a wooden post against the side of a wooden dock.

This lake will freeze over in winter, releasing its destructive force, but the dock's adjustable post brackets allow it to be taken apart—leg by leg and section by section—for removal at summer's end.

docks that could have you adding blocks and shims to correct it. Imagine making a significant height change to a dock whereby its position is held by through-bolting. It would be a big job to back bolts out of the wood and then reinstall them in another spot. The post and bracket method, however, will knock the effort and time down by simply loosening the bracket's grip on the post. If you're in a climate with severe ice that requires dock structures to be taken apart and removed before winter, the brackets' clamps can be loosened for quick removal of the posts and takedown of the sections. Whether you're in a warm or cold climate, though, all will appreciate the advantages of adjustability.

Suppliers for the post bracket usually offer other related parts that facilitate the use of 4x4 (76- by 76-millimeter) posts as dock legs. They include:

- **Post feet** that mount to the bottom of the post to prevent settling into silty beds. The same feet have a square hole in the middle so that the post can be pointed and will pass through the foot to be driven into the bed.
- **Brace clamps** hold a cross brace to the post so that you won't have to drill and bolt through the post. This is especially helpful when attaching braces underwater.
- **J-brackets** are specialty parts that facilitate the attachment of an adjoining dock section.
- **Corner irons** are bolted into a butt joint for reinforcement.

   A word about quality: The specialty hardware components that I'm mostly experienced with have been made from extruded marine-grade aluminum. I was never disappointed with the functioning, strength, and corrosion-resistance these parts offered. Spoken from a true dock builder, "There is no time on the jobsite for hardware to prematurely fail. There are too many other surprises that can come up; poorly made parts are ones that no one needs." Therefore, choosing good quality parts for my customers was always a top priority. Upon developing any new part meant for wood dock construction, I found it satisfying to test to the breaking point. A component would pass its test if the wood broke first. Let me encourage you, don't skimp on the quality of these parts. Wherever you find them, do your best to compare product offerings and choose what will be up to the task, providing years of trouble-free service.

Finding these parts: If your local building supply centers do not carry the parts, you can find them online and the manufacturers may ship directly to you. In this book, I've provided a source index to help you (see page 249).

The maximum depth for a post and bracket dock: Just like the permanent post dock, the post and bracket dock can be installed in depths up to 4 feet (1.22 meters). I would never tell you that you can't go deeper. Just remember, the deeper you go, the more resistance you'll get from buoyancy in the posts when pushed underwater. Just as a test, take a long wooden 4x4 (76- by 76-millimeter) post out in the water—either from a dinghy or another dock—and hold it vertically while pushing underwater. Get a feel for the maximum depth you'll be comfortable installing them into.

Getting Started

Let's look at the special brackets needed to assemble this dock properly. As with most of the previous methods, I'll use dock sections that feature synthetic, pre-panelized, perforated decking.

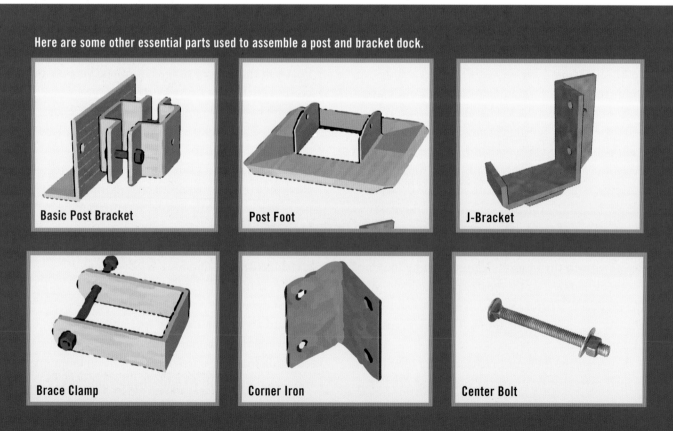

Here are some other essential parts used to assemble a post and bracket dock.

Basic Post Bracket

Post Foot

J-Bracket

Brace Clamp

Corner Iron

Center Bolt

Preparing the Post and Bracket Dock

Have a copy of your plan in hand and use it as your guide to place the hardware components. Beginning with your dock sections, the building blocks to any plan, turn them over so that you can easily access the underside for fastening hardware. I recommend that all hardware should be fastened with through bolts, not lags.

For the Dock Sections:

Reinforce the backside of each exterior corner butt joint with a corner iron.

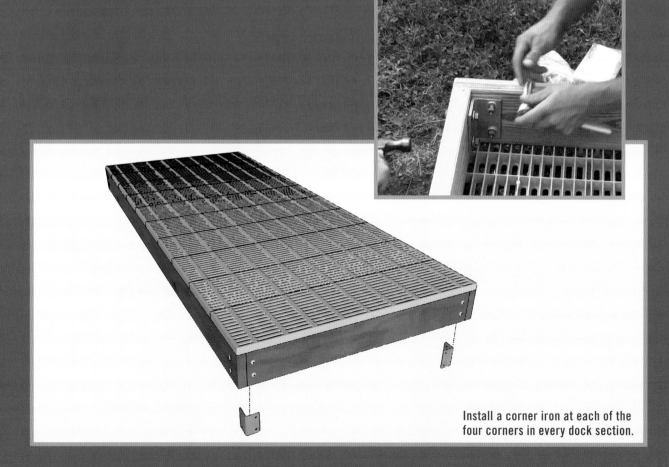

Install a corner iron at each of the four corners in every dock section.

The first dock section usually stands off the shore on four legs, much like a table. Attach four post brackets on the first section, one near each corner, according to your dock plan.

Attach J-brackets to the outbound end and the inbound end of the first dock section. Place them, through-bolted, about a hand's length in from each end.

Each additional dock section that continues the dock straight out will have two post brackets and two J-brackets on the outbound end. The last section out will not need the J-brackets.

Where there is an "L" or "T" section connecting, attach J-brackets at the proper outbound end or side so that it is ready to receive the adjoining dock section during installation. Seams where sections join need a minimum of two J-brackets. For seems that exceed 4 feet (61 centimeters), add one J-bracket for every additional 2 feet (30 centimeters) of seam.

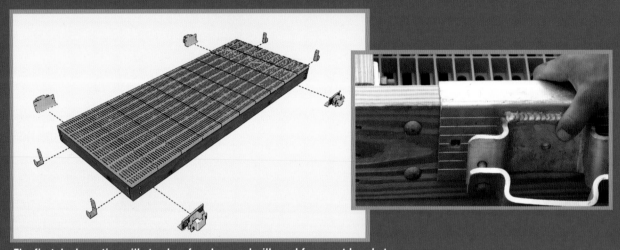

The first dock section will stand on four legs and will need four post brackets attached as shown. J-brackets attach at each end of the first section for adjoining additional dock sections, including one used as a ramp to reach the shore.

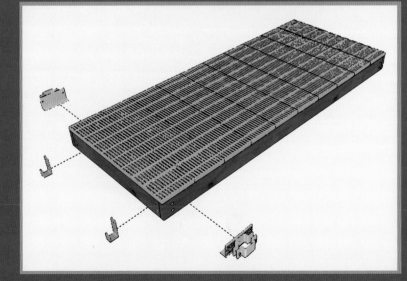

On the second dock section, only two post brackets are required, fastened at its outbound end. The end without post brackets will be supported at the J-brackets on the previously installed dock section. For every dock section you plan to add, attach J-brackets to the one before it.

Add J-brackets where you anticipate adjoining another dock section.

Parts Arrangement for Adding an "L" Section

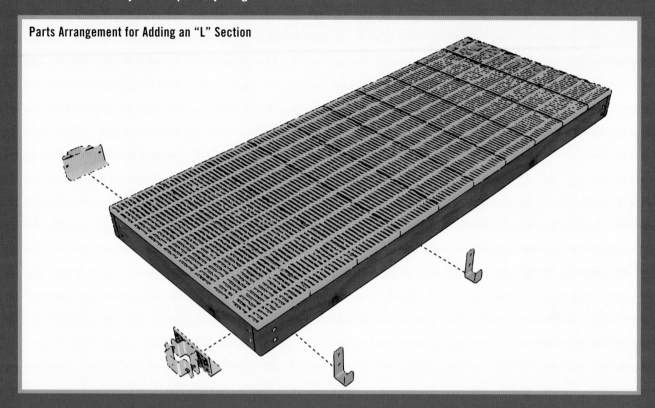

Parts Arrangement for Adding a "T" Section

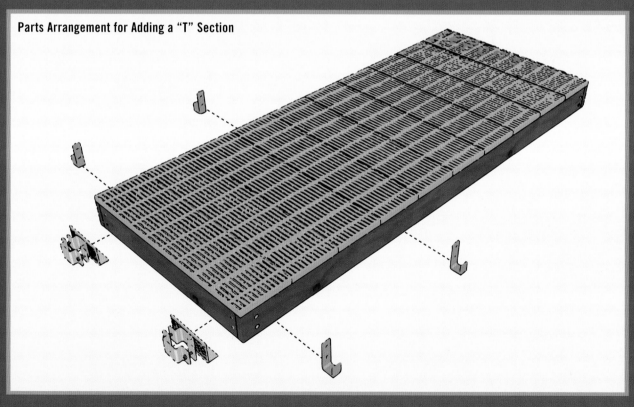

For the Posts:

Your plan from the site survey should indicate all the posts and depths where each of them stand. To prepare the length of each post, start with the water depth and add to it the amount you set, if any, into the bed beneath the water. Then add the distance from the waterline to the decking. Be sure there is enough height off the water for the largest anticipated wave to clear under the frame. Finally, add something for height above the decking.

If you plan to drive the posts into the bed versus letting them stand flat on the bed, use the sabre saw to cut a symmetrical point on the end of each post. If desired, attach the post foot, fastened with lag bolts, just above the point. I recommend numbering the posts and corresponding post brackets to match up during installation.

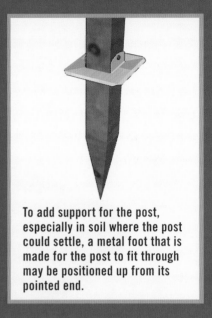

To add support for the post, especially in soil where the post could settle, a metal foot that is made for the post to fit through may be positioned up from its pointed end.

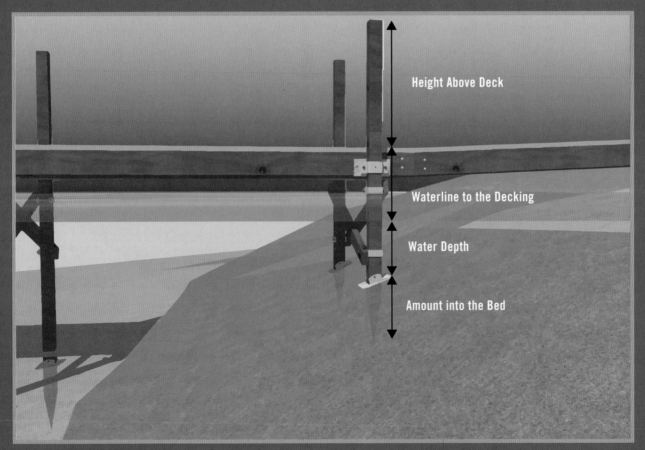

Height Above Deck

Waterline to the Decking

Water Depth

Amount into the Bed

Estimate the length for each post by adding up: 1) the amount to be set into the lake bed, riverbed, or seabed; 2) the water depth where the leg stands; 3) the height above the water's surface (enough so that the largest wave will clear below decking); and 4) any additional desired amount extending above the decking.

Installation of the Post and Bracket Dock

Please refer to the Special Safety Measures first (see page 12).

The First Dock Section—Bring the first dock section with four post brackets to the water. Place it on top of the temporary flotation to hold it off the water. Then drift into position so that the post brackets at the shore are over the location where you want the first pair of posts (dock legs) to set.

Insert one post at a time down through the bracket. If there are post feet to go on the

TOOLS REQUIRED
- Cordless drill for center bolts
- Cordless impact driver with socket adapter
- Drive cap
- Sledgehammer
- Ratchet wrench set
- Level
- Leveling winch
- Flotation for holding up the dock sections, such as a foam billet, canoe, or skiff

4x4 (76 x 76mm) Post Driving Cap

Leveling Winch

Pipe with Pipe Foot

Foam Billet

Jack Pole Extension

A foam billet, jack, or leveling winch on a jack pole offers temporary support for a dock section while posts are inserted through the post brackets and set into the lake bed, riverbed, or seabed. A driving cap over the post protects the wood while driving with a sledgehammer.

Installing the first dock section.

While the dock section is temporarily supported, the post bracket guides the post to its position into the lake bed, riverbed, or seabed.

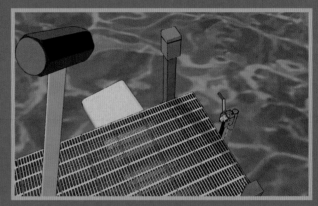
When possible, drive the posts into the lake bed, riverbed, or seabed. For light-duty installations on a firm bottom and shallow waters, a post may simply set undriven at the bottom.

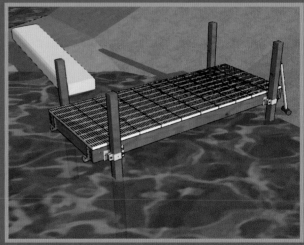
Finalize the dock section's height, and level after the posts are driven.

posts, open the clamp on the post bracket so that the post can go into the bracket. Then close the clamp over the post, but do not tighten.

Using a drive cap on top of the post to protect the wood, tap and drive each post into the bottom using a sledgehammer until refusal. A gas-powered post driver that has an adapter to fit over a post may also be used. While driving, check periodically to see that the post remains plumb.

Once the posts are all set, raise up the dock section on the posts to the desired height, one end at a time. Using the level across the deck, shift the dock section until it is level between adjacent posts. Proceed to the opposite end and repeat the raising and leveling procedure. The leveling winch can be used to assist with holding up the section. Once the dock section is level and all the post brackets tight, drift the flotation out of the way and prepare for the next dock section to be used as your ramp from the shore.

On the shore end of the first dock section, see that two additional J-brackets are in place that face the shore. Bring the dock section intended for the ramp, that we will call the "ramp section," to the shore.

The ideal J-bracket should have enough play in it so that the ramp section can be tilted if the elevation on the shore is different than that of the decking. If the fit is snug into the J-bracket when tilting the ramp section, choose a longer bolt for the bottom of the J-bracket and shim with washers as needed to angle the J-bracket.

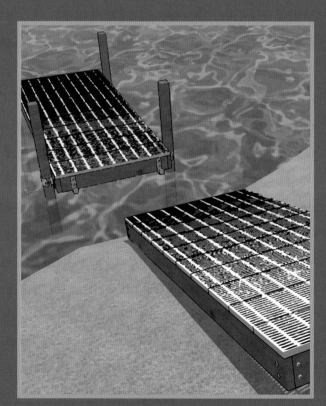

Prepare to attach a dock section as a ramp to shore.

If necessary, J-brackets can be shimmed to prevent binding from the ramp section's slant.

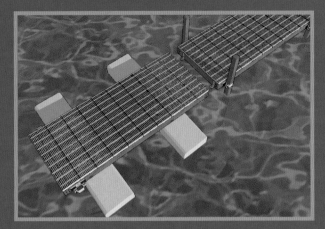

Adjoining an additional section of dock.

Before its posts are attached, an additional section is adjoined to the previously installed dock section while its outbound end is temporarily supported by a foam billet.

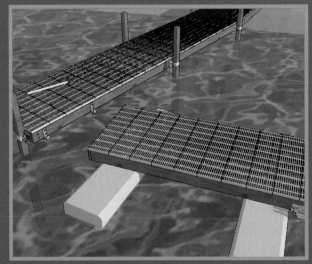

Adding a dock section to the side to make an "L" or a "T" shaped dock.

If continuing straight out, the second dock section will have only two post brackets on the outbound end. Bring it to the water and place over the temporary flotation. Drift into position and raise the inbound end onto the J-brackets.

With a cordless drill, bore a ⅜-inch (9.53-centimeter) hole near the center, through the headers of both dock sections where they meet. Install a ⅜-inch by 4-inch (9.53- by 101.60-centimeter) carriage bolt with nut and washer to secure the inbound end in place. Leave loose until the work on the outbound end is complete.

Install the posts on the outbound end the same way you did on the first dock section. Raise up the outbound end, level, and tighten the clamps and tighten the carriage bolt that secures the two sections together.

Repeat these steps for additional dock sections.

If there is wobble when walking upon the dock, apply cross bracing made with 2x4s (38 by 76 millimeters) to the posts. You may either attach using lags or use a brace clamp that holds it to the post. The brace clamp will not require pre-drilling the post underwater. You can learn more about bracing and stabilizing your post and bracket dock following the chapters on featured types of fixed docks (see page 36).

Trim the posts and finish with either a handsaw or cordless circular saw. Clean up the ends by sanding the edges or apply a finish cap.

Your post and bracket dock combines adjustability, durability, and charm all in one. One problem you might have while enjoying this dock is answering the call to come in for dinner. Dress this dock up with some of the ideas in this book, such as a ladder, bumpers, and solar lights.

Where the header of one section meets the header of another using J-brackets, they should be fastened together with a bolt that passes through both headers.

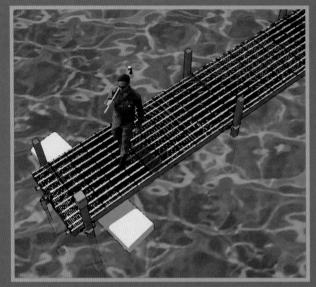

Completing installation of the second section.

Now the real fun begins.

Trim the posts as desired to finish.

Clamps made to fit around the wooden post can be pre-fastened to the wooden brace and installed in the water without power tools.

CHAPTER 9:
THE PIPE LEG DOCK

Amazingly sturdy, while made to knock down and store away before Old Man Winter's grip, the pipe leg dock is a DIY favorite in climates that experience severe ice. Every spring, the fixed dock gets re-erected and is relied on for yet another season of dependable service. The pipe leg is nothing more than standard-sized galvanized steel water pipe that can be bought at many home center, plumbing, or fence supply stores. Unlike the buoyant wooden post that resists your effort to set into the lake bed, riverbed, or seabed, a pipe leg cooperates fully, making it easier to install into deeper water.

Having to face the task of reinstalling every year, it's no wonder DIYers like the pipe. Its slender cylindrical shape facilitates driving into the bottom, a practice that pins the dock in place like staking a circus tent. The driven pipes stiffen, adding to the dock's stability while providing a solid structure to moor the boat against. In the fall when it's time to remove the dock, pipes will pull up with the turn of a pipe wrench.

A fixed dock properly installed on pipe legs provides a solid port for tying off.

Pipe legs may nest into stabilized rocks or be driven into a firm, gravelly bed.

Pipes cannot take all the credit for the dock's durability and ease of portability. Specialty hardware fittings that hold the pipe leg to the wooden dock section have setscrews or, sometimes, a clamp that grabs and holds on to the pipe at your desired height.

Companies that manufacture the basic pipe bracket for docks usually offer a host of parts that fit onto the pipe for various functions. Some of the parts you can expect to find would include leg bracing, brackets for accessory attachment, and pipe leg contact with the bottom. Though the offerings vary from company to company, they should have a broad enough line to help you get the essential dock completed. Expect each manufacturer to provide information about their alloy, process they use, coating type (if it is steel), and gauge or thickness. Comparing these kinds of details often explains the price disparity between brands. Not always, but too often, a choice based on lowest price is a choice toward aggravation later that is not worth the money you saved in the beginning. If seeing is

believing, build confidence in the product you're interested in by looking for the manufacturer's website gallery. Pictures that boast many examples of their products in use may be a clue as to how serious they are about their quality.

The hardware I mainly used in my work was made of either hot-dip galvanized, welded steel, or welded marine-grade extruded aluminum. As for the size of pipe to use, dock pipe components are on the market to fit 1¼-inch, 1½-inch, and 2-inch (32-, 38-, and 51-millimeter) pipe. I chose 1½-inch (38-millimeter) pipe, schedule #40, that measures 1⅞ inches (47 millimeters) O.D.—a good "middle of the road" size that wasn't overkill nor too light to handle the job.

Most of the docks I made using pipe legs were typical residential or light commercial grade and would hold any recreational boat under normal use. With all the challenges I could possibly run into from job to job, I always believed that the hardware should never be the root of a problem; therefore,

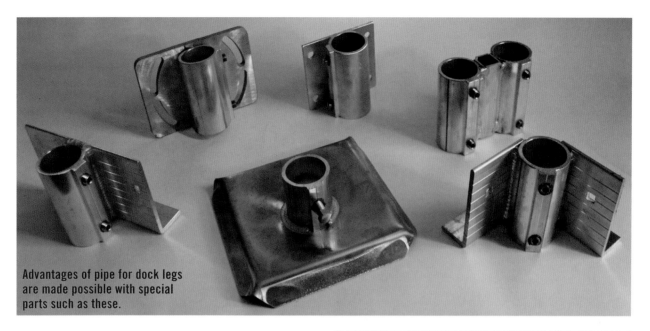

Advantages of pipe for dock legs are made possible with special parts such as these.

good hardware was something I committed to. The hardware should never break under normal use and should always make the job go easier. Here are some added hardware pointers to keep in mind.

1. Look at the different pipe sizes at a local hardware store before you buy the dock hardware to get a feel for what you're willing to handle and what will stand up to the job. For most applications, I stuck with 1½ inches (38 millimeters), schedule #40.

2. Be sure to use the appropriate size pipe for the hardware you bought.

3. I recommend hardware that has nothing protruding out into the expected path of a person or a boat. Setscrews, for example, should be on the side of a pipe bracket where they are less likely to gouge something or somebody.

4. I recommend that the setscrews on the pipe hardware be case hardened with a cup point that will cut into the pipe for a tight grip.

5. See to it that the butt joints at the exterior corners of every dock section get reinforced with a through bolted corner iron. Some pipe brackets are made to fit at the corner to reinforce the butt joint so you get the pipe bracket and corner iron all in one.

A steel galvanized pipe that is referred to as 1½" (38mm) in size has an outside diameter that nominally measures 1⅞" (48mm). The parts manufacturer should specify the size pipe to use with their parts.

The success of a dock supported on pipe legs and special parts depends on the set screw's hold. A cup point on the end of a set screw has a grip like no other.

When supporting a dock on pipe legs, reinforcement at the corners of a section of dock prevents butt joints from pulling apart.

While holding the dock section onto the pipe leg, this bracket also reinforces the corner butt joint.

What You're Investing In

It's easy to recognize that the pipe leg dock, with the cost of the pipe and parts, comes with a higher price than building with wood posts that just bolt on. It's important to keep in mind that you're buying the ease of set-up and or take-down, a necessity for docks in colder climates. There is undoubtedly a great value in the right product to make this process go smoother. The instructions that follow will give excellent guidance toward getting a dock that will perform and look good for years to come, but it will likely require a full commitment, including enough of the right parts into the job. Leaving parts out or skimping on crucial details because they weren't in the budget could result in a compromise for the dock's ease of handling and longevity. I've always found that the advantages gained by using the right amount of good parts more than justify their cost.

Getting Started

Let's walk through the assembly and installation process to completing your pipe leg dock. Begin with choosing your dock section sizes that are detailed in your plan.

For this exercise, I will choose sections with removable deck panels for improved ease of portability.

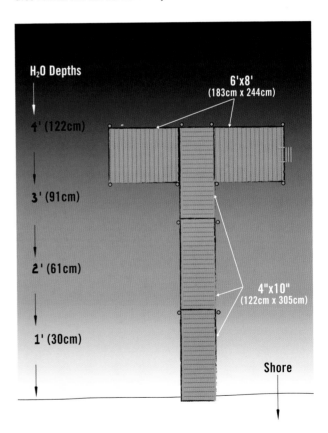

Here is a sample plan of a dock in sections that might resemble yours. It indicates where the pipe legs will be on each of the dock sections.

Preparing the Pipe Leg Dock

Every manufacturer of pipe leg hardware should have the common pipe bracket that holds a pipe leg to the side of a dock section. Though I've provided an illustration of what that can look like, you'll find they vary in appearance from brand to brand.

From my experience, the one I have been most pleased with fits onto the corner of a dock section and reinforces the butt joint while providing the leg socket. This is the pipe bracket I have featured in my instructions, just ahead, that I refer to as a corner socket.

PARTS REQUIRED
- Pipe brackets or corner sockets
- Corner irons
- J-brackets
- Center bolts
- Pipe feet
- Brace kits

Common pipe socket.

Corner socket.

Common pipe socket.

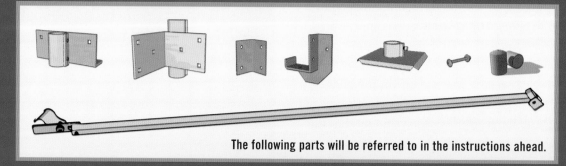
The following parts will be referred to in the instructions ahead.

Have a copy of your plan in hand and use it as your guide to place the hardware components onto the dock sections.

Though the illustrations ahead show the dock sections in the upright position, it will help you to turn them over for easy access while attaching the hardware. I recommend that all hardware should be fastened with through bolts, not lags.

TOOLS REQUIRED
- Cordless drill with bits
- Ratchet wrench set
- Pipe cutter
- Hammer (to tap bolts)

For the Dock Sections:

Reinforce the backside of each exterior corner butt joint with a corner iron. If using corner sockets, you may omit corner irons where the corner socket is used.

The first dock section usually stands off the shore on four legs, much like a table. Attach four corner sockets on the first section, one near or on each corner, according to your dock plan.

Attach J-brackets to the outbound end of the first dock section. If you'll be using another dock section as a ramp to bridge from the first dock section back to shore, attach J-brackets to the inbound end of the first dock section as well.

Each additional dock section that continues the dock straight out will need two pipe brackets or two corner sockets and two J-brackets on the outbound end. The last section out will not need the J-brackets.

Turning sections of dock over while attaching parts enables full access for securing fasteners.

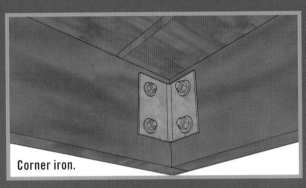

Corner iron.

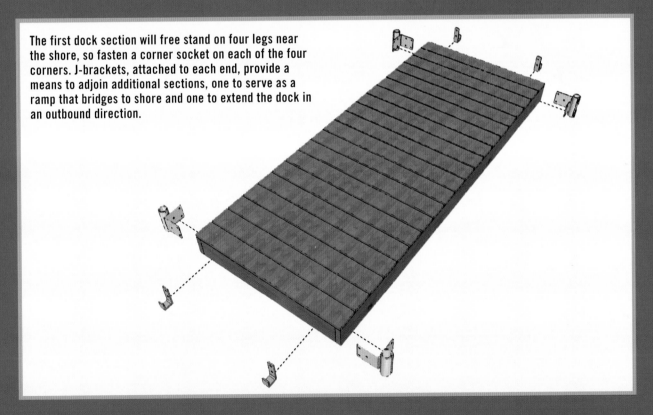

The first dock section will free stand on four legs near the shore, so fasten a corner socket on each of the four corners. J-brackets, attached to each end, provide a means to adjoin additional sections, one to serve as a ramp that bridges to shore and one to extend the dock in an outbound direction.

Where there is an "L" or "T" section, attach J-brackets at the proper outbound end or side so that it is ready to receive the adjoining dock section during installation. Where dock sections come together, typically two J-brackets are enough at the seam. If a seam is greater than 4 feet (1.22 meters) because the sections are wider, then another J-bracket should be added, one for every additional 2 feet (60.96 centimeters) of seam.

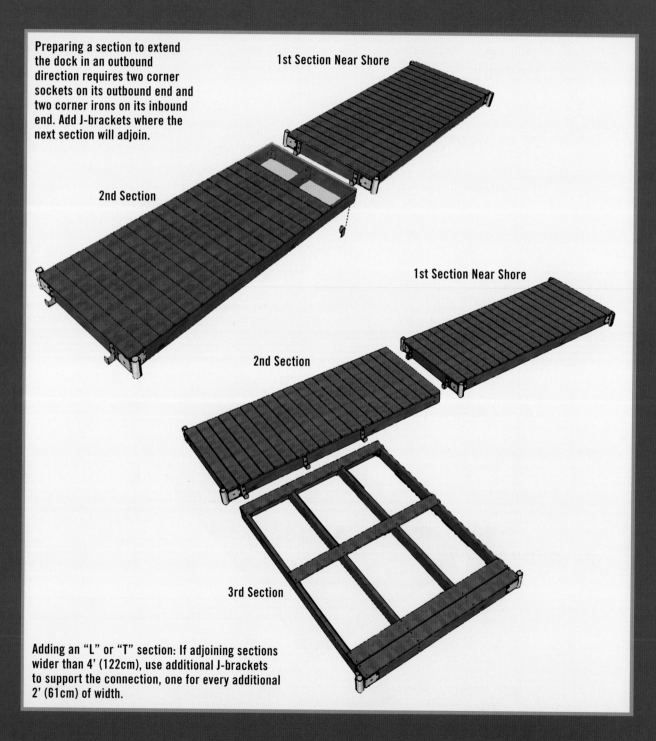

Preparing a section to extend the dock in an outbound direction requires two corner sockets on its outbound end and two corner irons on its inbound end. Add J-brackets where the next section will adjoin.

1st Section Near Shore

2nd Section

1st Section Near Shore

2nd Section

3rd Section

Adding an "L" or "T" section: If adjoining sections wider than 4' (122cm), use additional J-brackets to support the connection, one for every additional 2' (61cm) of width.

When all the dock hardware has been mounted onto the dock sections, we can begin transitioning toward installing them into the water.

Determine Your Pipe Lengths

Your plan from the site survey should indicate all the pipe legs and depths where each of them stand. Affecting your overall length of each pipe leg will be your decision to drive them into the bed by 1 to 2 feet (30 to 60 centimeters) versus not driving them. Driving them will improve the dock's stability while walking upon and capacity for holding your larger boats moored alongside. At dock removal time in the autumn, pipes must be removed from the bed and up through the sockets so that dock sections can be easily brought ashore. The turn of a plumber's pipe wrench will break the suction if needed. An alternative for easier installation and removal would be to apply a pipe foot to each pipe leg and let it nest into the bed. Though this is less work than driving and pulling pipes out every year, the dock will only moor light boats, such as dinghies and kayaks. A combination of driving pipe and using the feet is possible if the pipe foot is adjustable, made so that the leg can pass through it. The foot should

have a setscrew that allows you to adjust the position on the leg where desired. You'll be driving the leg into the bed to a modest distance with relative ease until the foot seats into the bed. Removing the leg will be less work when the time comes.

To prepare the length of each pipe leg, start with the water depth and add to it the amount you expect to drive, if any, into the bed beneath the water. Depending on the density of the bed, this could be a range of up to 2 feet (60 centimeters) more per leg. If the bottom is extra-soft sand or on the mucky side, then plan on using adjustable pipe feet set to your predetermined height on the leg so that you're not driving more than 2 feet (60 centimeters) into the bed. Since the pipe may not reach a firm base, such as clay or gravel, the pipe foot will prevent it from settling. Then add the distance from the waterline to the decking. Be sure there is enough height off the water for the largest anticipated wave to clear under the frame. Finally, add something for height above the decking; I typically add 30 inches (75 centimeters), give or take. This allows for adjusting the dock higher if needed or attaching dock bumpers and other helpful accessories.

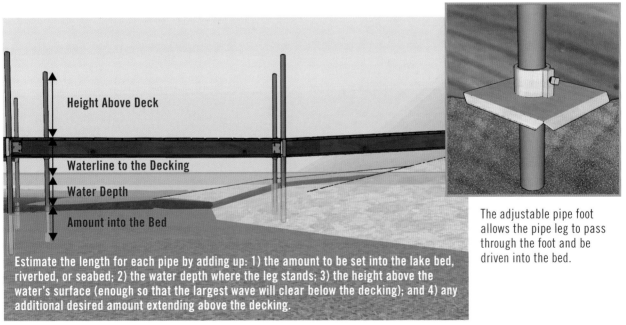

Height Above Deck

Waterline to the Decking

Water Depth

Amount into the Bed

Estimate the length for each pipe by adding up: 1) the amount to be set into the lake bed, riverbed, or seabed; 2) the water depth where the leg stands; 3) the height above the water's surface (enough so that the largest wave will clear below the decking); and 4) any additional desired amount extending above the decking.

The adjustable pipe foot allows the pipe leg to pass through the foot and be driven into the bed.

Installation of the Pipe Leg Dock

My recommendation for the temporary flotation is a swim raft, preferably an 8x8 (2.5- by 2.5-meter) or 8x10 (2.5- by 3-meter) to provide plenty of standing area on each side of the dock while you are preparing to support it by the pipe legs.

Please refer to the Special Safety Measures on page 12 before installing.

TOOLS REQUIRED

- Cordless drill for center bolts
- Cordless impact driver with socket adapter
- Drive cap
- Sledgehammer
- Ratchet wrench set
- Level
- Leveling winch
- Flotation for holding up the dock sections, such as a foam billet, canoe, or skiff

Special tools that will come in handy for installing a fixed dock on pipe legs.

Leveling Winch   Adjustable Jack Pole for the Winch   Driving Cap

A swim raft can make a great tool for floating dock sections into position while serving as a work platform.

The First Dock Section

Bring the first dock section with four pipe brackets or corner sockets to the water. Place on top of the temporary flotation to hold it above the water, then drift it into position so that the pipe brackets or corner sockets near the shore are over the location where you want the first pair of pipe legs to set.

Insert one pipe leg at a time down through the pipe bracket/corner sockets. If there are pipe feet to be used on the legs, put them on after you pass the leg through the pipe bracket.

Using a drive cap on top of the pipe leg to prevent damage to it, tap and drive each pipe leg into the bottom using a sledgehammer until refusal or until the pipe is tight in the bed. A gas-powered post driver may be used in place of a drive cap and sledgehammer. Just be careful not to unnecessarily over-drive the pipe legs, making them difficult to remove before winter. While driving, check periodically to see that the pipe remains plumb.

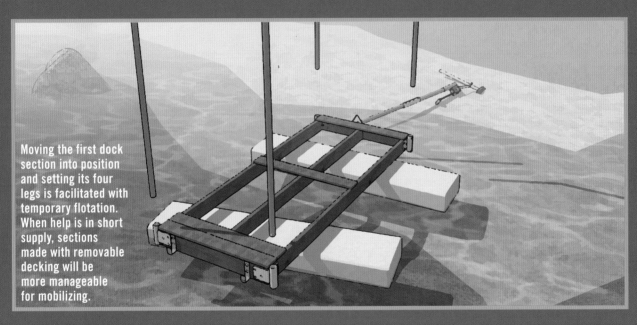

Moving the first dock section into position and setting its four legs is facilitated with temporary flotation. When help is in short supply, sections made with removable decking will be more manageable for mobilizing.

If pipe feet on the legs are desired, attach in place once the pipe leg is passed through the pipe socket.

When driving the pipe into the bed with a sledgehammer, place a driving cap over the top end of the pipe to prevent damage while striking.

Once the pipe legs are all set, raise up the dock section on the pipes to the desired height, one end at a time. Using the level across the deck, shift the dock section until it is level between adjacent pipe legs. Proceed to the opposite end and repeat the raising and leveling procedure. The leveling winch comes in handy by holding up the dock section before the pipe legs are in place. Once the dock section is level and all the pipe bracket's setscrews are tight to the pipe, drift the flotation out of the way and prepare for the next dock section to be used as your ramp from the shore.

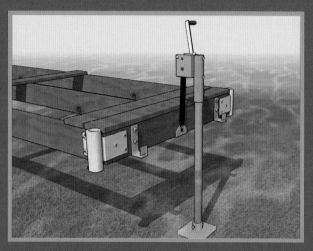

A leveling winch mounted to a spare pipe leg or jack pole will hold up the end of a dock section while its pipe legs are being inserted into the sockets and driven into the bed.

Once the dock section is at the desired height and level on the pipe legs, the setscrews are tightened on the corner sockets before the leveling winch and jack pole are removed.

The Ramp Section to Shore

Bring the dock section intended for the ramp (ramp section) to the shore. On the end that will set into the J-brackets, there should be corner irons bolted into the backside of the corner butt joints. The ideal J-bracket should have enough play in it so that the ramp section can be tilted if the elevation on the shore is different than that of the decking. If the fit is too snug into the J-bracket when tilting the ramp section, choose a longer bolt for the bottom of the J-bracket and shim with washers as needed to angle the J-bracket.

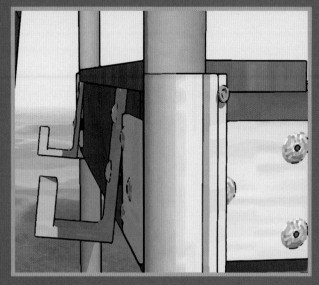

Prepare to attach a dock section as a ramp to shore.

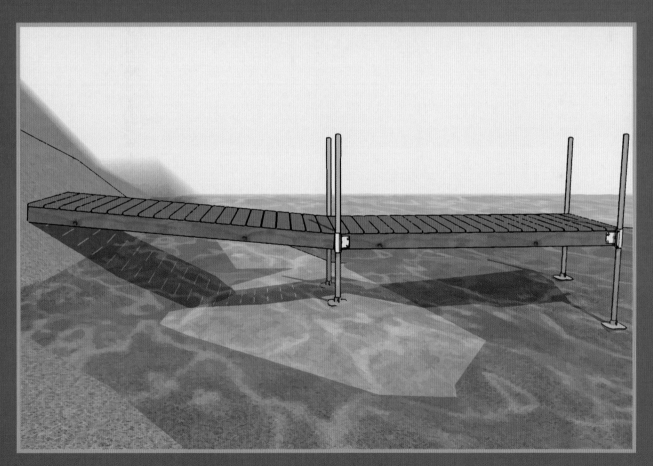

If necessary, J-brackets can be shimmed to prevent binding from the ramp section's slant.

Additional Dock Sections

If continuing the dock straight out, the second dock section will have only two pipe brackets on the outbound end. Bring it to the water and place on top of the temporary flotation. Drift into position and raise the inbound end onto the J-brackets.

With a cordless drill, just inside the edge on each side, bore a ⁷⁄₁₆-inch (11-millimeter) hole through the headers of both dock section where they meet. Install a ³⁄₈-inch by 4-inch (10- by 100-millimeter) carriage bolt with nut and washer to secure the inbound end in place. Do not tighten until the work on the outbound end is complete.

Install the pipe legs on the outbound end the same way you did on the first dock section. Raise up the outbound end, level, and tighten the pipe bracket's setscrews along with the carriage bolt that secures the two sections together.

Repeat these steps for additional dock sections.

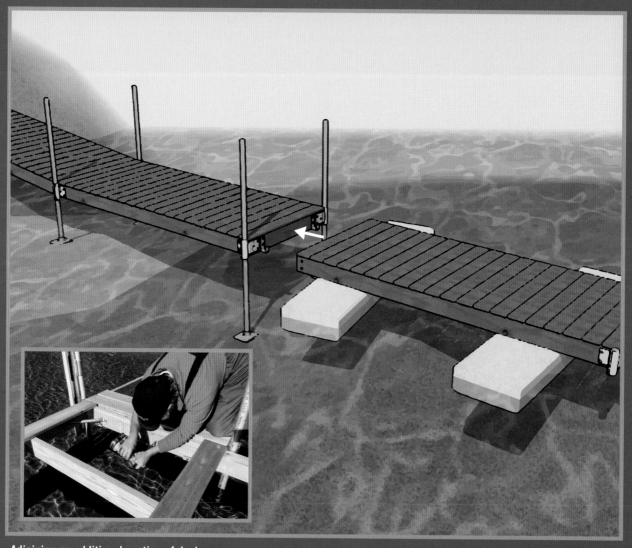

Adjoining an additional section of dock.

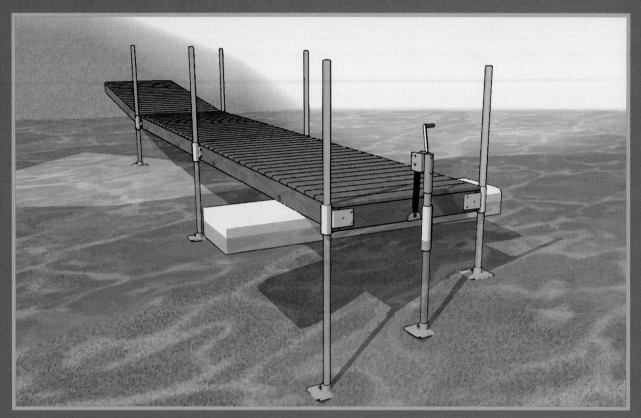

While the dock section is supported temporarily by a foam billet and/or leveling winch, pipe legs are installed at the outbound end.

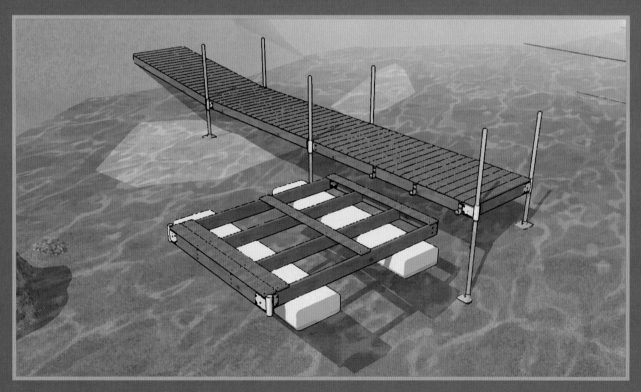

Apply Bracing and Finish

If the pipe legs are driven into the bed firmly and the dock is feeling solid, you may not need any cross bracing on the legs until you get into a depth of greater than 4 feet (1.2-meters). If bracing is needed, clamp them on to the pipe legs before adding the next section so that you have free access and plenty of room to work. You can learn more about bracing and stabilizing your pipe bracket dock following the chapters on featured types of fixed docks (page 36).

Trim the posts to an even height with either a plumber's pipe cutter or cordless reciprocating saw. Use a rasp to remove any sharp edges on the cut end to prevent injury. A fitted vinyl cap that slides over the top end of the pipe leg makes a fine finish.

Though pipe leg docks are ideal for setup and knock down under seasonal use, never underestimate how sturdy they can be. A properly built and installed one will perform much the same as a permanent dock. Not only do the pipes facilitate annual installation

Trim the tops of the pipe legs so that they all appear even. When finished, apply a vinyl cap over the tops for safety.

Attach bracing as needed.

and adjustments to temporary docks, they also provide a convenient way to easily attach accessories. When shopping among the suppliers for the pipe hardware, look for accessory parts that fit onto the pipe legs. Find things like bumpers to protect the boat with, solar lights made to fit the top of a pipe, and canoe/kayak arms for storing your favorite paddle craft off to the side. If you're serious about building this kind of dock, take time to explore the parts offered that may have multiple uses and let your imagination go.

Suppliers that offer basic parts for pipe leg support may offer accessory parts that also fit onto the pipes.

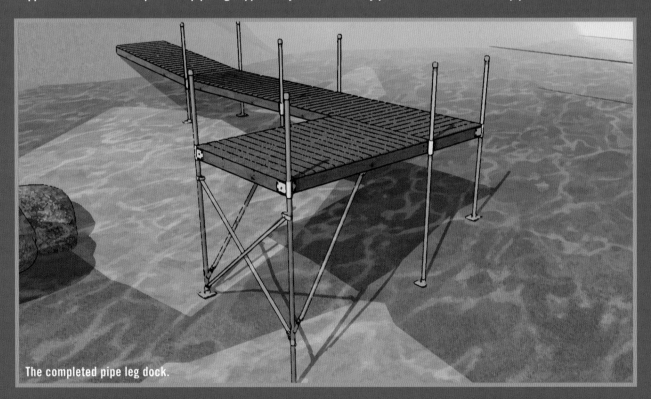

The completed pipe leg dock.

CHAPTER 10:
STABILIZING A FIXED DOCK

Walking along the length of your dock, do you feel it shake or shimmy? When you're standing still on the dock, do you feel that same motion while someone else is moving about? If it's to a point that could induce motion sickness or pitch your favorite in-law into the drink, then it likely has insufficient bracing. In this chapter, I'll describe the fundamentals of bracing a fixed dock that stops the unwanted motion. Understanding and applying what makes a good brace versus what doesn't will keep you in good standing with your relatives who come to visit you and your dock.

Motion in the Legs

The wobbly sensation you feel on a fixed dock begins with the amount of flex within the legs. Naturally, short legs are stiffer than tall legs of the same material, so a dock in shallow water will

Cross bracing from leg to leg stops unwanted motion.

feel more stable than in deep water. Likened to miscellaneous lengths of dried, uncooked spaghetti, the shortest piece is the most rigid while a full length is very flexible.

Therefore, the portions of dock in deep water requiring longer legs are usually subject to more complaints than portions over shallow water where legs are short. Lengthiness alone, however, is not the only contributor to flex. Differences in the girth, shape, and material of the legs can vary the amount of motion you're sensing. Here are some specific examples of differences that can matter.

- Skinny legs flex more than fat legs of the same material.
- Thinner wall legs, such as with pipe, flex more than thick wall of the same material.
- Round legs flex more than square legs of same material and thickness.
- Aluminum legs flex more than steel legs of same shape and dimensions.

I'm not suggesting that you choose thick, girthy, steel, square legs for your dock. I hope that you use legs that are practical for your application and fit within your installation abilities. Therefore, my emphasis is not about using legs that won't flex but, instead, removing flex from the legs upon installation or correcting a pre-existing condition in ANY dock leg to the point where your dock feels stable.

Eliminate Play, Top and Bottom

The first measure to reducing flex is to see that the joints where the legs meet the frame or the cap boards are all tight. Secondly, unless the dock is in shallow water and meant for light usage only, such as a canoe or kayak dock, set or drive the legs into the lake, river, or seabed. Even seasonal fixed docks that are removed before winter can have legs buried into the bottom, enough to significantly dampen any wobble. This is especially true for pipe legs made with steel pipe. They often drive with ease into sand or gravel to a practical distance of up to 2

Absence of bracing may cause unwanted or unsafe motion in a fixed dock.

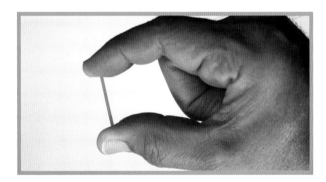

A short piece of spaghetti shows rigidity under compression.

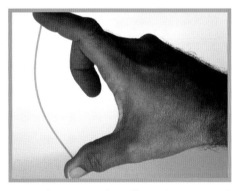

A long piece of spaghetti shows flex under compression.

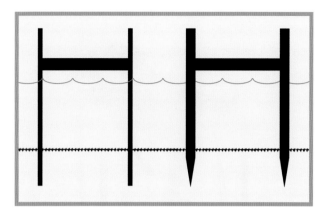

Setting legs into the lake bed, riverbed, or seabed will help to stabilize them and reduce motion.

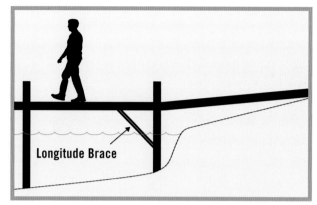

Longitude Brace

A longitudinal brace placed directionally with the length of the dock reduces longitudinal motion. If a dock is secured at the shore so that it cannot move in a forward or backward direction, longitudinal bracing may not be needed.

feet (60 centimeters). If in water depths less than 4 feet (1.22 meters), driving or burying legs into the bottom may stiffen things up enough so that no additional braces will be needed.

What you'll need to do will be up to your judgement. Just keep in mind, if there is a shimmy you've chosen to live with, over time, it can contribute to the loosening of joints where the legs and frame come together, exacerbating the motion. That said, though it may not bother you enough to feel the urge to take corrective measures now, I recommend "nipping it in the bud" so you're not revisiting a bigger problem later.

Longitudinal Bracing

The addition of braces to the legs is the next measure. If for whatever reason you can't or don't wish to set the legs into the bottom, braces will be the remedy for any unwanted motion. Directionally, there are two types of bracing on docks. The first one I'll describe is known as "longitudinal" bracing. Visualizing a typical dock that extends out perpendicular from shore, a longitude brace directionally runs parallel with the length of the dock. Unless the dock begins in deep water at the shore, requiring the first legs to be tall, or if the dock footprint branches off from the main dock, longitude braces are often not needed. When the legs, especially near shore in shallow water, are

driven into the bed, or the shore end is fastened to a seawall or something solid, the dock cannot wobble in the longitude direction, explaining why you don't see longitude braces on many docks. If the legs are not driven or set in and no solid connection is made at the shore, then longitude braces may be needed. When the footprint takes a turn from the main dock, to make a platform area, such as an "L" or "T" shape, then longitude braces will likely be needed to extend from the leg to the dock's frame.

Transverse Bracing

Bracing that runs across the width of the dock, commonly called "cross bracing" on opposing pipe legs, posts, or pilings, is known as "transverse" bracing. On a typical dock that extends perpendicular from shore, transverse bracing is often required on the taller legs, especially in deep water. The entire height from the bottom to the dock frame does not need to be braced, but the more you can do, the better. I aim to have a cross brace cover about two-thirds of the dock's height. On lakes where water levels drop over the course of summer and fixed adjustable docks will need a mid-season lowering, cross braces should be short enough and positioned below the point where the dock will be lowered.

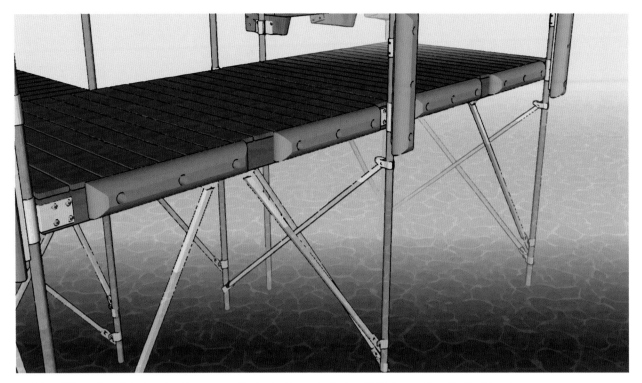

An "L" or "T" portion of dock, extending perpendicular to the main dock, will likely need longitudinal bracing to accompany cross bracing that extends across the width of the "L" or "T."

How Bracing Works

Civil engineers revere the triangle as their strongest shape. When you put braces on, from leg to leg or leg to frame, you're essentially making triangles, inserting the strongest shape inside of a rectangle to inhibit skewing or racking. Looking at the end of a dock with an elevation view, you see a rectangular area that receives alternating forces from the left and the right. This force is caused by movement on the dock from foot traffic and from boats tied alongside, either bumping into or tugging at it. The rectangle yields to the stress by skewing left then right, which is the shake and shimmy you feel. Attach one brace, diagonally across the rectangular area, and noticeable improvement will occur.

In the illustration (top right on page 106), when forces come from the top left, the brace is in tension or is resisting a force trying to stretch the brace. When forces come from the top right, the brace is in compression or is resisting a force trying to squeeze it. If the brace material can withstand the force without yielding, it will stop the skewing. Now, add another brace in the opposite direction and you have a brace in tension and a brace in compression at the same time, resisting forces that come from the left or right.

A Better Brace

A good brace doesn't bow when under compression. Using the dry stick of spaghetti again for a visual, try to stretch a full length between your fingertips and you'll see it resists very well. But, when you prop it between your palms and compress, it bows and gives way to the force. A thin brace, like a slender tube, rod, or flat bar that may make a good brace when in tension, does not resist compression as well. Cable or wire rope exemplifies this principal perfectly. It is only effective while in tension. Replace the cable brace with a rigid piece of pipe and you'll get the benefit of tension and compression resistance.

A transverse brace placed across the width of the dock from leg to leg reduces motion from side to side.

Brace A is in tension.
Brace B is in compression.

Depending on the direction it comes from, a force can put a brace in a state of tension or compression.

For pipe legs, 1-inch (25-millimeter) steel pipe or 1¼-inch (30 millimeter) square aluminum tube is sufficient. Wooden post docks that use 4x4s (76 by 76 millimeters) or 4x6s (76 by 140 millimeters) can be braced with wood 2x4s (38 by 76 millimeters).

Brace Attachment

Braces need to be firmly secured tight to the leg. If there is any slop or play, you don't have a good brace. Manufacturers of pipe leg hardware make either stanchions or clamps that hold a pipe brace to the pipe leg. During the installation of a pipe dock, the lower end of a brace could be clamped onto a pipe leg before lowering the leg to the bottom. That way, diving under to attach the lower end can be avoided.

The brace I use has a mechanism for the lower end that self-locks to the leg down low without the installer needing to dive. These are more expensive than a regular brace clamp, but ask a dock installer if it's worth it as he is about to immerse into chilling April water.

Suppliers of parts for docks supported on pipe legs should carry clamps to hold a brace to the pipe.

A self-locking brace connector for pipe legs can be attached without the installer getting into the water.

For docks standing on wooden 4x4 (76- by 76-millimeter) posts, there are manufactured brace clamps made to clamp a brace to the post. Using them will avoid the need to drill the post under water for brace attachment. Clamps may connect to a pipe brace or a mere piece of lumber, such as a 2x4 (38 by 76 millimeters). If you just want to bolt them onto a wooden post, pre-drill the posts down low before installing, so that your bolt hole for brace attachment is already done, avoiding underwater drilling.

A brace clamp that bolts to a wooden brace and clamps to a wooden post is much easier to move if height adjustments or dock leveling are needed later. Otherwise, a wooden brace can simply bolt directly to the post.

Bracing is extremely important to the safe use and longevity of a fixed dock. You've probably seen plenty of docks that lean and appear rickety, ready to fall over. Often, they're that way simply due to the lack of bracing, or the bracing that is there loosened up and complacency got in the way of its upkeep. Understanding that the unwanted motion in your dock often begins with flex in the legs and how a good brace works to correct it will point you in the best direction to correct the problem, prevent futile efforts, and keep everyone from getting shook up.

Maintenance of good bracing is key to the dock's sturdiness.

CHAPTER 11:
CRIB DOCKS

Once the rave when Romans ruled but far less popular today, crib docks continue to stand the test of time as can be seen in many parts of the world. Well, let me qualify that statement. The *idea* of the crib dock has survived, but the actual structures are often short lived, either removed by nature or replaced with more modern methods. Looking like they might have been around since the stone age, today, the crib is far from becoming a dinosaur in some regions and remains a reliable way of making a permanent support column for the dock or pier. Permanent is a relative word, of course. Many had expected their crib to last into the next century, were it not for the hard truth that manmade structures eventually succumb to the natural forces upon the Earth. Such crib docks have left their traces, as can be seen by the many submerged ruins that are cost prohibitive to completely remove before installing its replacement.

All over the northeast U.S. it is the unyielding ice that comes to their demise. Whether it be on a lake or brackish tidal inlet that can freeze, expanding ice on the water's surface will push with bulldozer force against what had hoped to be an invincible structure, leaving it with varying degrees of damage or complete destruction.

This crib dock, on Long Lake in Naples, Maine, was originally built at the start of the 20th century. Over 100 years later, having gone through routine maintenance and repairs from ice damage, it continues to serve as a reliable boat slip for its current owner.

A crib dock on brackish coastal water awaits reconstruction in the spring after a hard winter when ice formed and locked to it at low tide. The grip of ice floating on the rising tide caused this crib to flip.

Before summer's end, determination and an unwavering faith in crib docks saw to its restoration.

Sometimes, much more than docks may be riding on cribs.

Vulnerable as we understand them now, many owners of crib docks choose to faithfully repair them or replace when destroyed. I know of a marine contractor with a barge on Moosehead Lake in Maine who stays busy all summer repairing them for people. On some tidal waters, crib-supported piers remain a viable option where pilings cannot be installed due to ledge or extremely soft soil. The crib may be the best choice even with the threats that loom.

If you're interested in building a crib dock or restoring one, you should first investigate the permit requirements. Where I live, government codes do not permit new ones and a permit is required to work on your old one that is in disrepair. Some of the people I've met who own them have expressed to me that their crib dock adds tremendous value to their property for its perceived permanency and "grandfathered" status, versus having to annually

deal with a portable removable dock. I usually agree if they haven't had to re-build it every five to ten years. Crib docks are simple by design, but laborious to build or re-build if you've ever worked on one. During a time when the water is at its lowest level, square-like frames made with heavy timbers or logs are stacked, level by level and fastened together at the corners. With each frame that is positioned on the stack, rocks are piled up into the center. Some rocks overlap timbers along the edges, holding the frame down to counter buoyancy in the wood. Over time, the wood will become waterlogged and hopefully preserved, being oxygen deprived for most of the time. With every level, more rocks are placed into the middle until there are enough levels to support the framing and decking at the desired height. Cribs are slightly narrower than

summer. On occasion, over my career, I've met crib dock owners who were suddenly faced with a decision to re-build or bear the removal cost of their old cribs with little time before boating season begins. Some elected to leave the cribs and go with an all new fixed dock wide enough to straddle over the remnants of a dilapidated structure. This works so long as the cribs don't open and spread their guts out over a large area.

I recommend, if you're thinking about building an all new crib dock or restoring an existing one, that you check into the laws of nature and the laws of the land before going too far. If the cost and effort to restore a slightly damaged one is minimal, I'd keep patching and going with it. However, if major rebuilding from the bottom up is likely to be needed soon, I would seriously weigh the odds of its near future vulnerability before going deep.

the platforms that fasten upon them in hopes to be hidden from hulls. The builder may use dock sections or stick build in place, to span from crib to crib, affixing together with posts, beams, and bolts.

Cribs, with their weight in all the rock, make a superior dock with respect to stability and ability to withstand the jarring of a boat when bumped or tugged against. Their longevity depends on when and if Mother Nature decides to wreak havoc. Many bodies of water prone to freezing are drained down before winter so that cribs are protected from expanding ice. Other than lack of height adjustability that is sometimes desired, the crib dock works very well in the right conditions. It is quite common for people to add on to their crib dock, extending with a more modern method that affords them height adjustment, such as a floating dock.

But if the water uncontrollably rises from heavy rain or runoff during the winter, drifting ice or re-freezing at the higher water level can turn conditions into a lottery game of annihilation. Unfortunately, the revelation of destruction, come spring, doesn't leave much time to re-build before

A basic crib assembly for docks.

CHAPTER 12:
ROLL'N DOCKS

I n Maine, say the word "roll" and people light up at its sound because they think you mean lobster roll, one of the best ways to enjoy its succulent meat without all the work and mess. At the lake, a roll'n dock can be the best way to enjoy a waterfront when the dock is installed with ease, with no heavy lifting or getting wet. In climates where docks must be seasonal and removed before winter, waterfront property owners are often familiar with docks on wheels, be it repurposed iron ones from retired farm implements or durable plastic hollow wheels made for this kind of dock. Not only can they simplify

the annual in and out, but as water levels lower throughout the summer on some lakes, the roll'n dock can be easily moved out further into the lake.

Best Conditions

More commonly found on fixed docks but can be seen on floating docks as well, a clear, gradual slope to the water with only minor obstacles is the first condition for ease to be a reality. Keeping with a conventional floor plan such as a 4-foot (122-centimeter) wide, straight out dock **without** an "L" or "T" section will speed up the process. The

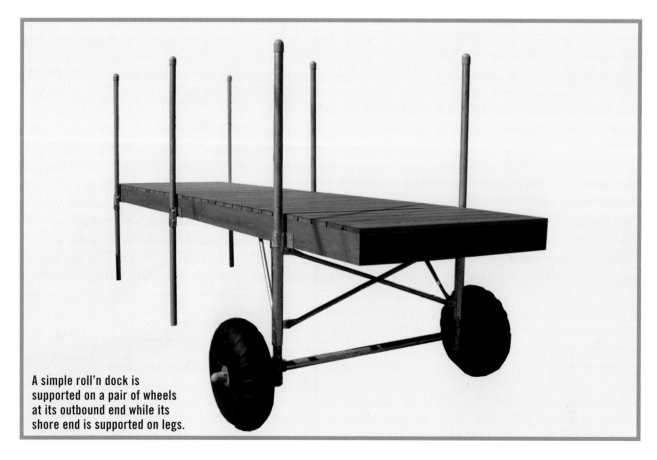

A simple roll'n dock is supported on a pair of wheels at its outbound end while its shore end is supported on legs.

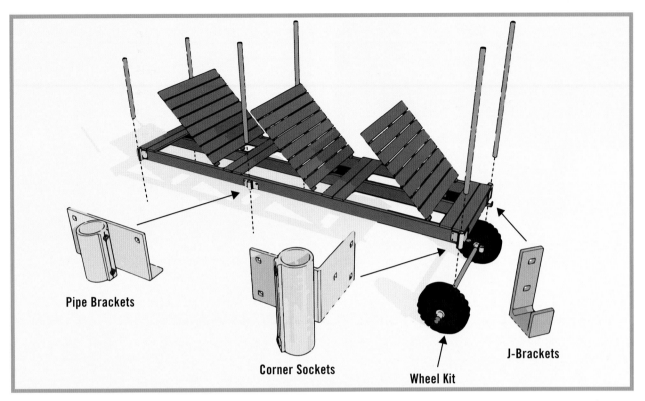

Pipe Brackets

Corner Sockets

Wheel Kit

J-Brackets

This assembly view of a roll'n dock section features decking in removable panels to lighten the load while underway. J-brackets fastened to the end allow easy attachment of another section to extend its length.

larger the roll'n, the more work it will be without the help of a tractor to push on install or pull on removal. The lake bed should be firm with sand or gravel; a mucky bottom will defeat the ease gained with wheels.

Movable Sizes

Make the basic section size 4 feet by 16 feet (122 by 488 centimeters) and you can go light as 2x6 (38 by 140 millimeters) on the framing, provided you include a support to the ground midway along the section. Increasing the section to have 2x8 (38- by 184-millimeter) framing will make it more rigid but will add less desirable weight. Plastic wheels that are molded for docks should be load rated. Usually, the heavier the rating, the higher the price. To keep the weight down while in transit, there is a plan you can follow in the Docks in Sections chapter (see page 24) that features removable decking panels.

If moving two or more sections joined together is difficult, they can be separated and moved independently. Always keep the speed of the roll very slow while watching that nothing gets hung up or binds. If moving them while joined together, I recommend the connection be made with J-brackets and center bolts that pass through the headers of each section. The center bolts should be loose enough while the dock is in motion for articulation over irregular terrain. Once the roll'n is parked and in position, center bolts should be tightened.

Anchor It Down

Bear in mind, this dock will not feel as solid as one with its legs driven into the lake bed. In areas of high wind exposure where a boat tied alongside could start bumping and tugging it, you might wish for something sturdier or use the roll'n as an access dock for temporary tie up only. I've known people

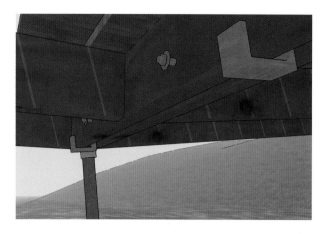

When two sections are left adjoined while rolling, center bolts are loosened to allow articulation over irregular terrain. Once the sections are installed and level, center bolts are retightened.

When there is enough help, rolling sections may remain connected. Otherwise, they can be separated and rolled into position one at a time.

Once satisfied with the roll'n dock's position, additional legs to reduce the section's span can be set into the lake bed to prevent it from rolling further on its own.

to add legs at the end that drive into the lake bed just to stake it down. If the slope of the lake bed is steep, I recommend driven legs at the shore end to prevent gravity from pulling it downhill and out into the lake. If you choose to add legs for anchoring or

rigidity, I recommend that the wheels stay in contact with the lake bed so they do not vibrate from waves rolling through.

On shorefronts with soft sand and incessant large waves from wind, assess if the sand moves about

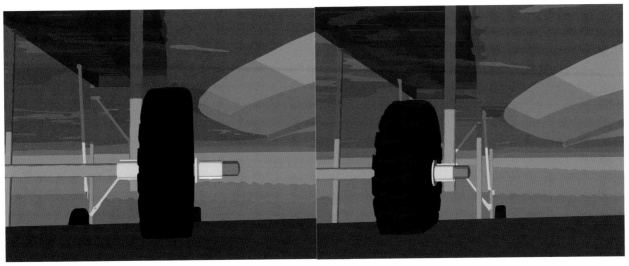

For maximum stability, wheels should be mounted outside the width of the dock. If the water is shallow, consider mounting the wheels just inside the dock width where they will clear hulls and avoid risking interference with boats tied alongside.

to any significance where the wheels would set. In places like this, the molded plastic wheels that are hollow will fill with sand, a harmless consequence other than adding unwanted weight upon moving. The more disappointing result is that wave action of this kind can undermine your wheels by putting the dock out of level and requiring ongoing adjustments.

Placement of Wheels and Bracing

Most wheels are set up so they are positioned outside the legs for maximum stability. This can interfere with the boat kept alongside if the water is extremely shallow. In this case, wheels can be turned to the inside of the legs. In deep enough water, keep the wheels on the outside of the legs to maximize stability.

Where the wheels will be parked in a depth of more than 3 feet (91.44 centimeters), you may want to put cross braces on the legs depending on how much shimmy occurs while walking upon the dock.

When installing your roll'n dock, a straight shot from the shore out will be easiest. If moving multiple sections that are connected, do not expect them to steer well. I built one on an occasion that needed good "steerability" to get around an

immovable rock pile. I put the wheels in the middle of the dock section instead of toward the outbound end. I was then able to maneuver each section on a dime. With deck panels removed from the frame, and the remaining weight easily balanced over the wheels, I found it very light and easy to handle.

With two sections on wheels, each 4 feet by 16 feet (122 by 488 centimeters), I rolled the first one effortlessly into position and set it off the shore about 8 feet (2.5 meters). Then I installed pipe legs at each end and leveled the section. The next roll'n section was a bit trickier as I jockeyed its position until satisfied with the alignment. Finally, I secured it to the first section's outbound J-brackets, installed the final pair of legs at the deep end, and leveled it out.

Wheels That Work

You can likely find some old iron hay rake wheels from a junk collector and rig them onto some posts. Just make sure the wheels are not outside the dock's width as they are not hull friendly. I recommend going with the plastic molded wheels. They won't rust and seize up and are less likely to hurt the boat should they ever make contact.

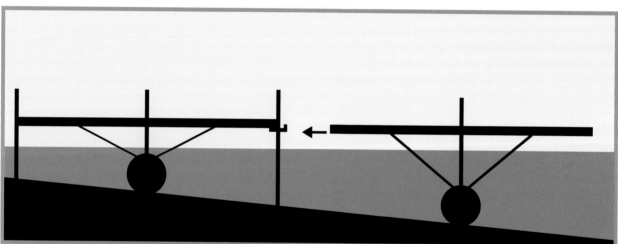

Wheels may be mounted at the center of a dock section if more maneuverability is desired.

There are a variety of companies that supply the molded plastic wheels and special brackets to put them on. Remember to watch for the load rating; go heavier if you have a choice. On most, the axle hole in the middle is 2 inches (51 millimeters), ideal for 1½-inch (38-millimeter) schedule #40 galvanized pipe that has an outside diameter of 1⅞ inch (47 millimeters). It can be purchased at a local hardware store. The pipe will need to be cut at the right length so that just enough extends beyond the wheel's hub for a cotter pin through a drilled hole. Brackets that join the axle to pipe legs may also be ordered from the company that supplies the wheels, along with bracket to hold pipe legs to your dock section. Should you choose to use 4x4 (100- by 100-millimeter) wooden posts for the legs instead of pipe, you'll need a bracket to hold the pipe axle to the post.

Accommodations

At your waterfront, see that you have room on the shore to park the size dock you have in mind. Sections joined together when bringing up on shore after the season may seem like parking a bus. There should be enough room so that the dock is completely out of harm's way when winter ice forms. Also, measure out from shore the depths where the wheels will set so you can plan your material requirements such as leg lengths and bracing. The roll'n dock in the right environment and application can be a real time saver and a non-issue where seasonal docks are required. If it sounds good to you, let's get rolling!

Until spring, the roll'n dock can be separated to fit into its winter storage spot, safe from the lake's ice.

A bracket may be purchased to attach the wheel kit axle to a pipe leg.

Made specifically for roll'n docks and available through dock hardware suppliers, large plastic wheels allow dock sections to roll with ease over soft sand or bumpy terrain. Drain holes allow the hollow wheels to sink upon entry.

CHAPTER 13:
FLOATING DOCKS

Benefits and Best Conditions

Logs, foam, barrels, pontoons, tanks, pipe, or poly drums likely do not cover all the things that have been commandeered at one place or another to support a floating dock. Diverse as the flotation is, so too is the level of performance among the host of floating creations. Just ahead, I'll show you how to plan and build a floating dock for DIYers using the techniques of a professional dock builder. First, let's look at why a floating dock may be right for you and the conditions that should be considered.

Fluctuating water levels, be it at a lake, river, or tidal shore, are likely the number one reason to consider building a floating dock. Fixed docks on a water body that varies its level within 1 or 2 feet (30 or 61 centimeters) can be tolerated, but at some point, the disparity between high and low levels range from difficult to impossible when climbing on or off the boat.

The floating dock sets at a constant and comfortable level above the water's surface.

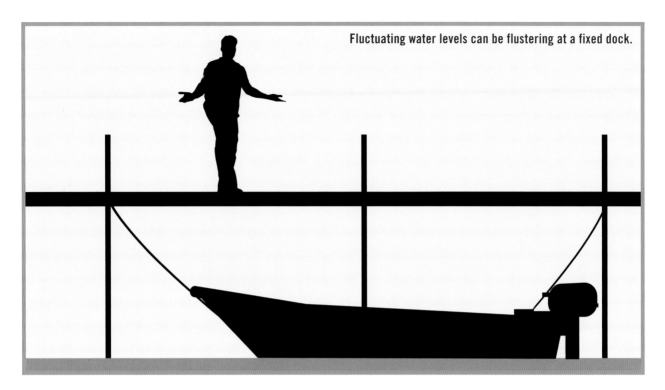

A floating dock that is stable and with the appropriate amount of freeboard against your boat provides a constant and reliable distance off the water. While floating docks are the "go to" remedy for varying water levels, let's look at some other reasons you should consider them over fixed docks.

- Water is too deep for a DIY fixed dock. A pipe leg dock in 8 feet (2.44 meters) of water is about the maximum depth you should go into before finding that the installation effort takes its toll on you and the stability on the dock will be less than satisfying. For deep water, I would consider the floating dock so that pipe legs, posts, and pilings are of no concern.

- Bottom conditions are too soft and soggy for the legs on a fixed dock to be firmly grounded. Leveling adjustments to the fixed dock could become a perpetual demand with each leg never fully settling. Posts or pipe legs on seasonal fixed docks that must get removed before winter's freeze will require a lot of patience when extracting against the suction. The floating dock over a mucky bottom avoids all that trouble.

Special types of watercraft can demand docks with a continuous bearing surface along the side and the absence of interfering posts or pilings.

- The "footprint" is large, and would require setting an undesirable number of posts, pilings, or pipe legs if opting for a fixed dock. This is especially important to think about for docks in severely cold climates that require annual reinstallation and removal. Floating docks that link together, section by section, go together over the water much faster than sections of fixed docks.
- Operators of special types of watercraft may prefer an approach to a dock that has fewer vertical lines. Wing struts on float planes and sail booms on small sailboats will likely smack into posts, pilings, or pipe legs that protrude above the decking on fixed docks. Floating docks may use a piling to hold the dock's position, but they usually don't need as many and can be placed selectively to avoid interference.

Regardless of the reason why a floating dock sounds like the right way to go, your level of satisfaction when it's complete will depend on the environment you've subjected it to and the method used to build it. Unlike a fixed dock, motion is expected on a floating dock, but it should be built stable enough for safe walking or standing upon with minimal tipping and swaying from side to side. For the best results from a floating dock, consider the following conditions.

Environmental Conditions to Consider

Shelter from wind is the first favorable condition I look for. To keep a floating dock in place and in good working order is much easier when not in the path of white-capped waves caused by prolonged winds. Constant wind at an exposed waterfront pushes on the floating dock and attached boats, straining all that holds the dock in place, such as hardware connections, pilings, and moorings. At the same time, the associated wave action puts torque on the wood frames, causing fasteners to loosen and fatigue. Articulating hardware joints are also at risk of premature wear and loosening while inflicting your neighbors with an incessant heavy-metal noise. A sheltered shore has a short fetch to the opposite shore or is buffered by a point of land that blocks predominant winds. Coves, inlets, and narrow canals

Floating docks perform best when installed where they are safe from white-capped waves caused by prolonged winds.

are usually safe places. If you're new to the property and not sure how wild the waterfront gets, ask a neighbor who is familiar with it. Your dream of a floating dock shouldn't be canceled just because you have some exposure to wind and waves. In many instances, your finished product can withstand a fair amount of abuse from wind chop by gauging what you build to the conditions. The key is your awareness of the severity level and your wisdom to discern if what you're capable of building will take the level of abuse that the wind will deliver.

Interminable boat chop has the same effect on a floating dock as wind chop. Torquing of the wood frame, wear, fatigue, and noise are all symptoms that are not helping and we'd rather do without, thank you. However, boat chop doesn't usually preclude building a floating dock if on all other points a floating dock is the best option. You'll have to decide if you can live with the added motion when walking on the dock, but the structural maintenance associated with boat chop is a matter that many accept as an inherent necessity.

Scattered boulders in the water add character to a water body, but they must be reckoned with when placing a floating dock nearby. Make sure as the water fluctuates it doesn't lower a dock to where its flotation is chafing on a boulder. If you can't move an interfering boulder due to environmental codes or its size, you may be able to jog the footprint of the dock so that it meanders around the obstruction. Sometimes a fixed dock is used to bridge boulders in the shallows near shore before transitioning into a depth where there is sufficient clearance for a floating dock portion. I will visit this topic again in Fixed to Floating Dock (page 178).

Rivers that swell suddenly from rain storms move swiftly with a sweeping effect, purging debris along the riverbanks into the current that can collect against a floating dock. A large enough pile of debris made up of branches, tree limbs, and possibly entire trees can exert enough pressure to wipe out any dock. The outside curve in a riverbend is usually the most vulnerable. Awareness of the risks on a river like this should guide your decision before you

Scattered boulders just under the surface pose a challenge for positioning a floating dock.

Rivers with severe flooding can sweep their banks of trees, rocks, and floating docks, depositing them downstream.

invest. I would ask other property owners along the river about what you can expect. If you see a technique repeated in more than one dock in the neighborhood, it may be something to pay close attention to.

Getting the Drift on Floating Docks

If the advantages of a floating dock fit your needs and you find the environmental conditions favorable, then building a floating dock may be your next project. Whether it will be now or later, equip yourself with the knowledge of the right materials, methods for building, and installing it properly. Coming up on page 150, learn about dock flotation, specialty dock hardware, methods for anchoring the dock in place, and much more. Just as my instructions for fixed docks put emphasis on building in sections, so will the chapters ahead for floating docks. I will focus on the section as the building block to any floor plan. Choose a lightweight portable design for installations where brawny help is in short supply or choose a more robust design because the conditions demand it. Whatever your preference, use my plans as a starting

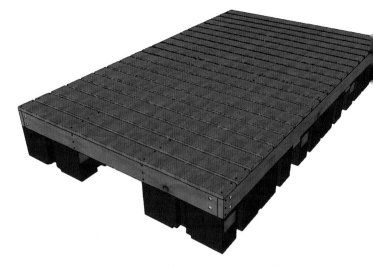

Think of your floating dock as being comprised of sections, the building blocks for any plan.

point and increase the timber size if a heavier dock is desired. DIYers appreciate the benefits that come with building out their docks one section at a time, whether in a garage, boat shed, or outside on sawhorses. With the help from some specialty hardware, such as hinges that provide the linkage between sections, all the sections can be mobilized from your shop to the shore and assembled into your dock configuration over the water. Here are some sample floor plans comprised of sectionalized floating docks to get you thinking.

These floor plans are all assembled by connecting 6'x12' (183 x 366cm) floating sections.

CHAPTER 14:
COMPLETING THE SITE SURVEY FOR A FLOATING DOCK

With your understanding of the best conditions for a floating dock, as detailed in the last chapter, you should apply your knowledge to conduct a survey on your own shoreline. Let's see if it has the right conditions for a floating dock. Perhaps you're familiar with the site, having a year or more experience there, and can make a fair assessment as to its viability. If not, then use this exercise fastidiously to learn about what you have for a waterfront.

Assessment of Wind Exposure

The leading deterrent for me when putting in a floating dock is a waterfront exposed to prolonged high winds over a wide span of water. If you recently acquired the property and are not familiar with its wind and wave potential, this should be your first order of business when thinking about a floating dock. A shoreline that can have wind-driven waist-high waves incessantly for hours at a time may not be suitable for your floating dock without putting more into to it than what you're prepared to do. If there is a long reach of say 1 mile (1.6 kilometers) or more to the opposite shore with no barrier in between, you can expect at least a moderate amount of exposure, especially if it channels the predominant wind. Get familiar with the exposure potential, if in question. Speaking with neighbors who have experience and know your shoreline is often a good place to start.

Selecting Your Dock's Location

After you've taken exposure into account, think about where on your shorefront you'd like to have the dock. In some cases, there is no choice if the code specifies where it goes or the lot is narrow, leaving with only one place the dock can go. Otherwise, if you have a choice, planning a new dock is an opportunity to do something different and better than what was done before. Keeping in mind your setbacks and privacy with neighbors, I would look for the lowest approach above the high-water level on shore so that steepness or length of the ramp between the shore and dock is minimized. See that the location provides the right depth for your boat and activities while being free of obstacles. If there is a barrier with a leeward side from wind and storms, take full advantage of it. The huge pine tree at the water's edge could offer shade for the dock if that's your thing, but it also rains sap and soot that's probably not your thing. A dock at the side of a swimming hole is preferred over a dock that is in the swimming hole. The same can be said for the scenic view, that it is better to keep the dock on the side rather in it. I guess that depends on what you'd rather look at, the dock and boat or the water and mountains behind them. Having it where you can see it without spoiling the vista would be

Right: When surveying a shoreline with options for a floating dock, seek the bank with a low approach, an outcropping wind buffer, favorable depths, and freedom from obstacles.

A shoreline exposed to choppy water kicked up by high winds is often a deterrent for putting out a floating dock.

Predominant wind

If there is a barrier with a leeward side from wind and storms, take full advantage of it.

Determine the Ramp Length

A transitional section of dock, usually referred to as a ramp, is what meets the shore and extends outward to the next floating section. A length must be chosen for the ramp that will be at a safe pitch to climb on if the shore end is at a higher elevation than the outbound end. Whether extending off a path at the shore, a seawall, or a fixed pier, use your judgment as to the length that will be safe and reasonable to manage.

Field Notes from the Water

Once the approach from shore is chosen and you know how long the ramp should be, continue your survey to the water. A canoe, kayak, or rowboat—something you're good with and won't spill out of—will come in handy. This will go better if you choose a time when the wind is calm and visibility is good. Bring along a 100-foot (30-meter) tape measure and a long pole such as a 1½-inch by

my objective. Finally, make sure you include your significant other on this desicion. It's much easier to move an idea than it is to move the real thing.

A gently sloped ramp transitions the approach from a fixed to a floating dock.

10-foot (3.81- by 305-centimeter) length of PVC pipe, marked for measuring depths. If you can get a helper, he or she can hold the hooked end of the 100-foot (30-meter) tape measure where you want the dock's ramp to meet the shore. At the same time, your helper can write down any notes that you wish to call out. With you in the boat and the coiled end of the tape measure in hand, paddle, or pole away, extending the tape to the length of the ramp. Cooperating with your helper, use the tape to simulate the ramps position and slope. This will help you visualize the ramp's steepness and to see if the length you're thinking about appears safe. Along with a safe slope, the length should span enough to get across obstacles, such as boulders, debris, and water too shallow for the dock. If the distance is too great for a practical length

A ramp makes the transition between a fixed point, such as the shore or a fixed dock on legs, to the floating dock beyond.

ramp to reach, you may need to begin with a fixed dock that transitions to floating. If there is plenty of water and clearance from obstacles, continue surveying for the floating dock.

As you move out from shore in the boat, use your PVC pole to check the bottom for hardness, determining if pipes or pilings can be driven as an option for anchoring the dock. Also, take note of the depths at various distances from shore so you'll know how far out you can use driven pipes for anchoring (not to exceed depths of 5 feet [1.5 meters]). Depths taken every 10 feet (3 meters) from shore will give you a picture of the bottom slope while revealing where you have depth enough for boats, a dock ladder, and safe diving. Should you plan to use moorings at the outbound end, take depth measurements there to project the total length

of chain required. Before you're through, seek out any obstructions under the surface, such as hidden boulders that could interfere with the dock flotation or other activities at the dock.

Drawing Up the Plan

Finally, after you've exited the water, go for a clean sheet of graph paper. From a bird's eye view, plot out your water depth to scale on the graph paper, beginning at the shore and then moving out. Draw in the dock, beginning with the ramp at the shore, then section by section until it is all mapped out.

A small boat that paddles is best for surveying over the water. Measuring out from the desired starting point on shore, record depths over the dock's anticipated footprint and the presence of obstacles at their respective distances.

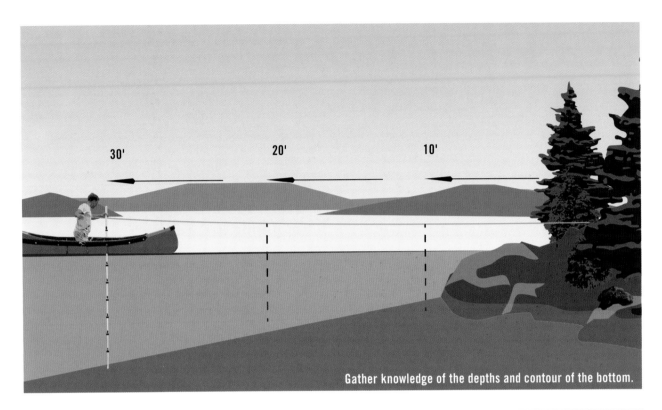

30' 20' 10'

Gather knowledge of the depths and contour of the bottom.

Add in any obstacles or landmarks that may be important to you. Indicate anything to help with installing the dock, the landmark on the opposite shore you're aiming it toward, and a landmark on the shore where the dock should start. At this point you have the basics down. Add more details if you'd like. Show where the swim ladder or the cleats are supposed to go and where each boat gets moored to the dock. **This is your plan.** However, if you intend to use this survey drawing for a permit application, keep the one with all the extras for yourself. Make a separate drawing that only includes the details asked for within the permit application instructions.

When sketching your plan, record all relevant information, including the sections of dock to scale in the desired footprint, depths, obstacles, and any landmarks worth noting.

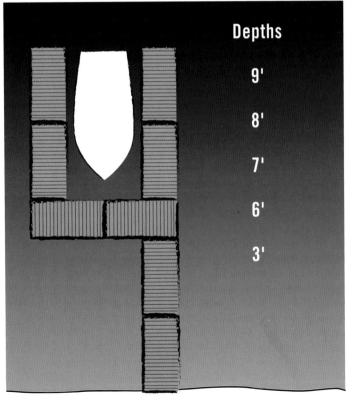

Depths

9'

8'

7'

6'

3'

CHAPTER 15:
DOCK SECTIONS THAT FLOAT

The exciting subject of a rectangle that you learned about by age three and mastered in high school geometry is revisited here. This not-so-sexy figure, yet extremely versatile equiangular quadrilateral, represents our basic building block to any floating dock floor plan.

As you visualize your dock's overall shape and position with the shore, imagine it comprised of rectangles or in sections that connect, one by one. Though we have been on this topic as it relates to sections for fixed docks, here we will go into some specific details important to making sections that float.

Take the dock sections that are detailed for fixed docks and convert them to floating—you will be asking quite a bit more of them. Fixed docks are not impacted by motion the way floating docks are. Forces from waves, current, load movement/shifting, and boat contact put strain on the structure of a floating dock differently. Furthermore, these forces will challenge the stability for people upon a floating dock in ways that a fixed dock is immune from. So, while imagining your rectangles required for mapping out your floating dock, let's be thinking about what should go into them to resist strain and instability.

Completing the Box

Have you ever appreciated the sturdiness of a cardboard box? At an early age, one time or two, you might have played in one and had more fun with it than some of your best toys. Imagine it with the top opened and you sitting inside, against the bottom flaps that are secured with shipping tape, and I think you'd agree that the cardboard is quite strong for what it is.

Now, imagine the top flaps being closed and sealed with shipping tape. You can stay in or get out first, your choice. Though strong enough to play with before and able to withstand some abuse, the cardboard box with all its flaps closed and sealed is exponentially stronger, enough to mail its contents across the globe. Building a dock section is very

Though seemingly dull-looking, mapping out your dock plan by connecting rectangles keeps the planning phase simple and easy to change.

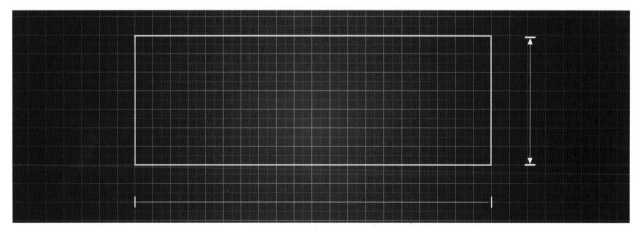

This beautiful floating dock originated from sketching
a series of connected rectangles.

Left: Though the box is open, we can expect it to have a useful amount of strength.

Right: Based on our familiarity with cardboard boxes, we can expect the closed box to be significantly stronger than the open box.

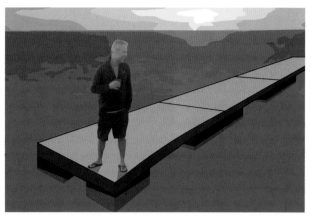

A twist in this floating dock section occurs when an off-centered load moves over the corner, revealing a weakness in its torsional strength. This is a sign of an incomplete box.

much the same way. Complete it with six sides, and you'll have a rugged dock.

Torsional Strain

Torsional strain comes from flexing of the section, between one end and the other. This occurs under the sections' own weight while waves roll below from an oblique direction, causing its support to be uneven. The section will appear to twist, alternating clockwise and counterclockwise. The flex also occurs when loads move about upon the section, especially when concentrated to one corner. The flexibility, inherited from its past while in the form of a tree, should be viewed as a plus actually, useful in dock construction to distribute shock and prevent breaks from stress. Controlling the flex, however, is what we want to do to reduce uncomfortable twisting motion on the dock. It should also be dampened to protect nails and screws from fatigue while stopping bolts from loosening. Nail heads that creep up through the decking are a result of flex.

Lateral Strain

Loads from a horizontal direction, such as wind or the weight of a boat bearing into the side of a dock, are lateral forces that can cause a dock section to rack. A dock section that started out with all

four corners at 90 degrees can go askew without bracing in the frame to resist these forces. Before getting too concerned about going the extra mile to prevent racking, all the plans for floating dock sections included here inherently have a great deal of resistance to lateral strain. If your exposure to these forces is greater because you're tying up an extra-large boat to this dock or you're in an area that receives more than your share of wind, then extra bracing should be considered.

About Stability

Building your dock sections to counter strain will at the same time improve stability for anyone walking upon the dock. But there is more to stability than resistance to torsional and lateral strain. Since stability is perhaps one of the most important

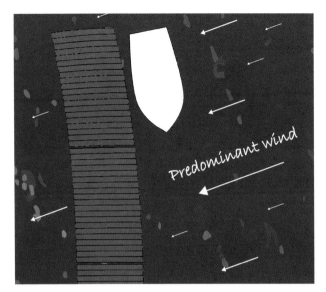

Sections of floating dock may rack or skew when subjected to lateral forces unless adequate bracing within the structure is present to resist the forces.

topics related to floating docks, let's look at other contributions. Understanding the key factors before you build will affect how you make some of your decisions that will bear on the outcome.

Dock Weight

Beginning with the weight of a floating dock, the heavier you build, the less it will budge when bumped by a boat. Weight in the materials provides ballast. Ballast reduces tipping caused by waves or people moving about (live loads) atop the dock. Picture two plastic bottles floating on the water, one sealed with just air, the other is half filled with water. Notice the one that is all air making quick, jerky motions upon the ripples while the one half-filled with water moves slower and is more at ease.

The heavy versus light dock behaves the same way but on a bigger scale. For the DIYer who wants light and manageable, especially for docks that must be hauled out before winter, this is not exactly what you want to hear. My suggestion is that you consider a lighter method and be prepared to add ballasts beneath the dock, such as weights suspended by chain that can be removed before hauling.

Length and Width of a Section

The length and width of a floating dock section matters perhaps more than the weight. When waves roll through from one end of a dock section to the other, the longer dock section will pitch significantly less than a shorter section. The same is true for the wider dock. When waves roll into its side, the oscillation or yaw will be less than that of a narrow dock. Your experience riding waves in boats of different sizes demonstrates very well how much more stable the larger boat is.

Added weight or ballast that comes with more width will also matter to stability. This can be seen when someone will stand on the edge at the side of a floating dock to board a boat. The narrow 4-foot (122-centimeter) wide floating dock has 50 percent less counterweight in dock material than the 6-foot (183-centimeter) wide floating dock, so the difference in the amount of tilt experienced is significant just by making the dock a little wider.

Incoming Wave Direction

It also helps to think about the predominant direction waves roll in from, whether caused by wind or boats. Since the sections link together via a hinge and can be connected at right angles to each other (to make an "L" or "T" shape), the yaw can be drastic when connecting the added section off the end versus the side of another section. Floating docks that are made narrow, such as 3 or

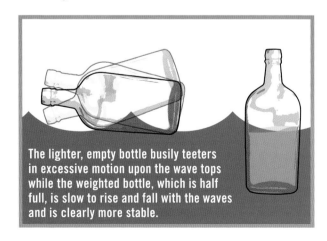

The lighter, empty bottle busily teeters in excessive motion upon the wave tops while the weighted bottle, which is half full, is slow to rise and fall with the waves and is clearly more stable.

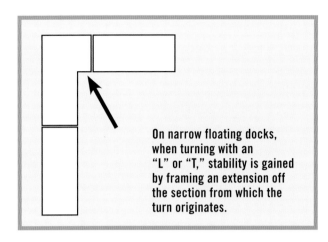

On narrow floating docks, when turning with an "L" or "T," stability is gained by framing an extension off the section from which the turn originates.

Width adds stability.

The narrow "L" section at the very end of this dock has a severe yaw or tilt as it rides the slope of incoming waves. This is a result of the "L" section's shorter dimension being turned perpendicular to the wave, while the hinge connection does not inhibit the tilt. In contrast, the "L" section to the right has its short dimension perpendicular to the wave, but its hinge connections at the end, rather than the side, provide a significant advantage.

4 feet (100 or 122 centimeters) wide are inherently the tippiest when taking waves from the broad side. For narrow docks such as these, beginning a turn that makes an "L" or "T" should be framed as an extension off the section from which the turn originates. This moves the hinge away from the corner and adds the stability you would experience in a wider section.

Choice of Flotation

Flotation holds a lot of weight when it comes to stability. The shape of the flotation and amount of its buoyancy will have a lot to do with your level of satisfaction when walking upon it. Flotation that is boxy in shape, such as black plastic dock floats

The shape of flotation can make significant differences in stability.

made specifically for docks, have nearly uniform displacement from top to bottom. In contrast, cylindrical flotation that lays in water horizontally, such as round pontoons and barrels, do not have uniform displacement. Since the greater amount of displacement is found near the centerline of a barrel or pontoon, an abrupt tilt from shifting live loads on a dock may be experienced simply because the barrel must sink a bit before the better part of its displacement goes to work. Though barrels are an affordable way to float a dock, the shape does not lend itself to the best stability. They do, however, offer a great deal of buoyancy. Whether you use barrels or the dock floats, put enough into the job so that a lack of buoyancy is not the cause of instability.

Condition of Connecting Hardware

Connecting methods for joining float sections may either lock them together rigidly or allow them to articulate. Though locking together improves stability, a hinged joint that can move is often necessary to release wave energy traveling through the dock sections. Allowing wave energy to escape between the sections alleviates flexing and strain on all the materials that go into the dock. Since most hinge connections are made of metal, their eyelets where a pin or rod inserts will enlarge from wear over time and result in unwanted play. Extra play in the hinge allows the dock sections to tip side to side. A small amount of added play can feel like a lot when you're

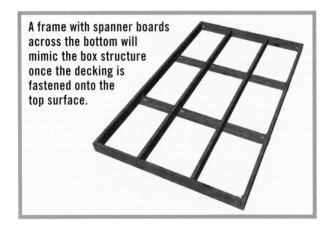

A frame with spanner boards across the bottom will mimic the box structure once the decking is fastened onto the top surface.

Shown here is a common hinge method that links one floating dock section to another.

standing upon the dock. Wearing hinges and pins can be kept after. Like most things, they have their life and should be replaced as needed.

Finally, when we think back to the point about completing the box, you'll see in some of my plans that I've included what is referred to as a spanner board. A spanner board is fastened across the underside of the stringers on a float section. On small sections to be kept lightweight, adding only a couple spread at even distances apart will help complete the box, adding torsional strength.

Just ahead, I've provided plans for common-size float sections that are considered residential or light commercial grade. They were designed with the DIYer in mind who would rather avoid unnecessarily overbuilding and overspending on material, especially when it comes to mobilizing sections to and/or from the water. If, however, your exposure to wind and chop demands a heavier design, consider using my plans as a guide and simply increase the timber size in the frame, possibly doubling the thickness around the perimeter if necessary. Where exposure requires you to step up the timber sizes, I recommend that you also step up the size of dock hardware that secures the section's butt joints and braces its corners. In the next chapter, you'll see examples of heavier connecting and reinforcement hardware (pages 142 and 143) commonly used on sections subjected to greater exposure.

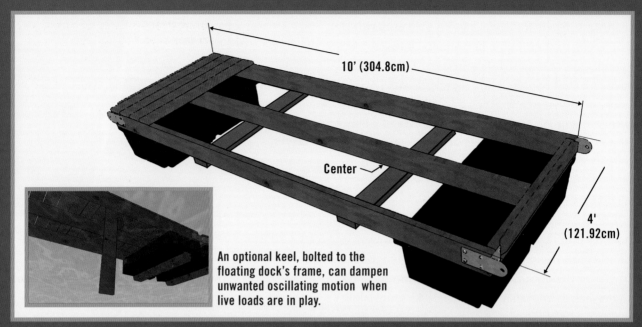

10' (304.8cm)

Center

4' (121.92cm)

An optional keel, bolted to the floating dock's frame, can dampen unwanted oscillating motion when live loads are in play.

A narrow section may be used to conserve space over the water or reduce cost. Since narrow floating docks are often known to be less stable, this section will serve best when used as an economical walkway to other sections that are wider or sections that connect alongside at right angles. Improve stability by using flotation that keeps one's center of gravity low and by adding more flotation than what is shown here.

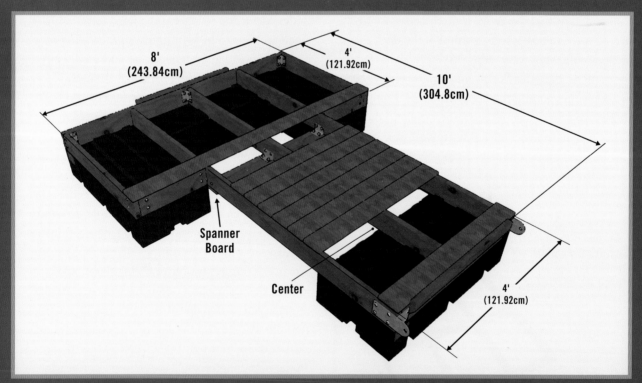

8' (243.84cm)

4' (121.92cm)

10' (304.8cm)

Spanner Board

Center

4' (121.92cm)

Used to stabilize narrow floating docks, this section, shown with some of its decking removed, features outrigger flotation to help stabilize the end of a ramp that leads to shore or a fixed dock. This section may also be used along a main walkway for added stability, providing a convenient place to join other narrow sections at right angles with the addition of connecting hardware.

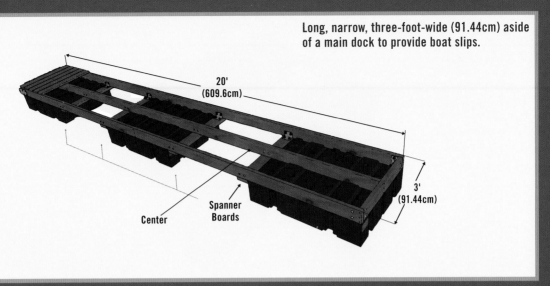

Long, narrow, three-foot-wide (91.44cm) aside of a main dock to provide boat slips.

20'
(609.6cm)

3'
(91.44cm)

Center

Spanner
Boards

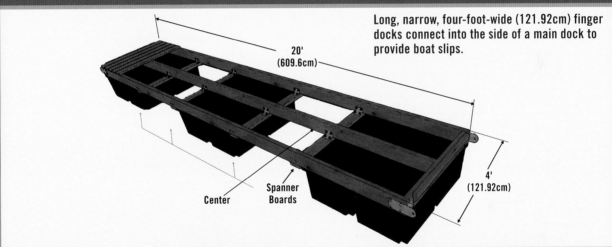

Long, narrow, four-foot-wide (121.92cm) finger docks connect into the side of a main dock to provide boat slips.

20'
(609.6cm)

4'
(121.92cm)

Center

Spanner
Boards

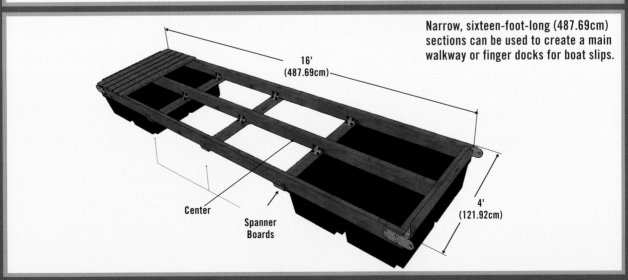

Narrow, sixteen-foot-long (487.69cm) sections can be used to create a main walkway or finger docks for boat slips.

16'
(487.69cm)

4'
(121.92cm)

Center

Spanner
Boards

Float sections
that are
6' (60.96cm) wide
and over provide
a stability and
comfort level that
is accepted more
broadly than docks
that are narrower.

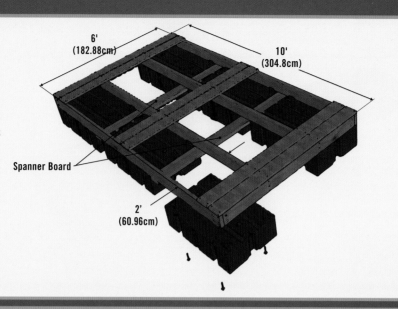

6'
(182.88cm)

10'
(304.8cm)

Spanner Board

2'
(60.96cm)

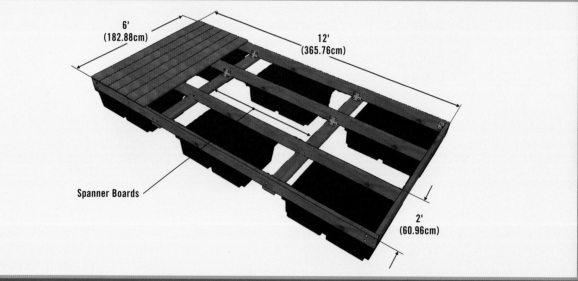

6'
(182.88cm)

12'
(365.76cm)

Spanner Boards

2'
(60.96cm)

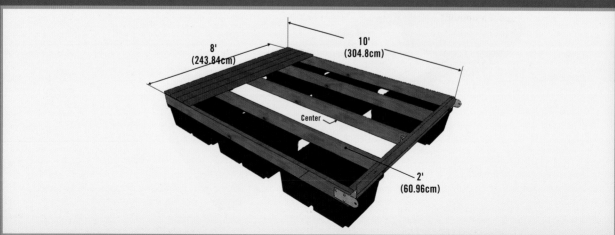

8'
(243.84cm)

10'
(304.8cm)

Center

2'
(60.96cm)

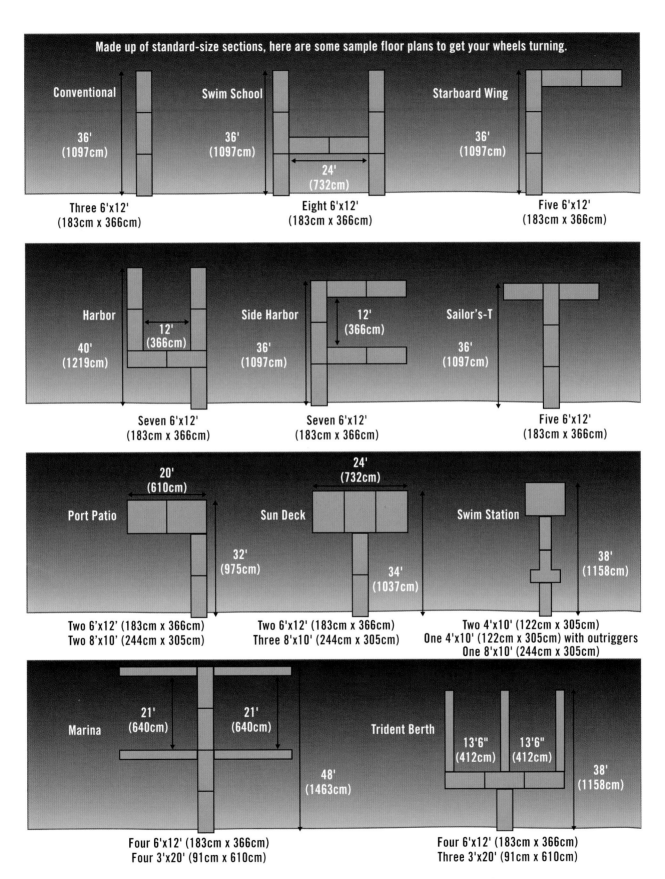

Made up of standard-size sections, here are some sample floor plans to get your wheels turning.

Conventional
36' (1097cm)
Three 6'x12' (183cm x 366cm)

Swim School
36' (1097cm)
24' (732cm)
Eight 6'x12' (183cm x 366cm)

Starboard Wing
36' (1097cm)
Five 6'x12' (183cm x 366cm)

Harbor
40' (1219cm)
12' (366cm)
Seven 6'x12' (183cm x 366cm)

Side Harbor
36' (1097cm)
12' (366cm)
Seven 6'x12' (183cm x 366cm)

Sailor's-T
36' (1097cm)
Five 6'x12' (183cm x 366cm)

Port Patio
20' (610cm)
32' (975cm)
Two 6'x12' (183cm x 366cm)
Two 8'x10' (244cm x 305cm)

Sun Deck
24' (732cm)
34' (1037cm)
Two 6'x12' (183cm x 366cm)
Three 8'x10' (244cm x 305cm)

Swim Station
38' (1158cm)
Two 4'x10' (122cm x 305cm)
One 4'x10' (122cm x 305cm) with outriggers
One 8'x10' (244cm x 305cm)

Marina
21' (640cm)
21' (640cm)
48' (1463cm)
Four 6'x12' (183cm x 366cm)
Four 3'x20' (91cm x 610cm)

Trident Berth
13'6" (412cm)
13'6" (412cm)
38' (1158cm)
Four 6'x12' (183cm x 366cm)
Three 3'x20' (91cm x 610cm)

CHAPTER 16:
CONNECTIONS OF SECTIONS

If you're thinking about building or improving a floating dock, and you've stuck with me over the last few chapters, then I trust that you're connecting with me through the topics of this book. Bringing your ambition, skillsets, and imagination together with my guidance will do great things for your dock. In this chapter, you'll find the tried and true methods for connecting your floating dock sections together.

No matter the method you employ to join your sections, the connections deserve your attention toward a result that has your complete confidence. The possibility of it coming apart unintentionally is most often a result of neglect, such as ignoring a worn or loose connection before it eventually failed. Rare, but on occasion, I've seen methods fail that were underbuilt for the level of exposure and abuse. Just ahead, we'll look at special hardware and measures to be taken that will prevent connections from failing.

Two sections of floating dock are drifted into each other for a connection that will lock them rigidly together.

Sections of floating dock are jointed where they connect to each other, allowing them to articulate as waves roll through.

Articulating and Non-Articulating Joints

The common hinged joint between sections not only provides a convenient way to connect, but its articulating motion allows wave energy to escape that may otherwise cause fatigue and damage to the dock. The alternative—bringing them together rigidly so that they don't articulate—offers improved stability, especially for sections that have been made short to keep them light and portable. Sometimes a combination is used to get the benefits of both.

An old method for making a connecting dock hinge uses shouldered eye-bolts, fastened to the adjoining ends where sections meet. They are aligned and held together by an iron rod that passes through all the eyelets. Linchpins and washers are at each end of the rod to retain the linkage. Traditionally, a short wooden post such as a 4x4 (100 by 100 millimeters) or 6x6 (140 by 140 millimeters) is bolted into the four corners to secure the butt joint together. The post, in each corner, extended above the decking will serve a secondary purpose as a tie-off bit for boats. Popular as this method

A traditional method of connecting sections uses eye-bolts lining up with a rod passing through.

has been, the holes through the wood frame where the eye-bolts are fastened become oblong from strain, causing them to loosen and fall out. Though enhancements help, such as fabricated washer plates and liquid thread lock, many DIYers have moved away from this method to dock hardware made for this purpose that requires less maintenance.

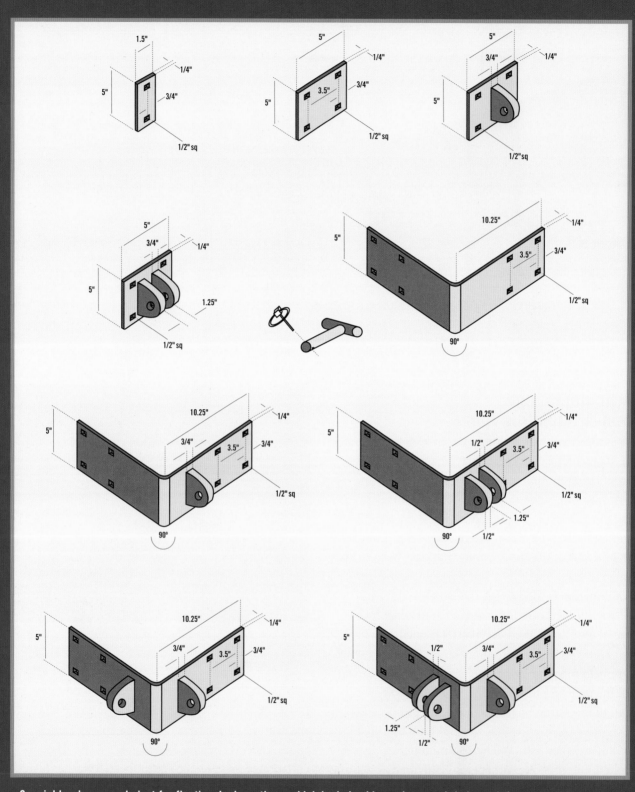

Special hardware made just for floating dock sections, which includes hinge plates and timber reinforcement irons, are commonly used by DIYers today, a substantial improvement over the old eye-bolt connection method. These hardware components are made to fit on framing that is 2x8 (38 x 184mm) and larger.

For decades now, career dock builders and many DIYers have come to trust in a manufactured or fabricated dock hinge that replaces the old eye-bolt method. During all my years in the business, I came to rely on hardware made from steel plate that firmly secures to the wood section with a grouping of bolts. For corrosion resistance, the steel is preferably powder coated or hot-dip galvanized. To distinguish them from the many eye-bolt hinges that were still present years ago, dock builders in my region assigned the name "hinge plates." Depending on the manufacturer or part of the world you're in, expect other names, but in this book, the hinge plate is what I will refer to them as. For joining sections end to end, a typical hinge plate would fit around the corner and through-bolt to both sides of the butt joint. While reinforcing the wooden frame, the hinge plate's steel pad-eye extends forward with its hole for the hinge pin and aligns with the pad-eye from the adjoining section. Some hinge plates have a male to female connection as do fittings for plumbing. The male has a single pad-eye that lines up between two pad-eyes on the female. There are a handful of manufacturers in the U.S. alone that make these hinge plates, all similar

in design utilizing 5-inch (127-millimeter) wide plate and available to contractors and DIYers alike. The standard hole pattern on these parts is made for framing that uses 2x8 (38- by 184-millimeter) lumber or bigger.

In climates that experience severe ice, requiring docks to be removed from lakes and ponds before winter, DIYers for many years have accepted dock framing made with 2x6 (38- by 140-millimeter) lumber. Though easier on the back, it is dimensionally too small for all the hinge plates on the market that use 5-inch (127-millimeter) steel plates. If you're planning on using lumber of this size, be sure the hardware you're looking to buy is sized right for the width of your lumber. When the lumber I'm using limits me to smaller hinge plates, I use a product made of ¼-inch (6-millimeter) thick plate, 4-inch (10-centimeter) wide, including the pad-eye without a male-female connection. Simple, yet rugged, the dock sections mate with pad-eyes lapping and leaving an inconspicuous offset. The hinge pin that I use for the hinge plates to pivot on is a simple ¾-inch by 1 ½-inch (19- by 38-millimeter) hex bolt, secured with a locking nut.

For smaller size framing, such as 2x6 (38 x 140mm), look for hardware components that are of proper size, having a bolt pattern that will be well within the dimensional borders of the board.

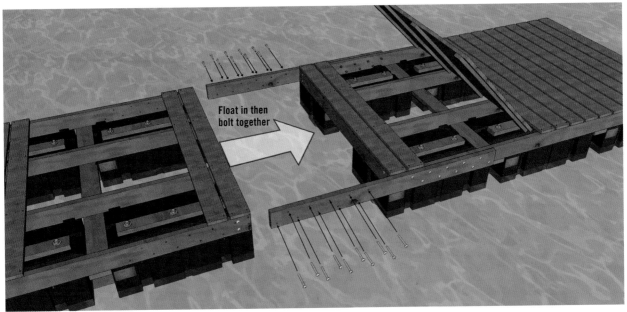

Float in then bolt together

A non-articulating joint may be made using two heavy planks along each side of adjoining float sections. Removable decking allows complete access to the fasteners for assembling and disassembling while over the water.

For joining dock sections where articulation is not wanted (a rigid connection), a splice may be made using heavy planks that through-bolt along the outside, holding the two sections tight at the seam. To aid in securing the two sections together, through-bolts should pass through the headers of the adjoining sections. If the joint needs to be separated later, some of the decking can be panelized and removable for full access to the fasteners. With this method, all butt joints in the frame should be reinforced with a corner iron and through-bolts.

Another way to join sections together for a rigid connection is with dock hardware made for this purpose. The same manufacturers that make the hinge plates provide similar hardware that use a pin or bolt at the top and bottom of the plate. Much of this hardware, again, is made for framing that uses 2x8 (38- by 184-millimeter) lumber or bigger.

For docks framed with 2x6 (38 by 140 millimeters), I use a rigid float connector that resembles a hinge plate. It has a square pad-eye extending forward on one plate that nests into a

A simple method to make a non-articulating joint on sections framed with 2x8 (38 x 184mm) or larger utilized this hardware kit.

For float sections framed with 2x6 (38 x 140mm), a non-articulating joint can be made with a hardware kit like this.

square channel on the opposing plate. One square set tight inside the other locks the two sections together so they will not articulate.

Let me just caution you on the use of dock hardware made for a rigid connection. It is best to use it on sections that are short in length or where connecting two sections at the broad side with each other. Recognize that rolling waves passing through the floating dock put leverage on the rigid connection and stress the hardware at the joint. The longer the section, the more leverage there will be. In calm protected waters, this is less of a concern, but where chop is common through a dock with multiple sections, I recommend that every other joint to be hinged.

Keep It Together

Any place where butt joints in the frame could pull apart should have a corner iron, through-bolted in place to reinforce and keep it together. Where the end of one section connects into the side of another, the outside stringer on the side that connects will be

A hinge connection that is away from the end of a float section should be reinforced with blocking. The blocking should be secured with bolted-in corner irons, as shown.

stressed by the two sections as forces push together and pull apart. In this case, the outside stringer that is being stressed should be reinforced by blocking that fits between the stringers, secured with through-bolted corner irons at every joint.

Reinforcing butt joints with corner irons is especially needed for sections that are joined without an articulating connection.

While a hinged joint allows wave energy to escape between sections, a locked joint will trap the wave energy, forcing it to dissipate through the dock's materials. Give it time and the energy effectively will make its own hinge by loosening fasteners and joints that once held everything tight together.

Using hinge plates that reinforce the corners and adding corner irons at other critical points adds tremendous strength and life to the dock, but it wouldn't hurt you to take it one step further. By now, you may have a pretty good idea of what is happening to a floating dock section when put in service. While under the stress of torsional and lateral strain, from wind, boats, and shifting loads, just to name a few, we can expect while on duty 24/7 that the fasteners may loosen in time. I recommend applying a liquid thread lock to the bolt threads to keep the nuts from backing off. You can choose between a formula that locks permanently or one that lets you remove the fasteners if needed. Another remedy is to use RTV silicone on the threads. Either of these products prevent vibration from sneaking up on you, the scourge responsible for important parts loosening and failing. Finally, your vigilance is required. Everyone and everything has its lifespan, so be watchful when something is worn and ready to be repaired or replaced. From my experience, the root cause was often neglect, ignoring a part that had exceeded its life expectancy or the replacement of missing bolts.

Gap Coverage

Connecting hardware, whether articulating or non-articulating, made by manufactured dock hardware results in a gap between float sections that varies depending on the product. It could be 3 or 4 inches (7 or 10 centimeters), but either way, gaps of this size should be reduced to prevent stepping into

Hinge plates often leave a significant gap between the sections while the floating dock sections are connected. A gap is required so that binding doesn't occur, but it must be reduced to prevent trips and falls.

One method to reduce the resulting gap from hinge plates uses two filler strips of wood, fastened to the end and flush to the decking where the two sections meet. Leave just enough gap, such as ¾" (2cm) to prevent binding or pinching as joint articulates.

Make a filler that secures to one side of the gap using a slender piece of decking called the cap. Its cut width should reduce the gap to ¾" (2cm) when fastened to one of the sections. A supporting piece of lumber to the cap is first mounted flush to the top of the frame. The cap is then fastened with deck screws to its support.

Filling or covering the gap can be done by extending the deck board, cantilevering it beyond the edge of the frame. Otherwise, you could make filler strips to reduce the gap that can be made with wood that fastens flush to the decking along the end of the floating dock section.

My preferred method is to make a removable cap that runs along the length of the gap. The ability to remove the cap allows clear access to the connecting hardware. For this method, fasten some support blocks—short pieces of 2x6 (38 by 140 millimeters)—onto the end of one float section between the connecting hardware, keeping the top edge flush with the top edge of the header or stringer. Do not mount any to the adjoining section. Using the same decking as what is used on the dock section, cut a length that matches the length of the gap. On a table saw, rip the deck board's width down so that it is ¾ inches (20 millimeters) less than the width of the gap. This will be the cap. When the sections are brought together in the

or tripping. Closing in the gap to about an inch (a couple of centimeters) will significantly reduce hazards, yet will allow the float sections to pitch into a wave while leaving a gap big enough so that binding or pinching does not occur. If you over-fill the gap, potential pinching results and could cause an injury while the float sections articulate together.

If you're sensitive to noise that may come from dock hinges, a durable plastic washer, such as nylon, positioned where hinge plates rub is known to help.

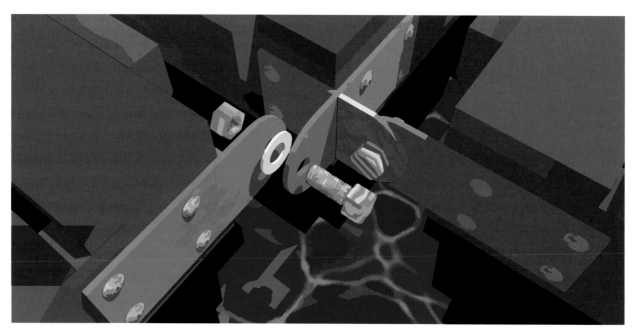

Shown here, a small floating marina reopens in early spring with all-new dock sections connected, one to another, with hinge plates.

water, joined at the hinge, apply the cap on top of the support blocks, tight to the edge of the decking. Pre-drill with a countersink through the cap and into the support blocks. Then fasten with a 3-inch (76-millimeter), number 8 flathead stainless screw. The cap can be removed by backing out the screws when the connecting hardware needs to be accessed.

Noise Control

At one time in your life perhaps you were drawn to heavy metal noise, just not the kind made by a floating dock. Quite often DIYers ask how to stop the squeaking made by the hinged connection. Mostly it comes from two metal surfaces bearing together, likely the pad-eyes. The easiest remedy is to apply lithium grease, preferably formulated for marine environments such as an outboard grease. This, of course, will need to be reapplied on occasion. If the hinge pin or hinge bolt has enough

length, nylon flat washers large enough for the diameter of the pin or hinge bolt can be applied where the pad-eyes are rubbing. Use an adhesive on one side of the washer to hold it onto the pad-eye while connecting the adjoining dock section. If using hinge bolts and locking nuts for the pin, do not over-tighten the locking nut as this will surely make unwanted noise. By backing off the pressure until there is play between the pad-eyes, you should notice an obvious improvement.

Sourcing Parts

If you're in a region where floating docks are popular and there is always a dock project going on, you may find dock hardware conveniently on the shelves at nearby hardware or marine supply stores. If not, then many companies offer the products online. For your convenience, I've listed some of the suppliers in a source index at the back of this book (page 249).

CHAPTER 17:
FLOTATION SENSATION

As you're forming a plan in your mind for components to use on the upcoming dock project, whether for new or rehab construction, some basic knowledge on flotation options will be helpful in advance. I'm going to float three different options by you: foam billets, plastic barrels, and float drums.

Foam Billets

I have never been a fan of foam, specifically unencapsulated foam as a flotation for docks. Not only have I seen pieces of it littering the shoreline but sound alternatives have been around for decades now that are not only better for the environment but also deliver a better performance overall.

Beginning with unencapsulated foam billets, that peaked out in popularity decades ago, some contractors and DIYers continue to choose them over more modern options, so long as regulations allow. Before building with foam billets, check your local codes to see if they have been banned in your area. The foam's vulnerability to breaking apart is common knowledge to many dock users and environmentalists who support its restriction. Aside from code compliance concerns, a couple other deterrents that may move you toward other options include its attraction to burrowing rodents seeking a "foam home" and water absorption between the foam's cells. Both conditions steal away your dock's buoyancy, leaving less than when the foam billet was new. If that doesn't discourage you, at least choose a foam that is made for dock flotation and box it in for containment that will protect your environment. Remember that foam is not foam. If it is specified for dock flotation, the manufacturer should boldly

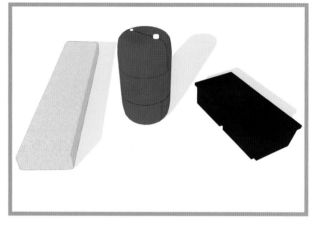

Represented here are three common choices of flotation used under docks: the foam billet, plastic barrel, and float drum.

make claims about its product's resistance to absorption and degradation from ultraviolet light.

There are two kinds of foam commonly used to float docks that I'm familiar with. One is an extruded product specifically for docks made by Dow Chemical® that is sold through retail lumberyards or stores that specialize in dock building materials. Its pale blue rigid structure consists of tiny plastic bubbles or air pockets that yield the light weight buoyancy. Available in two thicknesses, 7 inches (18 centimeters) and 10 inches (25 centimeters), a width of 20 inches (51 centimeters), and a length of 96 inches (244 centimeters), they can be easily cut to length for your custom size dock using a simple handsaw. Dow Chemical's website, *www.Dow.com*, provides information on their foam and free plans on how to build a floating dock with their product.

The other kind of dock foam usually found is made from expanded polystyrene (EPS).

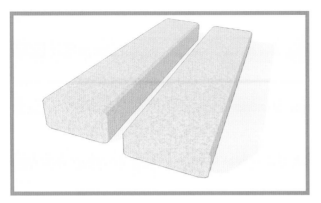

Dow Chemical's extruded foam billets contain tiny plastic bubbles or air pockets.

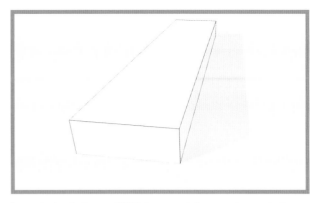

Expanded polystyrene (EPS) foam contains very buoyant, tiny white beads that stick to each other.

Instead of an extruded process, EPS foam begins as a polystyrene bead that puffs up when its manufacturer exposes it to steam. While hot under steam, the expanded beads stick together in a mold that forms large, white, lightweight, and buoyant blocks. They can be cut to size with a handsaw or better yet with a hot wire to cure their surfaces. EPS foam block manufacturers may sell direct or through building material supply houses.

Plastic Barrels Repurposed

The plastic barrel that once contained food products, either 30 or 55 gallon (114 or 208 liters), deserves honorable mention, regardless that it would not be my first pick in most instances due to its unstable curved surface. Nevertheless, the barrel does have its benefits, mainly, a low-cost advantage and that its repurpose is a commendable form of recycling. It may also be the best choice where docks are at a substantial risk of being wiped out by nature's wrath. I can think of a few places where investments into expensive dock materials would not be wise. One such place close to my home is in a mountain valley river that is notorious for flooding. An inch (a couple of centimeters) of rain in nearby mountains means the river will rise 8 feet (2.44 meters). With that comes a great purge along its banks of loose boulders, tree limbs, stumps, and even whole trees. Docks don't stand a chance there,

though people keep putting them back, on the cheap, of course.

I have faith that you would never choose barrels that contained toxic chemicals. I recommend that you wash out the inside of any food product residue to prevent fermentation and bloating. A DIYer once told me a story about a barrel under his dock that swelled with gas buildup until it exploded in the heat of summer: "Went off like a bomb, sending pieces of plastic everywhere," he said. I'm glad nobody was close by when it went. Barrels should be inspected for damage and the bungs or plugs should be sealed with RTV silicone. Choose black or blue barrels over white as the darker pigment has better resistance to UV degradation. A 55-gallon (208-liter) barrel will support close to an impressive 450 pounds (204 kilograms), but the round shape will be a compromise for optimal stability, noticeably more on docks under 8 feet (2.44 meters) wide. A 6-foot (1.83-meter) wide will feel like it's about 4 feet wide (122 centimeters) when you step near the edge. Stability on narrow floating walkways, in widths of 3 or 4 feet (100 or 122 centimeters), can be improved by including a section of dock with outrigger flotation, as seen on pages 136 and 152.

Float Drums

Float drums made specifically for dock flotation are what I recommend to most DIYers. Though more

Known for its low cost, but not its stability on the water, the plastic barrel can be cradled into a dock section's framing, as shown here, to provide a substantial amount of buoyancy. Seatbelt or tie-down straps for securing the barrel in place are cut to a length that can be screwed to the cradle blocks while stretched around the barrel.

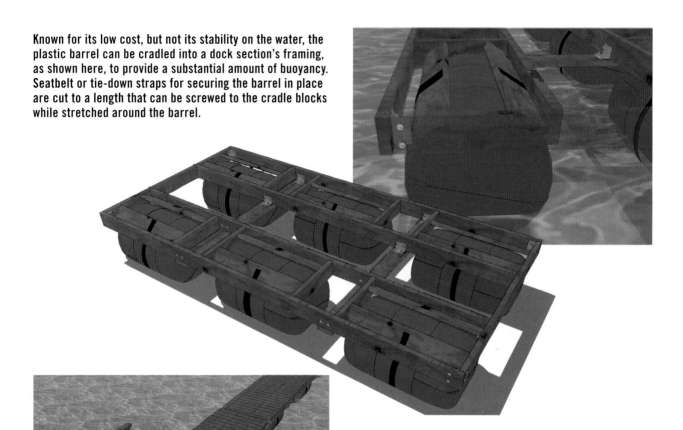

Framing a floating section in the shape of a "T" allows flotation to be placed further away from the main dock, serving as an outrigger for added stability. This is especially important for narrow docks that are floating on plastic barrels. Shown here, a ramp is extended from shore with its outbound end resting on the "T," giving it a generous amount of stability.

expensive than foam or barrels, they are made for durability, stability, and ease of installation while also better for the environment. Most of the time, they are truly what you need to do the job right. On the market today, there are a handful of choices made by companies that use any one of the following processes: rotational molding, thermoforming, and blow molding. All these processes use polyethylene for the outer shell, typically black as it is the most resistant to UV degradation.

Choices: Size, Shape, and Value

Whether you have a nearby retailer where you can buy float drums or you'll be shopping online, there are some basic tips I can help you with to understand the value in various options out there. I'll begin with size… well, it does matter. Every float drum comes with a buoyancy rating that tells the weight it will hold, and every float drum comes with a price. To understand the value in what the float drum will support, you'll want to know the price per pound (per kilogram) of support. Simply divide the price of the float drum by the weight in pounds (kilograms) that it supports for the answer. Though not always the case, usually the bigger the float drum, the lower the cost per pound (kilogram) of support. Perhaps the most popular and available sizes for DIYers is 12 inches high, 24 inches by 36 inches (30 by 61 by 91 centimeters) and 12-inch high, 24 inches by 48 inches (30 by 61 by 122 centimeters). These sizes are versatile for most home projects and are UPS® and FedEx® shippable to your door.

Let's keep going. Though at a glance, float drum brands and models may all look alike, discovering up close what appears to be slight variations can mean significant differences in performance. A float drum that is wider at its top than its bottom or is broadly rounded on the bottom will often deflect passing debris and allow current flow to sweep underneath with less drag than a float drum that has straight sides and right-angle corners.

By contrast, a float drum comparable in size, under comparable loading that does not have a taper or rounded bottom, will not be as quick to dip down when a live load moves over it. Its more block-like shape with uniform displacement makes it a more stable model.

Even the type of mounting flange can make a big impact. A continuous flange around the top perimeter offers liberty for placement and quantity of fasteners, but its convenience compromises capacity when comparing to a float drum of the same overall dimensions that does not have a continuous flange. For example, a float drum that measures at a full 12 inches by 24 inches by 48 inches (30 by 61 by 122 centimeters) has a buoyancy rating of 450 pounds (204 kilograms). A similar float drum that has the same overall dimensions but with a flange that measures 1 ½ inches (38 millimeters) all around the top will forfeit close to 75 pounds (34 kilograms) or 16 percent of its support.

Wall thickness should be questioned as there is added value in having more polyethylene in the outer shell. This characteristic alone can explain a price disparity between brands. Wall thickness is especially important at the corners and edges along the underside, including the bottom surface. A uniform wall thickness of ⁵⁄₃₂ inches (4 millimeters) is what I would look for at a minimum. This is especially important for docks that get handled more in climates where ice requires annual removal. I

recognize that it is not that easy to verify a product's claims online when you can't see the product firsthand. Since the float drums could be the single greatest investment in your project, speak with a knowledgeable representative at the company where the product is made. When you purchase it, keep a copy of the product claims and the warranty on file.

Most float drums on the market today are filled with expanded polystyrene foam (EPS), the little white beads that can make a big mess if not encapsulated. I find that most people assume that foam filling is insurance, should the outer shell rupture or become punctured, to keep things floating. Well, they wouldn't be wrong, but just as importantly, the black polyethylene shell needs a solid filling to keep it from collapsing under the weight of a dock—and the foam does that job very

Float drums are molded with a durable polyethylene shell. Many brands and models include EPS foam filling.

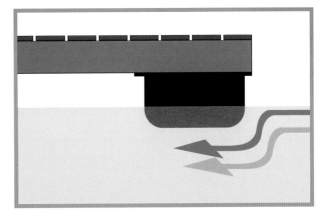

On water that has a swift current, as in a river, the float drum with a rounded bottom may have less drag while the water flows beneath it.

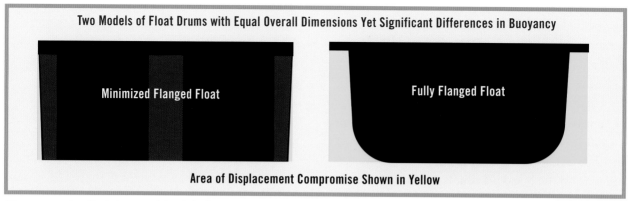

Two Models of Float Drums with Equal Overall Dimensions Yet Significant Differences in Buoyancy

Minimized Flanged Float

Fully Flanged Float

Area of Displacement Compromise Shown in Yellow

When comparing float drum models of similar overall dimensions, the optimal amount of buoyancy is in the one with boxy corners and smaller mounting flanges.

well. As for the insurance part, foam certainly keeps the float drum floating if punctured, but I wouldn't expect it to keep the water out. If water goes into the foam, significant listing and undesirable weight that becomes trapped in the shell may be irreversible. I can't say enough about having a good, thick shell; the best insurance against water getting in is not the foam, but the quality of the shell.

If you're interested in a float drum that doesn't use foam at all, consider one that has a heavy rotationally molded shell with internal posts for its structure. This was the float drum that I used for most of my career. I began using it back when the float drum industry was small and struggling to put out a product that didn't leak and absorb water into the foam. I reasoned then that all shells on float drums, foam filled or not, are subject to damage and that water-absorbed foam-filled float drums were not exempt from repair or replacement. I found that foam-less was easier to repair since I could drain all the water out and repair the shell.

By no means are my tips here intended to scare anyone away from float drums. All the brands and models I've looked at or tried are an improvement over the old ways, so you really can't go wrong. But your ability to navigate through all the choices will go better for you now that you're armed with some knowledge and understanding how to spot value.

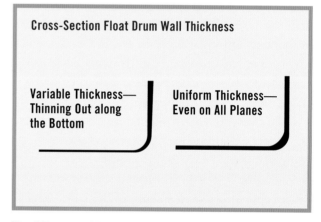

Cross-Section Float Drum Wall Thickness

Variable Thickness—
Thinning Out along
the Bottom

Uniform Thickness—
Even on All Planes

The different molding processes employed to make float drums can be expected to turn out varying characteristics in the wall structure. The process to make the wall consistently thick will likely come at a higher cost than for a wall that varies from thick to thin.

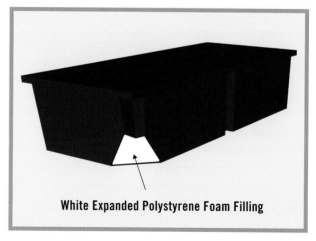

White Expanded Polystyrene Foam Filling

A cutaway view reveals the float drum's white EPS foam filling.

How Many Float Drums Does It Take?

A very good question for DIYers asks how many float drums should be used in a dock section. The best way to answer that is to know the total weight you want to hold. This would include the weight of materials in the dock along with fixtures and live loads expected to be upon the dock. For light docks that use 2x6 (38- by 140-millimeter) framing, a range between 25 and 32 pounds per square foot is usually required. For heavier framing, such as 2x8 or 2x10, I would use a weight of 40 pounds per square foot.

Multiply the square footage (meters) in the dock section by the weight demand per square foot (meters) to get the total weight you want to support. Applying the float drum's buoyancy rating available within the manufacturer's specifications, divide the total weight you want to support by the buoyancy in the float drum to reveal the quantity needed.

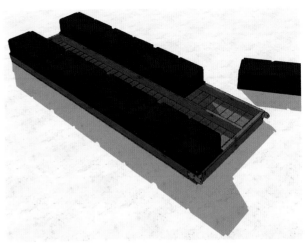

Manufacturers of float drums rate each model with respect to buoyancy. Determine the total weight you wish to support, including the weight of all the materials in the dock, the attached fixtures, and the maximum human weight that could be present. Use the buoyancy ratings of the float drum model to determine how many are needed to generously exceed your minimal requirement.

Imperial System

For example, a 6x16 dock section has 96 square feet. To support 40 pounds per square foot, the total weight to be supported is 3,840 pounds. A 12-inch by 24-inch by 48-inch float drum supports 450 pounds. Divide 3840 pounds by 450 to realize that you'll need eight to nine float drums.

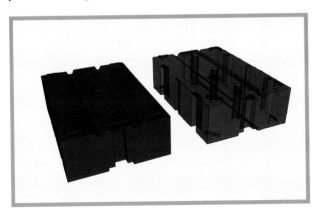

A model for environmental sensitivity that does not demand foam, the dragon float relies on its molded internal posts for rigidity instead of foam filling. Its posts are hollow and allow the passage of long bolts to hold an optional skid board along the bottom.

Metric System

For example, a 1.83 by 4.88 square meter dock section has 8.93 square meters. To support 18.14 kilograms per square meter, the total weight to be supported is 1,741 kilograms. A 30- by 61- by 122-centimeter float drum supports 204 kilograms. Divide 1,741 kilograms by 204 to realize that you'll need eight to nine float drums.

Keep Your Options Open

By now, you've gained some helpful insight as to the merits and demerits on three of the most popular choices for dock flotation. Perhaps you've already made up your mind toward the flotation that is right for you. For DIYers who choose to go the economical route and use foam or plastic barrels instead of the more expensive float drums, I recommend that you space your wood framing for a standard-size 2-foot (61-centimeter) wide float drum. That way, if you decide to upgrade someday to the float drums, your dock sections will conveniently accept them with ease.

CHAPTER 18:
SHORE TRANSITION AND ANCHORING FOR FLOATING DOCKS

Whether pondering improvements to your current floating dock or formulating a plan to build an all new floating dock, there are no pertinent topics more essential than how it should transition to shore and the best methods for its anchoring. A safe and sensible transition consummates your floor plan while a dependable anchoring method instills confidence that your investment will stay where you intended. The attributes from these two interrelated features that I've brought together in this chapter can make or break the overall success of the dock depending on your choice of methods. Therefore, let's pay special attention to details within the most popular methods of choice so that you may match up the best one for your dock's environment.

A floating dock transitions smoothly to its adjacent rocky shore.

Make It a Shore Thing (Marrying-Up to Dry Land)

Unless your floating dock is meant to be an island, somehow it must transition to dry land or a fixed point that adjoins to dry land such as a fixed dock or boardwalk. In the first part of this chapter, let's look at the portion of dock that will be brought into play for the transition, followed by shoreline situations that may resemble yours. From these examples, you may visualize a method best suited for your floating dock and shorefront.

Ramping Up

The transition segment that bridges between a floating dock and a fixed dock, seawall, or a natural shore-scape will be referred to in this chapter as a ramp. A ramp, often sloping while hinged between the floating and fixed points, may simply be a section of floating dock that is devoid of flotation at its shore end.

The Ramp as a Shore Anchor

If built rugged enough, a ramp may be used to hold the floating dock away from the fixed point. This will engage the fixed point where the ramp connects to serve as an anchor, holding the shore end of the floating dock in position. Under these circumstances, lateral forces against the opposite end of the floating dock will transfer back to the ramp where much will be asked of it. Diagonal members across the bottom of the ramp's frame will help to resist added forces that could cause its structure to become racked or skewed.

An alternative to using the ramp as a means of anchoring the shore end is for it to merely bridge over and support loads that cross, while some other method is employed to hold the shore end of the floating dock in place. No matter how much you ask of the ramp, its width and length should be an appropriate fit for where it will be installed and for safe passage of people and pets.

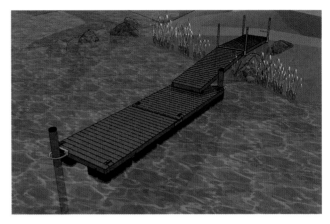

While transitioning to shore with the help of a ramp, this floating dock's anchorage depends solely on its yoke with nearby pilings.

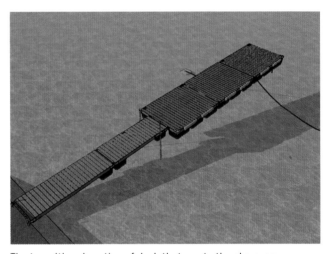

The transitional section of dock that meets the shore may sometimes play a role in the dock's anchoring.

A section of floating dock becomes a ramp and transitional section as it hinges directly to a fixed point.

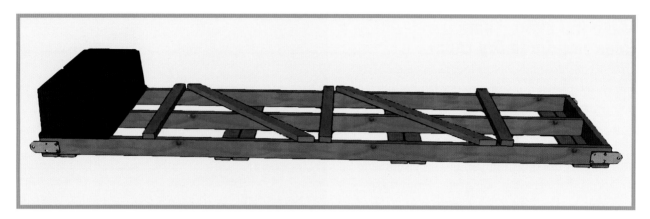

A ramp may be used to hold or anchor the position at the floating dock's shore end. The added strain it's under while doing this job may demand reinforcement to its frame. Notice here that the ramp is shown turned over for the addition of diagonal boards fastened along the bottom for its added strength.

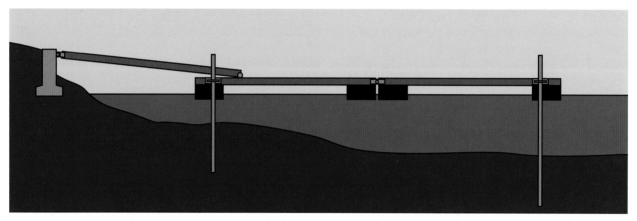

A floating dock is anchored off the shore, yoked to pilings, and does not need the ramp as a linkage to hold the dock's position. The ramp's role then is to simply bridge the gap to shore.

Deciding the Ramp's Length

Where water level fluctuations are negligible and the floating dock can be positioned close to shore, a small ramp may fit the bill comfortably.

By contrast, a floating dock that must be kept further from the shore or is much lower in elevation than the fixed point it connects with will need a longer ramp. I make it a habit of cautioning DIYers not to build the ramp too short. In climates where they know the dock will have to be removed before winter, the tendency is to build small and lightweight. I'm sympathetic but I'd rather see the right length ramp in place. When planning its length, be sure to project its steepest slope at the time of low water. A maximum slope of 15 degrees is manageable for most people, and in places like the coast of Maine, mariners accept much steeper slopes due to extreme tide swings. For ramps that get steep at low water, the deck surface should have "ramp cleats" to put your heel against and hand railing to get your arms and hands into, for the climb.

I'm not surprised if all this length has you thinking about the weight and how you're going to move it. You can conserve on weight by framing with 2x6 (38- by 140-millimeter) stringers and 1x6 (2.54- by 140-millimeter) decking. Lumber to frame a 16-foot (4.87-meter) long ramp is readily available at your local lumberyard and

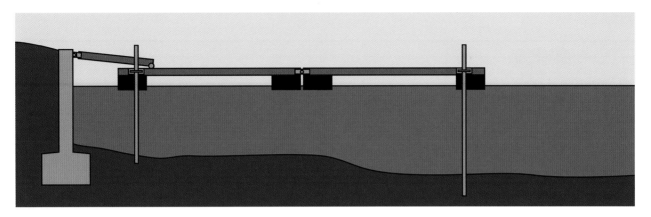

Provided lowering water levels don't make it too steep, a small ramp hinged to a seawall conserves space over the water.

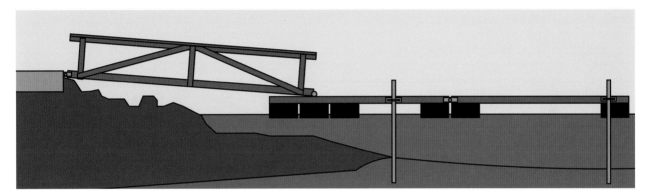

A long ramp allows the floating dock to set further offshore if needed.

even 20-foot (6.09-meter) long may be available with a special order. For ramps this long, 2x6 (38-by 140-millimeter) framing will still feel heavy, especially after you attach a rail along each side. If you don't have mechanical help for mobilizing it, consider panelizing the deck surface so it can be removed for lighter portability. For a ramp with a length up to 16 feet (4.87 meters), railing can be detachable by unfastening the bolts that hold them to the sides. Ramps longer than this should have a truss to improve the span, an added feature that won't be as desirable to handle without mechanical help. In regions that require ramps at greater lengths, there may be a fabricator who can build what you need with aluminum. Provided their workmanship has a good reputation, this may be a practical choice.

A ramp that can become steep should have rails to hold onto and ramp cleats to keep one's footing while making the climb.

A long ramp connects with a hinge near the shore. Its outbound end rests upon the deck of the floating dock.

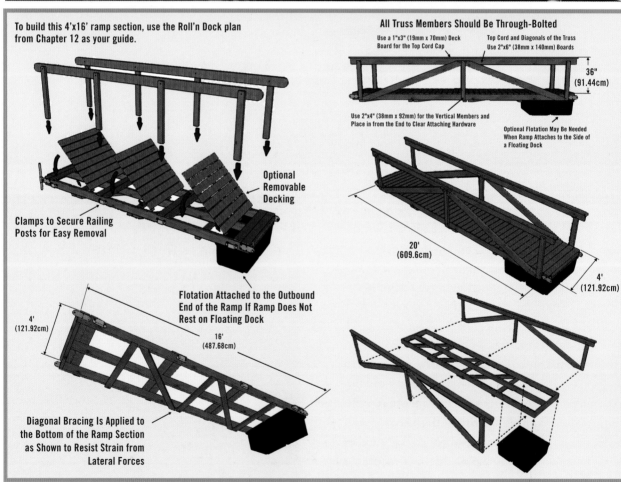

To build this 4'x16' ramp section, use the Roll'n Dock plan from Chapter 12 as your guide.

All Truss Members Should Be Through-Bolted

Use a 1"x3" (19mm x 70mm) Deck Board for the Top Cord Cap

Top Cord and Diagonals of the Truss Use 2"x6" (38mm x 140mm) Boards

36" (91.44cm)

Use 2"x4" (38mm x 92mm) for the Vertical Members and Place in from the End to Clear Attaching Hardware

Optional Flotation May Be Needed When Ramp Attaches to the Side of a Floating Dock

Optional Removable Decking

Clamps to Secure Railing Posts for Easy Removal

20' (609.6cm)

4' (121.92cm)

Flotation Attached to the Outbound End of the Ramp If Ramp Does Not Rest on Floating Dock

4' (121.92cm)

16' (487.68cm)

Diagonal Bracing Is Applied to the Bottom of the Ramp Section as Shown to Resist Strain from Lateral Forces

If a long ramp is necessary for your project, consider one of the plans presented here. To improve portability, you may opt to make the decking removable in panels, along with making the side railings removable. A ramp that is longer than 16' (487.68cm) should have a wooden truss along each side as part of the railing to prevent sagging. The truss I've featured in my plans includes three vertical posts to support the railing. Diagonal planks are to be cut and fitted between the center posts at the railing and the end posts at the ramp's frame. All fastening should be through-bolted.

Ramp Hardware

Ramps may utilize the same reinforcement and connecting hardware for floating dock sections, found in Chapter 16, Connections of Sections (see page 140). Sometimes a ramp needs to roll or slide at one end. If your ramp has lawnmower wheels, it is not the first. If you can't fashion something together homemade, there are companies eager to sell their version to you. Otherwise, a ramp may do better by sliding on a durable polymer strip, specifically, ultra-high molecular weight polyethylene (UHMW), fastened along the ramp's bottom edge.

Flotation Compensation for the Ramp

When a ramp is hinged at the side of a floating dock, additional flotation will be needed to support the ramp's weight, otherwise the dock section it connects to will list. Provided the ramp doesn't get too steep, a float drum fastened to the underside at the outbound end often does the trick. Just make sure you have enough buoyancy in the float drum(s) to support the ramp's weight. However, if you expect the ramp to steepen as water levels drop, the attached float drum(s) will rise out of the water due to the tilt, putting the ramp's weight burden on to the dock. If you anticipate this, plan on building with more flotation into the dock, under the end that connects to the ramp. This is also recommended when the ramp will be resting on top of the floating dock instead of attaching to its side. Since half of the ramp's weight will be supported at its shore end, the total buoyancy amount for its outbound end should be enough to support the floating dock section and the other half of the ramp's weight.

For narrow floating docks, especially in the range of 4 feet (122 centimeters) in width, the ramp and dock will be extremely tippy unless you include something called an outrigger float. This will add tremendous stability and help maintain your sober composure. Building the narrow floating dock section into the shape of a "T"—with its wide end

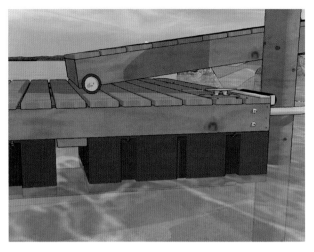

As the floating dock, held by pilings, rises and falls vertically during water level changes, the ramp resting upon it may move back and forth with the help of rollers or wheels.

Instead of rollers or wheels, a solid plastic board with a smooth slippery surface may be fastened along the bottom of the ramp, allowing it to slide. See to it that its screws are countersunk so there is nothing to gouge into the decking. This method can be improved upon if the deck boards in the area where the ramp will slide are made with a plastic resin base.

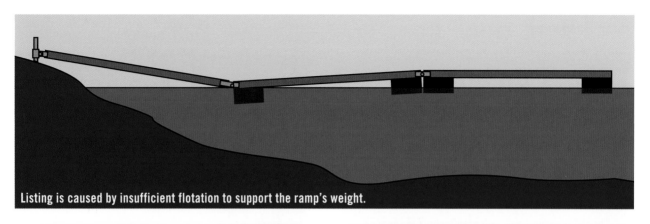
Listing is caused by insufficient flotation to support the ramp's weight.

Looking up from below, the floating dock's shore end can be seen with extra flotation, to compensate for the ramp's weight that rests upon it.

placed under the ramp—will yield the stability of a wide dock as it accommodates ample flotation for the ramp where it joins.

Shoreline Situations
Directly Connecting to Shore

So long as there is not a severe water level change expected, the first floating dock section—serving as the ramp, with flotation only present on its outbound end—can be hinged to a fixed point on the shore, such as a seawall, fixed dock, or anchor point on a natural shore-scape. The fixed point must be solid and there should be additional anchoring so that it will not budge from leverage exerted by lateral forces at the dock's outbound end. If pilings will be placed alongside to hold the outbound end

Find plans for building this outrigger section on page 136 in Chapter 15.

Upon a narrow floating dock, looking back toward the ramp, a "T" shape section offers room for the extra flotation needed to support the ramp's weight.

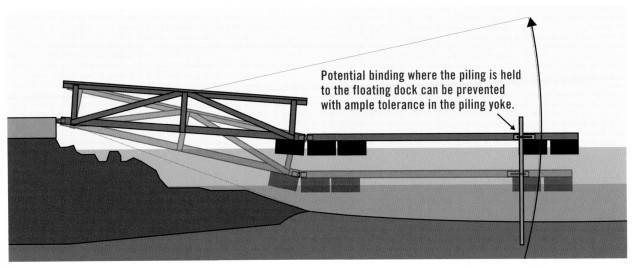

Potential binding where the piling is held to the floating dock can be prevented with ample tolerance in the piling yoke.

A ramp that is hinged at both ends and used to hold the floating dock off a fixed point will arc similarly to a circle compass as it rises and falls with water level changes. A piling used to anchor the floating dock's position must have ample room in its yoke to prevent binding as the dock arcs.

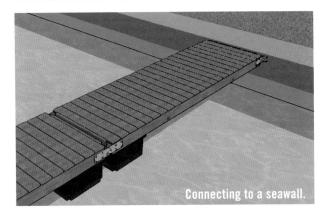

Connecting to a seawall.

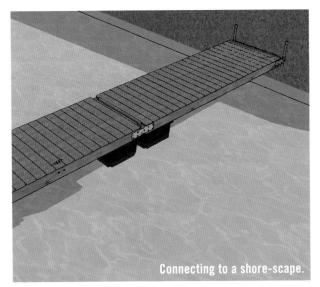

Connecting to a shore-scape.

Connecting to a fixed dock.

steady, keep their yokes loose enough to prevent binding during water fluctuations.

Do not depend on hollow concrete block walls for the shore connection and see that all face boards on fixed docks are reinforced with through-bolted corner irons. The result will be a firm connection to the shore that is steady to walk on as it stops all side-to-side tipping near the shore transition.

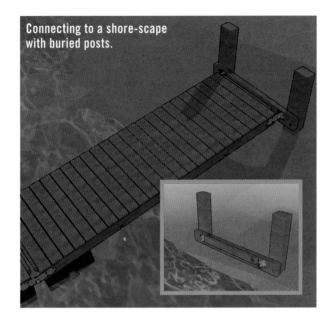

Connecting to a shore-scape with buried posts.

Ramp Resting Ashore

On a natural shore-scape, such as a gently sloped bank, the ramp that is hinged at the dock may simply rest its shore end on the ground without connecting to a fixed point. The ramp will creepily slide or roll longitudinally on the shore while the dock freely rises and falls with water level fluctuations. This method will work so long as the floating dock is held and guided sufficiently in position by pilings or moorings that minimize lateral movement.

Ramp Rests upon Dock

When the floating dock is held by pilings or moorings that limit the dock's freedom to move

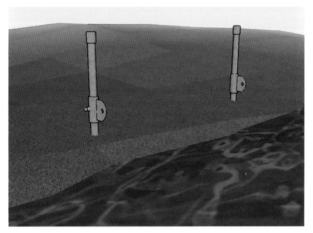

Pipes driven into the bank as an anchor for the shore end may install easier than wooden posts. A special sleeve held on the pipe with a setscrew links with the dock's ramp section.

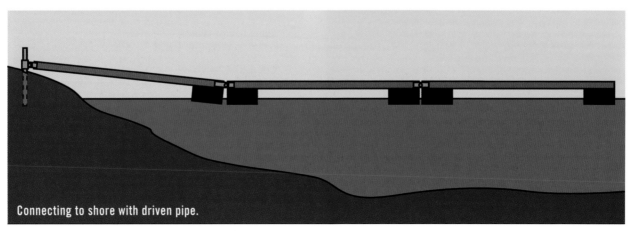

Connecting to shore with driven pipe.

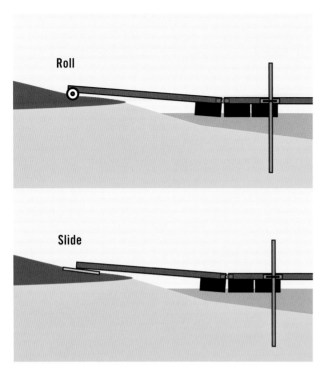

When the floating dock is anchored in place with pilings, the ramp may rest on the shore-scape and roll or slide.

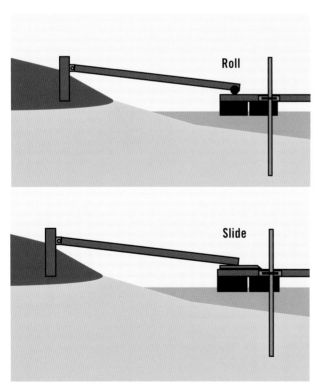

With the ramp hinged to a fixed point on shore, its outbound end may rest upon the floating dock and roll or slide.

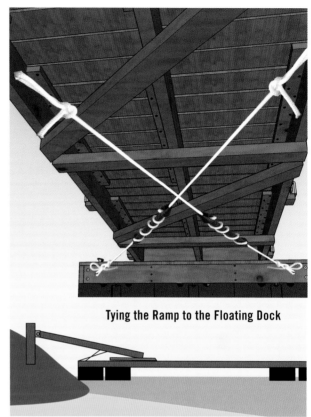

Tying the Ramp to the Floating Dock

Looking up at the underside of this ramp reveals how it may be tied to the shore end of the floating dock that it rests upon. A floating dock that is held in place with moorings has some freedom to move about. Tying the ramp to the floating dock will maintain the ramp's position and keep it from slipping off the edge.

laterally, a ramp, hinged at the shore at an elevation above the dock, spans across to simply rest atop the dock. As the dock rises and falls with water fluctuations, the ramp will slide or roll longitudinally on top of the dock.

Docks that are held and guided in position by moorings instead of pilings will likely have an undesirable amount of lateral motion. This can cause the ramp to eventually skid its way off the edge, presenting a situation that may induce an outcry of expletives beyond imaginable. To prevent this, the ramp can be unobtrusively tied down to the dock using heavy line, attached at the underside of the ramp. To alleviate tension in the lines, apply a line snubber for elasticity.

Transitions of Terror

Let me share with you some transition mistakes that I'd rather not see repeated.

1. Never attach a fully floated dock section directly to the end of a fixed dock. Flotation near the hinged joint, rising above the wave crests, will hoist the fixed dock's nearby legs or pilings out of the lake bed, riverbed, or seabed. Where a floating dock section or floating ramp section joins any fixed point with a hinge, there should only be flotation on the outbound end.
2. Positioning a floating dock section directly adjacent a fixed dock can pose a serious pinching or crushing hazard, especially if the deck surface to the floating dock is not far below the frame on the fixed dock. Always set the floating dock away from the fixed dock and transition with a ramp section.
3. A ramp that is too short may be too steep to climb. Anticipate what the maximum steepness of your proposed ramp length could be before deciding on its length.
4. When the water level drops, the ramp steepens toward the dock, narrowing its hinge gap until pinching occurs. Reduce the filler that shrinks the gap or install a dock hinge cover.

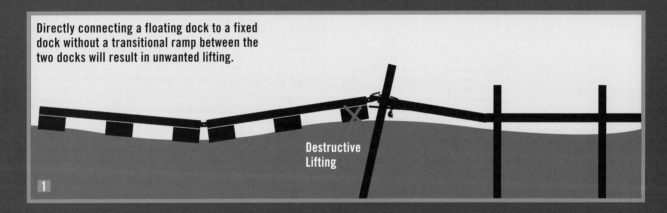

Directly connecting a floating dock to a fixed dock without a transitional ramp between the two docks will result in unwanted lifting.

Destructive Lifting

1

The convenient step down from a fixed to a floating dock can cause a pinching hazard. Prevent this by using a transitional ramp between the two docks.

AH!

CRUNCH!

2

5. What's worse than a ramp over sharp rocks? A ramp that is very narrow without a guard or railing to prevent falling off the side. Don't wait for someone to get hurt before attaching a secure railing.

6. A transition that falls short of reaching safe ground on shore should be rethought. Make sure there is enough length to safely bridge everyone over the treacherous surf and turf.

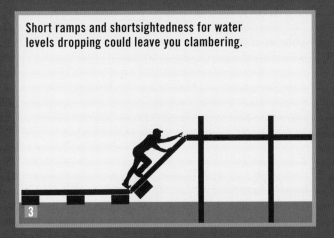

Short ramps and shortsightedness for water levels dropping could leave you clambering.

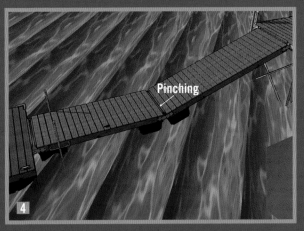

Pinching

Long and narrow ramps without railing are only for the nimble.

This transition is not making the grade.

Holding Steady (Anchoring for Peace of Mind)

Archimedes said, "Give me a place to stand and with a lever I will move the whole world." Think of a floating dock firmly held at the shore that extends out over the water. This is an Archimedes lever. The longer the dock, the longer the lever and the more force it will catch from wind, current, and boats that bear against it. All the forces that push at the dockside will naturally transfer back to shore where its hold will potentially be defeated without the aid of additional anchoring.

Undoubtedly, the method by which your floating dock is held in place carries a hefty responsibility. This is never truer where exposure to the elements

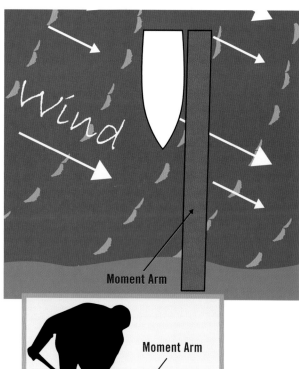

A floating dock that catches forces on one side becomes a moment arm that puts its anchorage to the test.

will put your method to the test. For the sake of your investment (the dock and its tethered boats), this is not a test you'd want to retake. To help with that, the remainder of this chapter is dedicated to this critical component for the success of your floating dock. Just ahead, we'll get into some ways and means you may employ to hold your dock steady and in place with complete confidence knowing that your investment is secure. Dock moorings, pipe or pilings, and stand-off arms are the three most tried-and-true methods that I have come to rely on as a dock builder. No matter what your level of familiarity is with any of them, I think you'll take something away from here that will put you ahead.

Moor Information

Dock moorings set to hold a floating dock in position are particularly popular in climates where ice requires their temporary removal during winter months. Once docks are detached and put up for winter, mooring tackle is flagged and left on the bottom, safe from ice damage. When in use, moorings for docks are often arranged in tandem or in pairs to counter forces that come from either side of a dock.

Before we consider where and how they might be used, let me describe the ingredients of a basic dock mooring followed by the principles of how they work.

Merely consisting of an anchor, chain, shackles, and an attachment point for the chain at the dock, I may not be revealing anything new to you. Many DIYers who know the right components, however, miss the understanding that a proper mooring has its anchor set a lengthy distance from where its chain attaches at the dock. I'm frequently asked, "How big should the anchor be to hold my dock?" This question often indicates an expectation that the burden of holding depends mainly on the anchor's weight. That wouldn't necessarily be wrong, but my reply to the question might be, "Make it so heavy that it would sink the dock section if placed upon it."

Moorings may be employed to hold the floating dock against forces that threaten its position.

My genuine answer is that a good anchor has more to do with its shape and the way it grabs into the bottom than making it heavy. Think of a boat anchor, light enough to toss over the side, but capable of holding all the boat's weight by its claw that digs into the bottom. Let me stop here and set your thoughts about the anchor aside for a moment while we consider the chain's length and associated weight that I'll refer to as a static anchor. Bear with my exaggeration, please, but imagine hypothetically if your mooring had a mile (kilometer) of heavy chain extended out windward in a straight line along the bottom.

Seriously, the buoyancy in a typical dock section may nearly support 1 ton (907 kilograms). Unless the anchor weighs more than the dock's lifting capacity, a strong wind or swift current against the dock can certainly drag its anchor, leaving your dock and its attachments in a mess. An anchor that size, of course, would be daunting to move, especially when the plan was to float the anchor on the dock as the means to get it launched.

You wouldn't need an anchor that sits static—attached at the other end. That much chain, though a costly proposition, would be heavy enough to do it all. Now visualize wind pushing against the dock, causing it to surge away from the chain upon the crest of each passing wave. But with so much weight strung incrementally, link by link, the chain's swag never straightens. Even as the wind intensifies, delivering more surge against the dock, the chain answers with more links, weighing down and pulling the dock back to its origin.

Enough weight in concrete is added to a section of floating dock until it begins to sink.

WIND

One chain is at rest while the other responds to wind and wave surges, returning the dock to its position.

Returning to reality, I'm not recommending that your dock moorings be made with super long chains, but the thought of it helps us to grasp how a chain's length and weight is capable of being a variable anchor, taking nearly all the burden from the static anchor. The static anchor, be it solid concrete, rock, or iron, should be set away and dug in so that the chain can have substantial length and weight lying between each end. In this way, any tugging on the static anchor is from a horizontal direction, less likely to break its grip, while the chain behaves like a shock absorber, an immeasurable attribute to every component in the mooring and the dock.

If the environment for your floating dock is a quiet, sheltered corner in the lake, dotted with lily pads, my sermon on moorings may seem like overkill or even hoopla. I couldn't agree more as there are countless circumstances where very little is needed for a dock mooring. By contrast, if your environment has exposure, and dock moorings are your preference for holding the dock's position, then applying the principles here will prove invaluable.

Anchors Away

Make sure that any anchor you buy or make does not have a high-profile feature potentially hazardous to swimmers and watercraft; otherwise, keep at a safe depth or distance.

DIYers like to use pre-cast products like cinder blocks chained together forming a large heavy heap. Though that may be okay for light anchor requirements, it wouldn't be my preference where there may be significant exposure. Round concrete pads with a rebar loop in the middle may be ready to take home from a stone center and they roll very conveniently from the pick-up bed to your shore, but

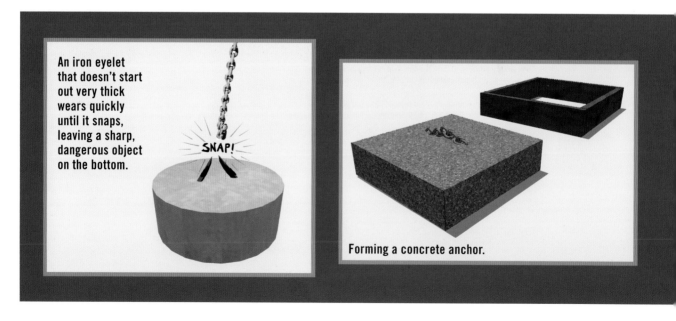

An iron eyelet that doesn't start out very thick wears quickly until it snaps, leaving a sharp, dangerous object on the bottom.

SNAP!

Forming a concrete anchor.

I have found them to be on the light side, especially since concrete loses about 40 percent of its weight when immersed. Yes, that's right, 40 percent. You should also beware of thin rebar loops that may be cast into round pads. The mooring chain shackle will wear through and snap it open, leaving two pencil point–shaped barbs standing upward for a swimmer to find. (Ouch!) And, unless the bottom is so mucky that an anchor will sink out of sight, I would avoid casting anchors with 5-gallon (19-liter) pales as they tend to roll and are not very dependable.

Making Your Own Concrete Anchor

Instead, I would make a square form using four pieces of 2x6 (38 by 140 millimeters), each 2 feet (61 centimeters) long. When nailed together at the corners, place the form onto a piece of poly on the ground. Use a bagged pre-mix concrete rated for 3500 psi (246.07 kilograms per centimeter squared). Pour the cement up to the brim of your form. With a trowel, smooth over the top and bevel the edges. Then, at the center of the square, sink a 3-foot (91-centimeter) length of ½ inch (13 millimeters) or bigger, galvanized mooring chain into the cement, leaving a chain loop exposed for the mooring chain connection point. Give the cement about two days for a full cure before moving off the poly. An anchor this size will weigh close to 300 pounds (136 kilograms) out of the water. Depending on how much dock you're going to hold, wind exposure, and density of the bed, you may need more than one concrete anchor of this size per mooring chain.

Making an anchor isn't rocket science, but maybe more like rock science. One of the best anchors you can use is a large dense rock cut in a rectangular slab that has a hole through it for the mooring chain attachment. Take granite, for example, that has a density weight of 171 pounds per cubic foot (2,691 kilograms per cubic meter) and is 15 percent heavier than concrete. This kind of anchor is what I prefer when sheer dead weight is needed, as when the lake bed, riverbed, or seabed is hardened clay or ledge where anchors can't settle themselves in.

For a sand or mud bottom, consider a helical anchor or mushroom anchor. Small helical anchors may be turned into mud or sand by hand, best done by a scuba diver when in deep water. In soft muck beds, be sure that the shank length is enough to bite into a firm base beneath the muck. Mushroom anchors lay sideways and usually settle into sand and mud over time, but digging them into the bed upon installation with the help of a scuba diver is wise.

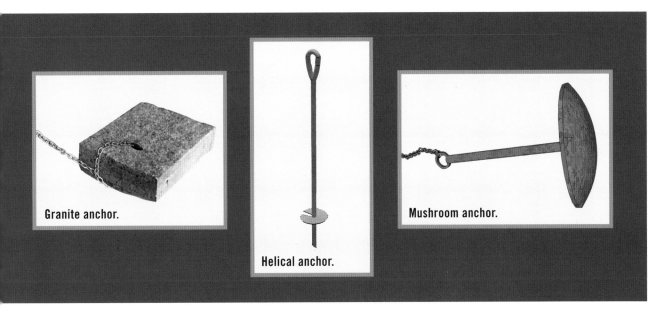

Granite anchor.

Helical anchor.

Mushroom anchor.

Make sure that the mushroom anchor's bell portion (that is shaped like a salad bowl) is at a safe depth away from swimmers.

Mooring Chain and Attachment

Chain for most non-commercial mooring applications should be ⅜ inch (9 millimeters) or greater, galvanized, and "long-linked" (if available) for the ease of fitting shackle bolts/pins through. The easiest link on a chain to put a shackle bolt/pin through is the end link. When you want to bring a shackle into any other link to adjust the length of a mooring, you'll appreciate the "long-link" as it provides extra room to make the connection with ease. Connecting a mooring chain to the dock can be done with a simple forged eye bolt, ½ inch (13 millimeters) or bigger, fastened through the wooden frame. Eye-bolts that are made from a rod that is bent to an eyelet shape are not as reliable for the strain by a mooring. A better connecting method is with a steel plate that has a keyhole-shaped chain slot or a chain retainer. Either of these special parts will allow length adjustments to the chain with greater ease.

Holding Steady with Ramp and Moorings

While a ramp hinged at both ends will hold the floating dock off a seawall, fixed dock, or shore-scape, its linkage to the solid object can make a very substantial anchorage for portions near the shore end. It would be a mistake, however, to expect a solid hold at the shore end to withstand the strain that comes from forces against the dock's outbound end. When straight on, forces put the dock in a state of compression, pushing it into the shore anchor. In this situation, the floating dock often takes it quite well as hinges between sections allow the dock to buckle, releasing energy from the force.

When forces push against either side of the dock, a proper mooring will limit how far the outbound end can be moved. Typically, the mooring anchors are placed at left and right sides near the dock's outbound end while chain that attaches from the dock to the anchor will be at a right angle to the main dock. Mooring chains that hold a dock to the anchors should be crossed underneath so that the chain doesn't interfere with the path of boats and swimmers. When the predominant wind comes off the water at an angle, say 30, 40, or 50 degrees, you may opt to set the mooring anchor and chain windward and well beyond the outbound end of the dock. Another mooring should be its mirror image for balance.

When placing the anchors, move them far enough away from the floating dock so that

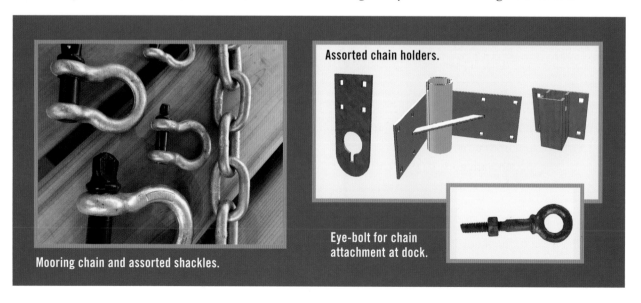

Mooring chain and assorted shackles.

Assorted chain holders.

Eye-bolt for chain attachment at dock.

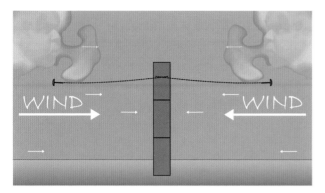

Moorings are attached to each side and crisscross beneath the outbound end of a floating dock. The mooring attached to the right side of the dock extends to the left and counters forces from the left. The mooring attached to the left side of the dock extends to the right and counters forces from the right. When there are no forces present, each mooring holds the dock centered and balanced.

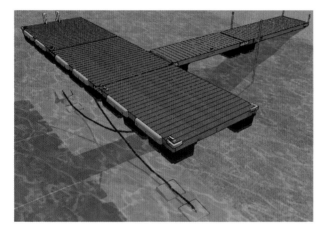

Crossing the mooring chains to their connection at the floating dock will help prevent interference with boats and swimmers. If possible, especially in shallow waters, take advantage of opportunities to position the anchors of moorings under portions of dock such as "L" or "T" sections.

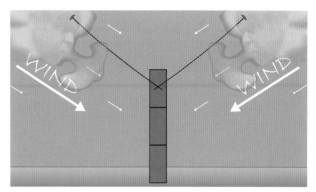

Though moorings are typically extended 90 degrees to the dock, consider extending them at the angle that is toward the predominant wind.

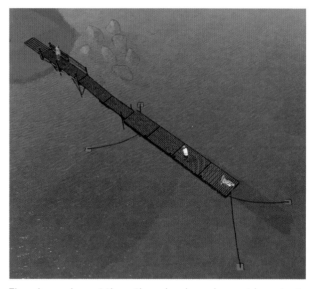

Though moorings at the outbound end may be most important to counter forces, floating docks with substantial length will likely need additional moorings at one or more midway points between each end depending on the dock's length and exposure.

swimmers who jump or dive from the dock are far from them. An "L" or "T" shape at the dock's outbound end sometimes provides the opportunity to place anchors underneath and out of the way. For docks that extend out with considerable length, additional moorings may be needed to keep mid sections from deviating out of their alignment. Remember, though, the moorings that do the most good and deserve the greater investment are the ones at the outbound end.

Holding Steady with Moorings Only

Suspended in the middle of four separate moorings, one off each corner, a floating dock can drift in small circular patterns without running away. Where setting pipes or pilings to help hold the dock in place is prohibitive, this mooring option has been employed and successful when careful attention is given to the placement, chain length, and weight of the moorings. Each mooring must have capacity to hold the floating dock and attached loads on its own. Two moorings are placed off the outbound corners at an outward angle and two off the shore end in the same manner. The longer the mooring chain and distance out from the dock, the more effective it will be. Mooring chains off the outbound end will cross each other and connect back from the left and right corners of the dock. Because of their distance out with lengthy and hefty chain, the outbound moorings will pull the dock away from shore. The shore-end mooring chains may be crossed or not, depending on your preference that might be based on available space near the shore end. They pull back toward shore putting the dock in a neutral position. Sometimes the shore-end mooring chains attach to the posts, crib or pilings of the fixed dock or pier that leads to the floating dock. Adjustment to the moorings' chain length and its swag between the anchor and dock are critical to minimizing range that the dock can drift. A ramp that bridges to the floating dock may be hinged or placed on top of the deck to slide or role. In the latter case, restricting the range of drift is especially crucial to preventing the ramp from slipping off the dock. This requires patience while monitoring the dock's motion. Tying the ramp to the floating dock will give some assurance that it will stay where it belongs.

Holding Steady with Pipes and Pilings

When anchoring in shallow waters of no greater than chest deep, galvanized iron pipe, 1½ inches or 2 inches (38 or 51 millimeters) in diameter, can be passed through an iron ring and driven into a sand/gravel bed. The DIYer uses a pipe cap and sledgehammer or gas-powered driver. Put these strategically around your floating dock for retention and a hold that minimizes lateral play. Just make sure the pipes are plumb while there is enough play in each guide so that binding doesn't occur during water level fluctuations. Pipes are most effective when driven until they feel solid. This could mean 2 to 3 feet (60 to 100 centimeters) into the sand/gravel bed. Avoid this method for greater depths where the dock's weight, bearing against the pipe would cause it to flex or bend over. If your dock begins in shallow water and extends where it is too deep for pipe anchoring, consider pipes to hold the shallow end while moorings hold the deep end.

If there is enough play in the ring, you may choose to slide a piece of gray PVC conduit pipe over the iron pipe to mitigate metal wear and clatter. In climates that require docks to be removed before winter ice sets in, pipes can easily be extracted with a turn and upward pull of a plumber's wrench.

A floating dock may be held in position exclusively with moorings. Moorings beyond the outbound end pull the dock away from shore, while moorings toward shore pull against the outbound moorings, keeping the dock balanced between. During mooring chain attachment to the floating dock, the chain's swag is adjusted until proper tension is found to minimize drifting off its center position.

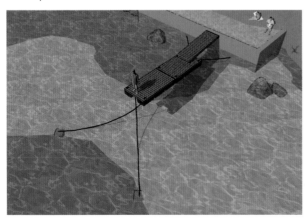
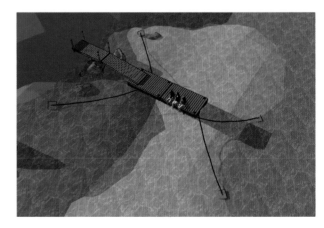

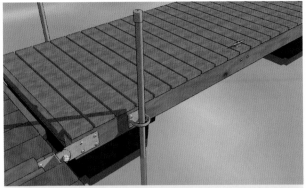

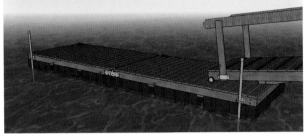

In shallow waters, slender pipes can be driven into the bed to a depth that holds them firm while yoked to the floating dock for anchoring. The dock's weight bearing against a pipe in depths greater than waist high may cause the pipe to flex.

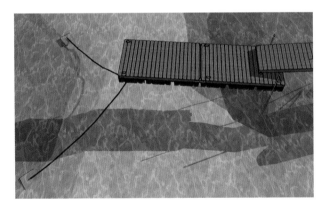

To anchor a floating dock from shallow to deep water, pipes may hold the shore end position while moorings hold the outbound end.

Where ice is not a problem, wooden pilings will work the same way (and even better when it comes to deeper water). Installing the pilings should be done by a marine contractor who has the proper equipment. Secure the floating dock to pilings using a guide that looks like an oversized U-bolt, available through dock hardware suppliers online. Otherwise,

PVC pipe fits over steel pipe to reduce noise and wear at the yoke.

a length of ⅜-inch (9-millimeter) chain will do, draped around the piling and fastened so that the piling is corralled to the side of your dock. Chain can be cut at a generous length to give added play if desired. Using a 1½-inch (38-millimeter) plastic pipe, dice it into 2-inch (51-millimeter) segments, about ten pieces total, to fit around the chain and help it slide along the piling. A sacrificial wear block of wood or preferably solid plastic lumber should be fastened to the side of the dock to buffer the piling.

When pipes or pilings are used to hold the floating dock in place, the guidance of a ring, hoop, or chain mainly allows the floating dock to rise and fall vertically while lateral motion is minimized during water level fluctuations. For this method of anchoring, refer to an earlier part of this chapter, Shoreline Situations (page 162), where I described proper transitioning to shore. Remember, a ramp may descend onto the deck of the floating dock and slide or roll during the dock's vertical motion. Otherwise, depending on your situation, a ramp may hinge at the dock at one end while resting on the ground at the shore end. If the ramp is hinged to the floating dock while also hinged to a fixed point at the shore end, binding could occur at the pipes or pilings without special provisions. To prevent this, pipes or pilings should be installed along lateral points and each guide that the pipe or piling passes through needs play enough to prevent binding.

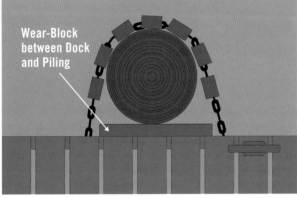

Wear-Block between Dock and Piling

A guide, which looks like a large U-bolt or a chain threaded through short pieces of plastic pipe, fits around a wooden piling to anchor the floating dock. A rubber roller or wear block made of plastic is fastened to the floating dock for the piling to rub against.

Holding Steady with Stand-Off Arms (AKA Stiff Arms)

In the same way that a ramp, hinged at each end, can be used to hold the floating dock off a fixed dock, seawall, or shore-scape, stand-off arms may also be used in this way to either share in the work that the ramp is bearing or alleviate the ramp entirely of anchoring. The ramp may then simply hinge at one end while the other slides or rolls. Stand-off Arms can be made with 4x6 wood timbers, hinged at each end, arranged as a pair, and cross braced with cables. Floating docks that run parallel to a fixed dock, seawall, or shore-scape may need multiple pairs. When two or more are working together they should all be the same length. Their hinge points along the dock should all be in alignment with each other and hinge points along the shore should all be in alignment with each other.

A 1½-inch or 2-inch (38- or 51-millimeter) galvanized pipe may also be used for stand-off arms, available at a fence or plumbing supply company that may have them up to 21-foot (6.4-meter) lengths. Shorter lengths can be found at a hardware or home center store. Special hardware that fastens to the pipe and joins it to the floating dock and fixed points can be ordered online from suppliers of commercial-grade components for floating docks.

For shorelines with greater exposure to wind and chop, I couldn't be happier with the pipe **swaying stand-off arms** that use trailer balls and couplers to hinge each end with. I have used some of these on turbulent waterfronts that would rip apart other methods, but the flexibility and play allowed by trailer balls that behave as a universal swivel, prevents leverage by wind and current from doing its thing. Using at least two 1½-inch (38-millimeter) pipes as a set of arms cut to your desired length, you'll find that standard 2-inch (51-millimeter) trailer couplers will fit over each end. Drilling through the pipe for fastening is required and fasteners should be secured with locking nuts. While drilling holes for the couplers, drill for a ½-inch by 2½-inch (13- by 64-millimeter) eye-bolt a few inches (several centimeters) back from each coupler. These will be used for connecting a rope brace. On the shore and dock, 2-inch (51-millimeter) trailer balls are mounted in an upright position that directly appose each other. Once the couplers are secured to the balls, a crisscross of heavy solid braid rope is tied to the eye-bolts between each pair of stand-off arms. The rope limits how far the arms can skew as wind and waves surge against the dock. Add a mooring line snubber to the ropes for enhanced elasticity and shock absorption. If docks nearby are not already using this method, you'll be the envy of the neighborhood, likely to get copied. This method is illustrated below and again in more detail in Chapter 19 on page 184.

Tying It All Together

When it comes to floating docks, shore transition and anchoring are two topics that I am most frequently asked about. So, if feeling challenged with these features, you're not alone and you're being wise to give them your keen attention. To fulfill a dock's purpose after all, it must include safe and smooth transitioning at the shore while serving as a dependable base for tie-up and other activities. Determining the best methods can seem difficult with all the choices at hand and uncertainty as to their outcome. I recommend that you examine your shorefront, becoming familiar with the exposure and features of its environment. Then match up your waterfront to the best fitting method described in this chapter. It usually helps to see other docks in the area with similar environments and talk with their owners. Look at both, the ones that appear to be a failure, noting the cause, while learning from the ones that are successful. Between the guidance offered in this chapter, your knowledge of the environment and ideas from neighbors gone before you, I bet you'll choose the best course.

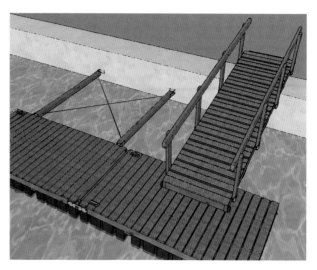

Along a seawall, a floating dock may be held in position with wooden stand-off arms.

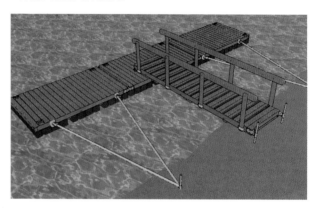

Pipe may be used as a stand-off arm instead of wood.

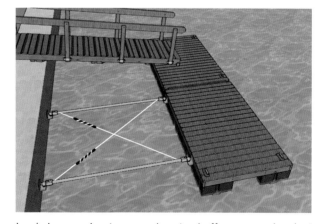

In wind-exposed waters, swaying stand-off arms can skew just enough with the surge of gusts and waves, allowing energy to pass without straining joints. Heavy nylon rope that is crossed and tied between the arms counters the energy that causes the skew, bringing the arms back to center between surges.

CHAPTER 19:
FIXED TO FLOATING DOCK

aving trouble making up your mind between a fixed or floating dock? Maybe what you need is both. Out of necessity, a combination may be the answer when all of one kind doesn't cut it. Here are some common reasons DIYers go with a fixed to floating dock.

- Often out of necessity, due to fluctuating water levels, a floating dock is the goal, but it takes a stretch of fixed dock to get out where the floating dock can begin. Obstacles such as stumps and boulders or lack of depth near the shore can make a floating dock prohibitive without a fixed dock to bridge over.
- The decision is to build a floating dock but a small portion of fixed dock near the shore will serve as the shore-end anchor.
- With a combination, dock users enjoy the best of both, the optimal stability on a fixed

A modest floating portion on a fixed to floating dock offers just enough space for boat access on a lake known for its water level fluctuations.

A fixed dock over rocky shallows transitions to floating where there is safe clearance for a boat.

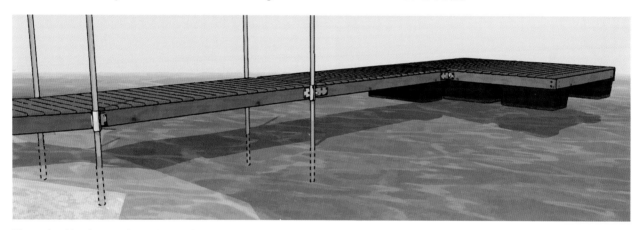

The main objective may be to have a floating dock, but a portion of fixed dock at the shore helps to anchor the floating dock's position.

The best value in a fixed to floating dock is realized when each portion has a specific purpose it optimally serves and no part of the dock is wasted.

The long dock over water that is prone to high winds and chop is less exposed when fixed above the wave height. If a floating dock is preferred, exposure is limited when keeping a small floating dock at the end of a fixed dock.

For a safe and reliable transition from a fixed to a floating dock, the ramp deserves your careful forethought and vision for how you want it to perform.

portion and low to the water accessibility on the floating portion.

• A combination can be found in an environment where a floating dock is desirable but seemingly more vulnerable to high winds or currents that may be present. To minimize exposure, the greater portion is fixed and safe above the water while a minimal portion is made to float and be subjected to the elements.

Do your needs or desires have anything in common with these fixed to floating situations? With the help you've acquired from the pointers in this book, you're better equipped than ever before to build both a fixed and floating dock. This chapter will help you bring the two together to achieve a smooth and secure transition. A site survey of your waterfront is a good place to begin, so refer to Chapters 5 and 14 (pages 40 and 124) to assess your environment while mapping out your proposed dock. Your knowledge from doing the survey, along with past years' experience that you might have at the site, will help you zero in on the method that will work best for your specific waterfront. The principles and methods described in Chapter 18 are key to putting a fixed dock together with a floating dock. I encourage you to compare your knowledge of the site with the methods I've described there, to guide yourself into the best choices.

Avoid Transitions of Terror

Whatever approach you take, pass the idea first through your mind's safety filter. When transitioning between fixed and floating, my list of "what not to do," shared in Chapter 18 (page 166), did not make it into this book without good cause and plenty of field experience. They are examples of someone's thought-out plans with all good intentions whereby the whole picture wasn't visible until it was done. Let's learn from their misfortune to thwart a bad investment that would lead to a costly and or painful failure.

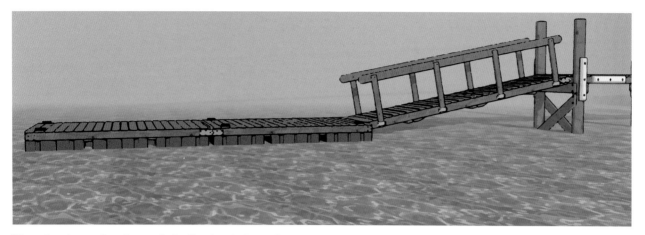

When choosing to directly attach the floating dock to a fixed dock, the fixed dock must be capable of withstanding strain transferred by the floating dock.

When choosing to directly attach the floating dock to a fixed dock, the fixed dock is not capable of withstanding strain transferred by an attached floating dock, see that the floating dock.

It's About the Ramp

Going from fixed to floating takes the ramp to do it right; therefore, the ramp is worthy to be a well thought out detail in your scheme. Consider its structural integrity, overall size, steepness, safety features, and any artistic expression you might want to add. Its complete purpose depends on your decision to have it hold the floating dock away, enduring leverage, or just bridging the divide between the two. This may be up to preference but compare the methods to your site's exposure. As you continue into this chapter, you'll find more tips for your ramp along with a recap from Chapter 18 of anchoring methods that interrelate with the ramp's purpose.

When the ramp is hinged at each end and used to connect the fixed to floating dock, it should be reinforced so that it doesn't rack. The bottom view of the ramp shows diagonal planks fastened to the underside of its frame for added rigidity.

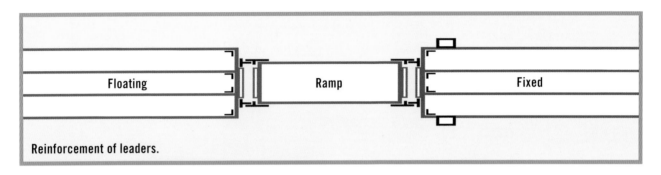

Reinforcement of leaders.

Corner irons reinforce the header on a dock section where it joins and is hinged to the ramp.

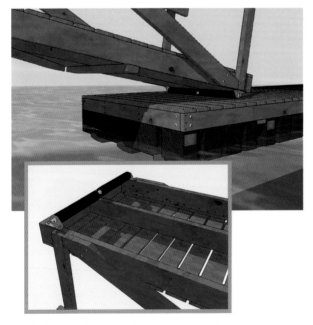

Upside down and upright views. As the floating dock rises and falls on waves and water fluctuations, rollers at the end of its ramp prevent wear at the point of contact.

Qualify the Fixed Dock

When you plan to use the fixed dock for anchoring the floating dock's shore end, you'll want to be confident in the fixed dock's ability to withstand any strain that is transferred to it from forces against the floating portion. Adequate moorings to resist strain on the floating dock will alleviate strain to the fixed dock but not entirely. The outbound end of the fixed dock should have its legs fully braced (see Chapter 10, page 102) and firmly set into the lake bed, riverbed, or seabed, securely holding its position. If cobble or ledge won't allow the legs to be set properly, then you may not want to attempt this arrangement. In that case it would be better to anchor the floating dock separately, using pipes, pilings, or with moorings only, as shown in Chapter 18. The ramp, hinged at the fixed dock, would simply rest atop the floating dock.

Reinforcing the Ramp

When moorings hold the floating dock at the outbound end while the ramp, hinged at both ends, is expected to hold the floating dock off the fixed dock, additional reinforcement for the ramp should be considered. Play that is in the moorings will let the floating dock sway to the side enough that the ramp may skew from its rectangular standing. For starters, the ramp's frame will be strengthened when using hinge plates that fit around each of the four corners, through bolting them on so that they secure the ends to the sides. But to truly stiffen and reinforce the ramp's frame, you should attach bracing across its underside.

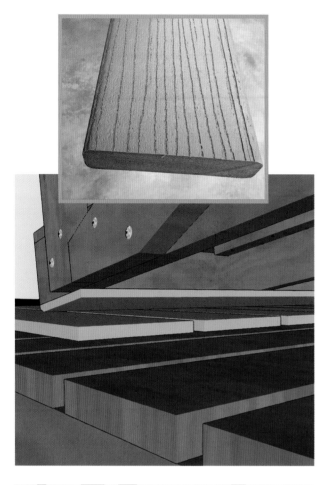

This will do wonders by adding years of life—and keeping all the corners square and tight. Just beware, everything has its limits, of course. Under severe wind and wave exposure, a reinforced ramp may not be trustworthy. You'd have better success with the swaying stand-off arms described in Chapter 18 (page 177), revisited on the next page.

Reinforcing the Headers

Where a hinge will be used to join the ramp to the fixed dock, the header that the hinge fastens to must be reinforced using corner irons and through bolts that will prevent the header from pulling off from the ramp's weight. By the same token, if the ramp joins the float with a hinge, the header on the float must be tied into its abutting stringers with corner irons and through bolts.

Ramp Rollers and Sliders

When the ramp has one end hinged to the fixed dock and the other sets atop the floating dock, it will need to slide or roll without wearing the deck or frame surfaces. If the floating dock is held by moorings, the ramp will need to slide slightly sideways as well. For this, a smooth, hard plastic roller with its ends eased over will likely cooperate avoiding stress on the ramp.

Though rollers are often the first thing thought of, consider a way to help the ramp slide freely. Using a plastic lumber made with polyethylene, make a 1-inch (25-millimeter)–thick pad area for the ramp to rest on. It should be wide enough so the ramp has room to slide in a controlled area without slipping off the pad. Its perimeter should have a 45-degree bevel. Fasten down to the decking with countersunk fasteners and the seams running with the direction of the ramp. For the ramp, use the same material, with radiused edges, cut to a length that will fit across the ramp's width along the bottom edge. When the ramp is over the pad with its smooth, plastic edge down, the ramp can slide smoothly on the pad.

Instead of rollers, a plank made of plastic lumber is fastened along the bottom at the end of a ramp. More plastic lumber is used to form a pad on the floating dock where the ramp bears its weight and glides. Beveling along the front edge of the pad will prevent a tripping hazard.

Shore Holding for Heavy Forces

The reinforced ramp described above sounds like it will be a tank carrier, but if your exposure includes relentless winds and rolling whitecaps, the conditions may overwhelm the ramp and cause it to break down. If the ramp manages to hold out for however long, you need to question the integrity of the fixed dock where the ramp is passing its forces to. Rather than attempting to build a ramp that won't rack or expect the fixed dock to stop the energy passed to it, a better way would be to roll with the forces, allowing them to dissipate between the floating dock and the fixed dock. This can be done with **swaying stand-off arms** as described in Chapter 18 (page 156). Using steel pipes as the arms that hold the floating dock away from the

fixed dock, hitched up to trailer balls with couplers at each end, allows the arms to sway, moving with the forces instead of bucking them. Heavy nylon line crisscrossed between parallel arms provides elasticity while limiting how far the arms can sway. Proper dock moorings (described in Chapter 18) at the outbound end of the floating dock will limit how far the floating dock can move off center while

In relentless winds and rolling whitecaps, swaying stand-off arms that hold the floating dock away from a fixed dock are jointed with a trailer ball and coupler connection. Their freedom to sway prevents strain and fatigue. Meanwhile, constant tension from moorings beyond the outbound end pulls the floating dock away from the fixed dock and minimizes the amount of its sway.

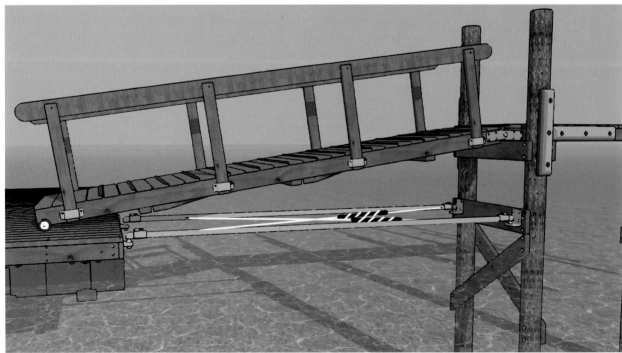

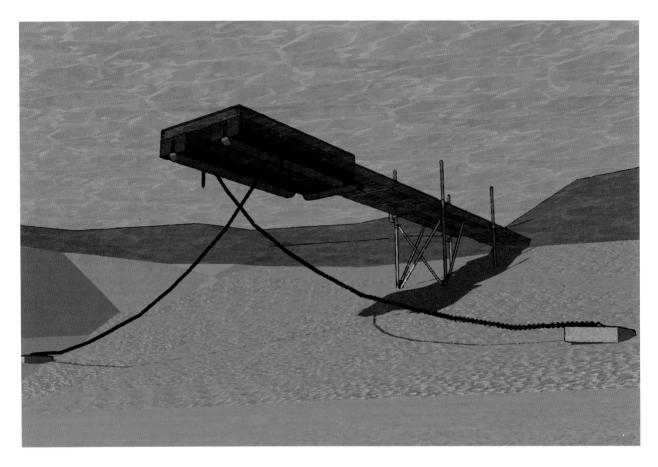

limiting the strain at the swaying stand-off arms. The ramp would be hinged to the fixed dock, resting its outbound end atop the floating dock where it will slightly slide as the floating dock sways left or right rising and falling.

Float Anchoring

Chapter 18 brings light to popular anchoring methods for floating docks, each with their own merits over the next. Though you may be fortunate to take your pick of choices, many DIYers will largely depend on what environmental or building codes allow, what the climate and exposure allow and what is available for resources to make the choice happen. Knowing where these boundaries lie should be the first order of business. Then think about each of the options—moorings or pipes and pilings, described in Chapter 18—for the one that fits within your boundaries.

Getting It Right

Success with a fixed to floating dock often depends on the amount of environmental exposure to be reckoned with. A small dock in a quiet protected cove offers forgiveness to the DIYer who does not have the knowledge that you have gained from this book. The challenge is greatest when faced with exposure, be it a large dock in heavy wind or current. If your fixed dock and floating dock are built solid, made to match the elements in your environment, the marriage between the two depends mainly on each holding their own while joined with a cooperative transition. One can help the other, but each must be able to stand or float on their own. Whether working on existing or building all new dock, a fixed to floating dock will certainly test your abilities in both arenas. Having come this far with me, just think how better equipped you are now to take it on.

CHAPTER 20:
TIDAL AND RIVER WATERS

The state of Maine is known by many around the world for its craggy and crooked coastline that if made straight would nearly extend along the entire U.S. Eastern Seaboard. While the best lobsters can be found in Maine, so can the most extreme tides in the world. I grew up in the southern end of the state where tides fluctuate about 12 feet (3.66 meters). Head northeast toward the Canadian border on the Bay of Fundy and tides there are about 20 feet (6 meters). Isn't that insane? Can you imagine that volume of water making its way in and out twice daily through convoluted inlets, islands, and estuaries? Unquestionably, it sparks intrigue while taking part in a profound and wonderful beauty. The people whose lives are connected to a shore with extreme tides make their choice to cope and deal with the daunting nature of it. Similarly, a riverfront may have a variable range of water levels that change from one extreme to another, just not with the daily influx as a tidal shore—unless, of course, it is a tidal river. These kinds of environments sometimes require docks to have unique methods for unique challenges. In this chapter, you will find information on some common tidal and river environments with topographical challenges that might sound like yours, while

A floating dock slowly rises with the incoming tide on Casco Bay in Maine.

At low tide, a floating dock lays on the mud for several hours until the water returns.

presenting common methods for the DIYer to meet those challenges.

Tied to Tide

Whenever I met with customers about a new dock on tidal water I always made my appointment for low tide. That way I could see how far a dock must extend outward to reach the remaining water. The reality for many Mainers is that it isn't feasible because the water's edge at low tide is too far out. There is a shore, just north of Portland, Maine, where every neighbor has a dock and the water's edge at low tide is a ½ mile (.8 kilometers) away. Though this example is on the extreme side, to some degree a similar situation is quite common. Waterfront users challenged by these tides accept nature with full cooperation, even if the window of time to swim or take the boat out seems short. At low tide, their floating dock and any boats attached will ground out on the sand or mud unless they are kept on a mooring off the shore where there is enough depth. Imagine, a boater under sail, paddle, or power must plan accordingly with the tide or

they won't be returning to their dock for several more hours. Tied to tide, dock users must be on their game.

Gradual Slopes

A gentle grade to the water that rising water creeps up on and slowly bleeds away from may be the simplest shore to build a dock for. Provided this method is permissible at your site, a floating dock in sections can start just above the high-water mark, extending out until reaching the low water. As the water level drops, one by one the sections ground out on the riverbed or seabed. Skids below the flotation should be included in your plan to prevent damage while chafing against the bottom over shallow water. Visit Chapter 18 (page 156) for shore transitions and anchoring.

Environmentally Sensitive Shorelines

When over terrain such as sand or cobble, there may not be significant environmental impact from a dock that grounds out at low water. A dock that would ground out on marsh grass vulnerable to

On a gradually sloped tidal shore, a floating dock made in sections like links of chain will lie on the seabed, one by one, as the water recedes.

Where crossing over sensitive areas, the use of perforated decking allows light to reach vegetation below.

erosion or in a habitat for wildlife, however, is not likely to get permitted. Instead, a fixed dock (aka an elevated boardwalk) may be permitted to span over the sensitive ground that will not crush and kill anything living beneath it. Set above the maximum high water-level, it must also be enough so that vegetation is not deprived of sunlight. The rule of thumb has been that the height above ground shall be no less than the boardwalk's width. To facilitate passage of light to the grass, resin-based perforated decking that reduces shading by about 40 percent can be purchased from suppliers online. The elevated boardwalk extends toward the low water until an attached ramp can reach a float that is safely away from the sensitive area. For building an elevated boardwalk, refer to any of my chapters about fixed docks. In climates where docks must be removed before winter, consider the fixed docks featured in Chapters 8 or 9.

A fixed dock or elevated boardwalk crosses over a sensitive marshland that floods at high tide. Its length reaches beyond the sensitive area before transitioning to a floating dock.

Protection for the Dock and Shellfish

Where a floating dock will ground out at low tide, skids along the bottom will protect from chafing that would otherwise shorten the life of your flotation. However, if there are shellfish at risk from the skids upon grounding out, you may opt for something called a float stop. To keep the clams

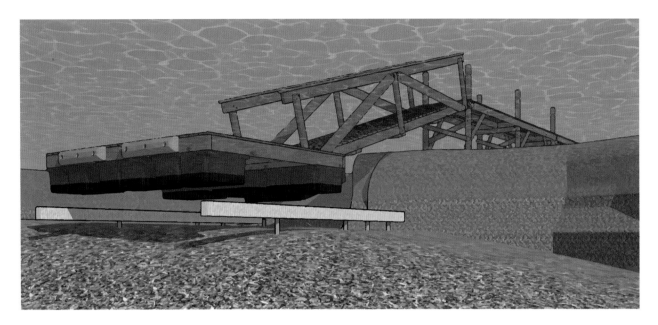

A float stop keeps a floating dock from grounding out on shell beds at low tide.

happy, heavy timbers slightly elevated above the shell beds are positioned and anchored where the float can come to rest at low tide. This will stop the float just above the shellfish. This method may be required where shellfish are present, under the terms of a dock permit.

Elevated Bank or Seawall

In tidal or river waters, elevated banks and seawalls demand a long ramp to reduce pitch when the water is low. Your elevation from the low water mark to the top of your bank or seawall will determine the length ramp you'll need. The ramp will hinge at the edge of a seawall or to an anchor point at the top of a bank. A fixed dock or pier may be required to position the ramp and float into deeper water. In places with extreme tides, like Maine and Oregon, fixed docks or piers may have to be set at a height that is not practical for many DIYers to tackle. The permanent pilings that are preferred are long and girthy, requiring a commercial pile driver to set. Sometimes a crib can be built in lieu of pilings, but even that can be a big bite to chew without the

Having completed a floating dock for the end of his pier, the DIYer chooses to use pilings and the help of a pile-driving contractor to anchor its position.

equipment of a marine contractor. Once you know the scope of your project requirements, from there you can sort out what parts you're best suited to do, leaving the rest to a marine contractor.

The Long Ramp

In Chapters 18 and 19, I have provided some details about long ramps, including plans that may be very useful for elevations no greater than 7 feet (2 meters). Where a longer ramp (over 20 feet [6 meters]) is

A ramp's length is determined by the elevation difference between the floating dock and its fixed dock at the lowest tide.

required, commercial dock builders and DIYers have trended toward aluminum ramps to reduce weight that burdens the float and the hands that must manage it.

Whether you choose to build your ramp with wood or buy an aluminum one, it is highly subject to racking from lateral movement when in service, especially while resting on a float that is held by moorings. Though the play that is inherent with moorings will prevent shock absorption, it requires the ramp's hinge to move laterally while articulating in a medial direction. DIYers sometimes hang the ramp in a dangling fashion from the fixed dock using chain or turnbuckles instead of using hinge plates. Though hinge plates allow the ramp to be articulated, they have no give when the ramp's opposite end swings left or right. Attaching with chain or turnbuckles seems a little sketchy, especially when you experience the peculiar motion while upon it, but it has been copied again and again as

A ramp is attached at its pier, suspended by a chain that allows it freedom to sway laterally while articulating in a medial direction.

a trusted method to alleviate strain from lateral movement or the lever affect. If you go to an experienced aluminum ramp fabricator, see that they have a hinge that is made to oscillate laterally while it can articulate as the ramp changes its pitch.

Where the ramp rests on the float, it may roll or slide, depending on your preference. Visit Chapters 18 and 19 (pages 156 and 178) to learn about how the ramp transitions to the float.

Anchoring the Float

In Chapter 18, several methods of anchoring are detailed for your reference. If your tidal site has extreme water fluctuations, float anchoring will likely be best with the use of pilings set by a commercial pile driver or moorings that you may choose to install yourself. Pilings are best for keeping the float tight to its desired position. Though the pilings themselves are costly (not to mention the cost of a contractor) they are solid and offer stability for the float. There is often a perception that the float is more secure when held to pilings rather than moorings when under wave turbulence. Through my own personal experience, however, I found that floats in turbulent waters pound against the pilings and cause costly damage. During one of the few hurricanes that I have experienced in my life, I watched my neighbor's floating dock self-destruct as it bashed incessantly into the pilings that held its position. Meanwhile, my floating dock that was held by moorings rode it out smoothly with only minor damage when it was over.

I've known many DIYers who chose moorings because they could use the opportunity at low tide to mobilize them into position, saving the cost of hiring a contractor with a barge. The helical anchor, available in varying lengths to reach a firm grip into the bed, has become popular for its portability and relative ease of installation by a DIYer. Where the bottom is extremely soft, demanding an extra-long anchor, a marine contractor may be more

A floating dock rises and falls with water fluctuations while yoked to a row of pilings and tethered to moorings.

A helical anchor to moor a floating dock is turned into a sandy seabed by a diver.

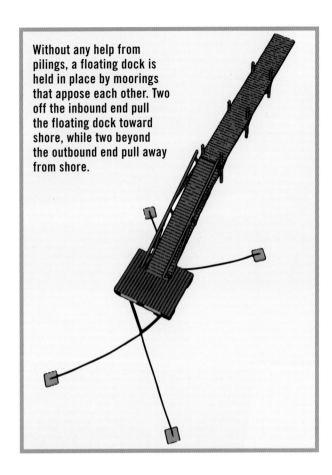

Without any help from pilings, a floating dock is held in place by moorings that appose each other. Two off the inbound end pull the floating dock toward shore, while two beyond the outbound end pull away from shore.

suited for the installation. However, there are many opportunities where conditions are right for shorter helical anchors that the DIYer can manage. If a scuba diver is needed to help with installing, his/her cost should be much less than the contractor with heavy equipment.

The method of using moorings only, described in Chapter 18 (page 156), is commonly relied on whereby the float is suspended within the confines of four moorings, one off each corner. The float can drift in small circles, but to a limited range by each of the moorings. The key is understanding the principles to a mooring so that it is installed properly. Especially with tidal shores that have significant daily water level changes, the moorings must be set a good distance away from the float. This prevents minimal chain slack changes over the course of the tide influx. Upon installation of the float with a ramp resting upon it, the DIYer must

adjust the swag on each mooring chain until the desired position and amount of play is achieved. The ramp should lay in far enough from the float's edge so that it can move in a limited range without falling off. As a fail-safe measure, the ramp may be tied with heavy rope to the float.

River Ready

Less frequently, but in some cases more severe, inland rivers are known to have the same challenges as a tidal shore. During the winter thaw or a profuse rain event, you know what this can mean if you're an experienced riverfront resident. The water is near the upper bank and moving swift unless you're in a backwater area. When water is low in the summer, the current slows to a peaceful and inviting pace, but the bank can be dangerous and daunting.

Some rivers are known to be so treacherous during spring high-water that a dock in the river's wrath will not stand a chance, especially while purged debris from banks upstream collect against the dock. For these rivers, I recommend that your dock is portable and kept out of use and high above the bank until things seemingly simmer for the summer.

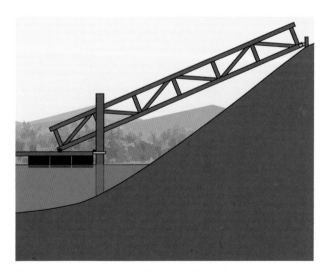

A long and steep riverbank is revealed at a time when the water level is low. A floating dock yoked to pilings is accessible via an extra-long ramp that is anchored atop the bank into stable ground.

A floating dock on a flowing river can trap drifting debris and drag the upstream side of the dock under. Unless the debris is routinely removed, it can rapidly pile up and put strain on the dock.

On a river with stable water levels, a short ramp on a low bank conserves the dock's distance into the river.

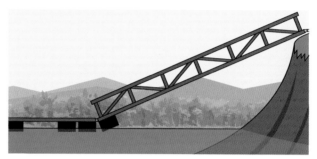

A ramp may be used to hold the floating dock off the riverbank.

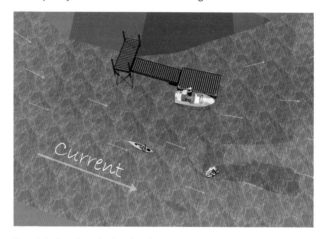

To minimize drag in the river's current, a fixed landing extends off the bank with its floating dock turned parallel to shore and trailing downstream.

Ramp and Float

Since rivers are known to fluctuate up and down, even during the summer, a float is held off the shore while a ramp extends to it from the bank. Sometimes, the ramp is used to hold the float off. For small rivers that have less fluctuation and lower banks, you may only need a short ramp of about 10 to 15 feet (3 to 4.5 meters). If the banks are high, naturally, you might consider a long ramp to help with the climb. On a small river with high banks, the ramp needed may push your float too far out into the river. In that case, a landing over the bank to position the ramp and float parallel to shore may be better. I'm not a big fan of this for rivers that can rise suddenly as the landing with its legs are vulnerable to debris and erosion. I would also avoid this when the bank is unstable and extraordinarily high.

Anchoring a River Dock

Extending directly off a bank, the ramp's shore end is sometimes chained to an anchor point on the bank to hold its position. While securing the ramp to the bank, the chain allows freedom to creep laterally, relieving stress from forces such as current and/or wind that push against the float. Landscape timbers may be used to cradle the ramp's shore end to prevent its eroding rub. The outbound end of a ramp may hinge to the float, serving as the method of holding the float off the bank. A heavy nylon line is secured to the float's corner, closest to shore on

Landscape timbers may be used to cradle the ramp's shore end to prevent its eroding rub, while chains connect to anchor points in the bank.

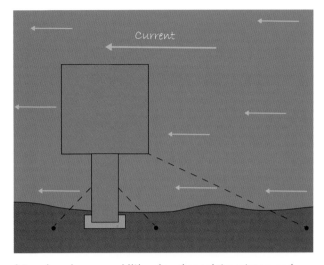

A top view shows an additional anchor point upstream and into the bank to hold the dock in the river's current.

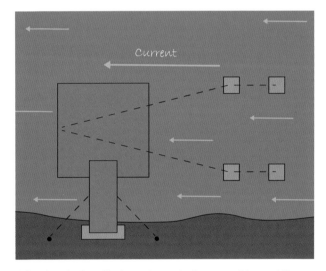

A floating dock trails downstream in the current beyond its moorings, where its ramp connects to the bank.

the upstream side and is tied off to an anchor point on the bank.

Depending on how well you know the river's nature, you may also secure the float with mooring anchors placed on the upstream side, tethered by chain. The float will trail downstream from the anchors. However, if your river is known to rise and pick up current speed from sudden rain storms, mooring chains may catch drifting debris floating through, resulting in a potentially unimaginable mess. I wouldn't take a chance with this method unless I was confident that the mooring chains would be risk-free.

Stairs Instead

For rivers that are known to remain tame during summer months, low-profile and low-cost stairs down over a long bank, not steeper than 35 degrees, may be less trouble than using a long ramp. At the bottom of the stairs, a much shorter manageable ramp could extend out to your float. At season's end, bring everything up to avoid winter and spring flooding.

Go Lean

On a river, especially where water levels could possibly rise and rage during summer, I recommend keeping a low profile with a dock. In other words, I wouldn't extend more out into the river than necessary given the risks. This is especially true if your shore is on the outside curve at a natural riverbend where purging debris is heavy and steep and eroding banks are a threat. Less dock will be less to manage and less to lose should Mother

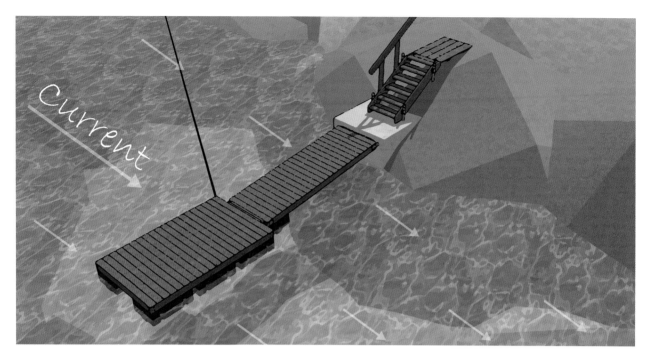

A stair on the riverbank positions the ramp's shore end at a lower elevation, allowing the ramp to be shorter and/or less steep.

Nature catch you off guard. Rivers prone to sudden flooding, where DIYers expect a high mortality rate for their docks, often go on the cheap since replacement may be a regular thing. For them, many are using plastic barrels for their flotation. Though not as stable as boxy flotation, they are low cost and easily replaced should damage or destruction come to the dock. Notably, the barrel's curvature, when its broadside is toward the current, will ride over the flow of moving water and debris quite well. A float that resembles a trapezoid with its beveled side facing upstream will also help to deflect passing debris.

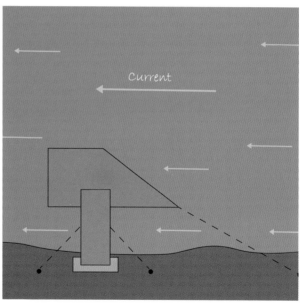

A unique trapezoid-shaped floating dock deflects passing river debris.

Before You Begin

Building a dock into tidal waters and rivers usually requires knowledge of unique characteristics and challenges inherent with the environment your shoreline is on. Experience and the knowledge of others around you is like gold. Before investing in any dock, seek the guidance and advice of others in your neighborhood for the best methods. Someone has gone before you and paid the price to find out what works and what doesn't. Take advantage of that while you apply any of the techniques found in this book.

CHAPTER 21:
SWIM RAFTS

Were you ever "King of the Raft" as a kid? Even if you never made kingship, it was fun trying. Moored away from the shore, swim rafts (aka swim floats) help make lots of good times and memories for kids and adults. Not only do they provide a destination for the swimmers in your family, they define the offshore limits for a swim area. As an added safety benefit, when moored a reasonable distance out they will usually discourage passing boaters from cutting between the swim raft and shore. Though you may already have a swim raft, this chapter reveals some methods that could improve what you have. If you're thinking of building one, let's get you ahead of the game with my experience to help make your project a smooth success. I've provided one plan to consider that has been built many times before and provided years and years of fun to countless families.

Size-Wise

For private use, an 8-foot by 8-foot (244- by 244-centimeter) swim raft is a practical size that suits most. I wouldn't make it much shorter in length and width for the sake of stability. It can be

A swim raft that is moored offshore, beyond your dock, defines the swimming area while providing a destination for swimmers.

When portability is required, lifting is easier when the decking is made into panels that can be removed separately.

framed with 2x6 (38 by 140 millimeters) and decked with 1x6 (25 by 140 millimeters). If the decking is treated yellow pine, cedar, or redwood, you can span up to 24 inches (61 centimeters) between stringers. When using a synthetic, such as a plastic deck panel or composite-like plank, you'll likely be closer to 16-inch (40-cemtimeter) spacing for the stringers. When the swim raft is in service, heaviness, constituted in part by its size, is a good thing for stability, but not so desirable when handling in climates that demand annual removal before winter. If portability is a concern, check out my plans to make wood decking in panels that will lift off the frame, knocking about one-third of the weight out before handling. Otherwise, if weight is not an issue, fasten down permanently. I would expect a raft this size with cedar decking, fastened permanently, to be between 300 and 350 pounds (136 and 159 kilograms).

Flotation

For stability and the least trouble, I recommend float drums, made specifically for docks (see Chapter 17, Flotation Sensation, page 150). Their boxy design will be far less tippy than round barrels, provided you choose a flotation height not to exceed 12 inches (30 centimeters). One on each corner, fastened onto the bottom of your frame, will hold the wood high enough to prevent waterlogging. Should you choose to use barrels, regardless, I recommend that the spacing of stringers be held to typical dimensions (22½ inches [57.15 centimeters] center to center) for float drums so that you can conveniently upgrade to them later.

Climbing Aboard

Before you go to any trouble building a ladder with wood, look at the many choices of dock ladders offered online that have nice features and are ready to install. If you're in a climate where swim rafts need to be removed annually before winter, choose one that will easily detach or swing up onto the deck so that it clears the bottom when moving to and from shore.

Diving Boards

Before you install a diving board onto a swim raft, let me stop you. They don't work well when trying to bounce and could lead to serious injury. A diving board is meant to be mounted on a solid, fixed platform such as a swimming pool deck. A swim raft is neither of these. Water beneath the swim raft's flotation absorbs the energy by a diver's impact on the board. As the board dips, so does the platform it is mounted to. The anticipated spring-back by the board does not compensate for the distance

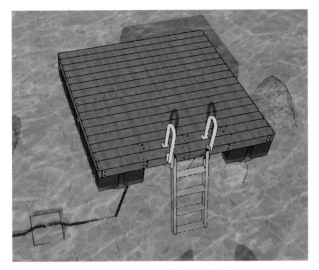

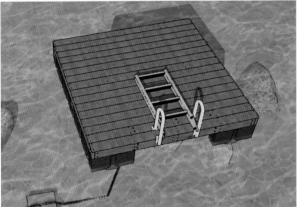

A ladder is essential for accessibility to the swim raft. If removal of the swim raft before winter is required, add convenience with a ladder that swings up and out of the way.

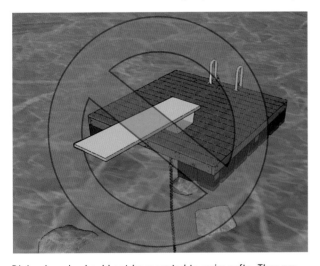

Diving boards should not be mounted to swim rafts. They are meant to go on fixed platforms only, over a safe depth.

the board has dipped, failing to spring a diver high enough for a proper dive. For the one who thinks a diving board is a pogo stick, while airborne he/she will discover that the swim raft rotates on the water, leaving them without a board squarely under their feet. . . . Ouch!

Optional Skids

If on tidal water where it may ground out at low tide, skids will buffer the flotation from abrasive damage. Skids are also important if you plan to drag your swim raft over abrasive ground during installation and removal time. For this, I recommend mounting a short piece of chain between the skids to hook your tow-line into.

Anchoring

Swim rafts that are to be moored offshore will need a solid anchor point underneath for a mooring chain connection. I recommend no less than ½ inch (13 millimeters) through-bolted, forged eye-bolt at an arm's reach distance in from the end opposite your ladder. It should be 3 inches (76 millimeters) in from the bottom of the stringer and secured with liquid thread lock. Another option for the anchor point is with a steel plate that has a chain slot. Should you choose the removable decking option upon construction, you'll appreciate the easy access to the mooring chain. The stringer that has the anchor point needs to be reinforced at each end where it fastens into the headers. In those locations, I would apply through bolted corner irons. I would also apply corner irons to the inside of the four exterior corners.

The simplest and most trouble-free mooring method is to use a single marine-grade chain, with links no lighter than 5⁄16 inch (8 millimeters), shackled from the attachment point under the swim raft to the mooring anchor. A chain swivel should be linked into the chain, about 2 yards (2 meters) down from the top end so that the swim raft can rotate without twisting up the mooring. This is also your

For mooring chain attachment, many raft builders rely on a heavy-duty eye-bolt under the swim raft. It should be fastened through the center of a stringer and secured with liquid thread lock.

Instead of an eye-bolt for chain attachment, a steel plate that has a chain slot through it adds ease of hook-up and adjustment of the chain's length. Looking up, from below the raft, notice that the stringer where the chain is attached has been reinforced with corner irons at each end.

A chain swivel allows the swim raft to spin freely in the wind without twisting the chain.

connection or disconnection point, retrievable with the help of a boat hook, and slack enough to access from the swim raft's surface.

In Chapter 18, I've described dock moorings as having lengthy chains that are to put the anchor a good distance from the dock. Since swim rafts are relatively small and without boats attached, their moorings usually do not need much scope. On a calm and sheltered body of water, using a deadweight anchor of about 300 pounds (136 kilograms), one and a half times the anchor's maximum depth for chain length, has always worked for me. If the exposure to wind or current is greater, you'll need to increase the chain's weight, its scope, and/or add another anchor tethered to the first one. During times of wind or current, the chain should not be so short or lightweight that it would become taut from end to end, potentially jarring the anchor loose from its bottom grip.

For the anchor(s), they should be low profile, that is with no part protruding upward that could cause injury to someone diving or jumping deep. Cinder blocks joined together are not dense and durable enough unless used where the water is always flat and calm. Avoid using 5-gallon (3.8-liter) buckets filled with concrete as they can roll on the bottom when tugged upon. See Anchors Away in Chapter 18 (page 170) to learn how to make a better anchor.

Unless conditions are very shallow, placement of the raft is usually less than 200 feet (60 meters) offshore, avoiding a navigable channel and centered with your swim area. Preferably, a depth of 10 to 15 feet (3 to 5 meters), clear of obstacles, should be under the swim raft for diving. Make sure that a permit isn't required before installing one. If so, see that you comply with the guidelines of the permit. White paint or stain around the four sides along with reflectors on the corners will help everyone see it at night. I put a solar light on mine.

Rafts That Rule

Now that you've got the best tips on making swim rafts, see what you can use from this chapter to improve the one you have. If beginning an all-new swim raft, make this one worth swimming for. Follow my plans and guidelines for a simple, great looking—yet sturdy—swim raft that will supply hours of safe, affordable fun.

Depending on wind or current exposure, an additional anchor may be needed.

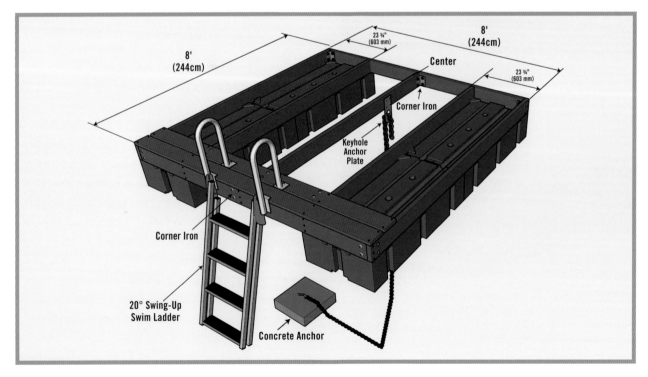

8' (244cm)

8' (244cm)

23 ¾" (603 mm)

23 ¾" (603 mm)

Center

Corner Iron

Keyhole Anchor Plate

Corner Iron

20° Swing-Up Swim Ladder

Concrete Anchor

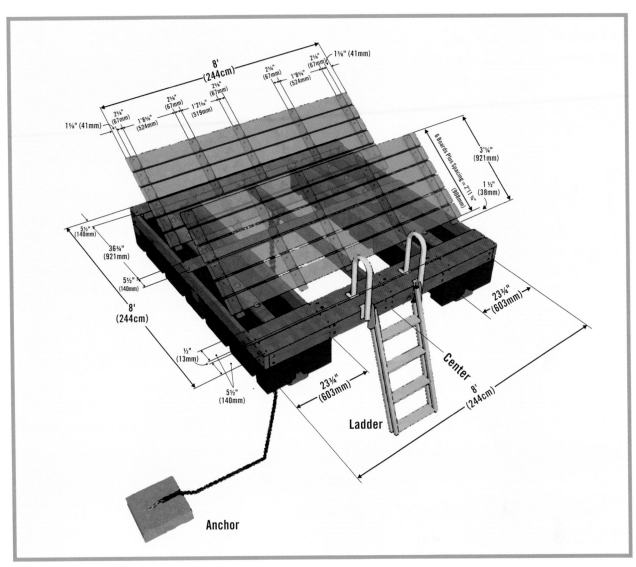

8'
(244cm)

2⅝"
(67mm)

1'8⅝"
(524mm)

2⅝"
(67mm)

1⅝" (41mm)

2⅝"
(67mm)

2⅝"
(67mm)

1'8⅝"
(524mm)

2⅝"
(67mm)

1'2⁷⁄₁₆"
(519mm)

2⅝"
(67mm)

1⅝" (41mm)

2⅝"
(67mm)

1'8⅝"
(524mm)

6 Boards Plus Spacing = 2'11 ¾"
(908mm)

3'1¼"
(921mm)

1 ½"
(38mm)

5½"
(140mm)

36¾"
(921mm)

5½"
(140mm)

8'
(244cm)

½"
(13mm)

5½"
(140mm)

23¾"
(603mm)

23¾"
(603mm)

Center

8'
(244cm)

Ladder

Anchor

Above: The swim raft plan shows dimensions for making the decking into removable panels. Notice that two boards are left permanent at one end for attachment of a ladder. One deck board is made permanent at the opposite end and another near the center.

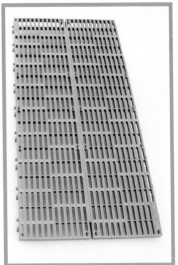

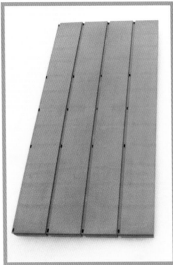

Right: Perforated synthetic decking in panels stay cool and allow dirt to easily wash through. Otherwise, for a more natural look, a solid synthetic panel may be considered. The manufacturers' framing specifications may be different than what the plan in this book shows.

CHAPTER 22:
CLUES FOR CLEATS

Could there be a more practical shape for a small vessel tie-up than the traditional horned cleat? Learn to make a simple cleat hitch with your lines and you'll see why the cleat's basic shape remains timeless while deserving of its iconic recognition. Since every dock should have a few cleats, innovators are busy bringing new choices to the market, nonetheless, seldom deviating far from the traditional design. As important as it is to choose cleats that function and fit your needs, this chapter's emphasis is mainly on proper installation. Though a quality cleat will come in handy to hold your boat, kite, a fugitive, or an alligator, let's make sure that cleat stays where you put it.

Choosing Your Cleat

When shopping cleats, don't let the many styles, shapes, and special features confuse you. Aside from durability, the correct size for your lines, and any "must have" feature, choosing one style over another will likely boil down to personal preference. Deserving honorable mention is the "fold down when not in use" cleat for klutzy feet and the solar rechargeable illuminated cleat for docking in the dark. Specialty cleats like these may only be offered in one length, ideal for line sizes typically used with smaller vessels. The manufacturer may provide specifications for the appropriate line diameter(s) that work best. If not, find out the horn length, as

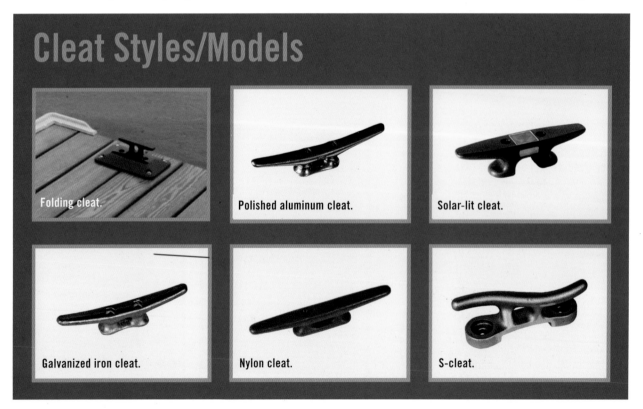

Cleat Styles/Models

Folding cleat.

Polished aluminum cleat.

Solar-lit cleat.

Galvanized iron cleat.

Nylon cleat.

S-cleat.

Making a Cleat

While exploring cleat options on the market, don't ignore the possibility of making your own from hardwood. Simply cut out the basic profile from the scraps of a 2-inch-thick (5-centimeter) plank, and round the edges over, sanding to a smooth finish. Though they require some time, wood cleats are simple to make and stunning to look at once in place.

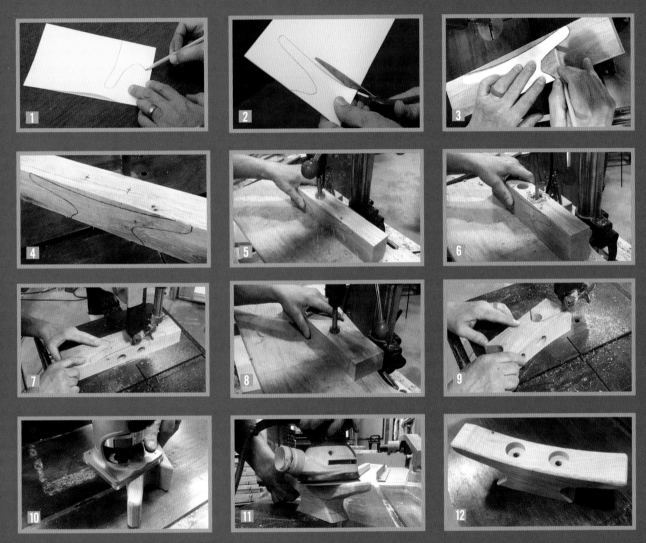

1. Make a tracing template for a homemade wooden cleat. From the fold line on a piece of paper, draw one half of a cleat.
2. Cut out your template from the sheet of paper.
3. Trace the cleat pattern onto a scrap piece of hardwood.
4. Measure and mark the top side for boring the bolt holes.
5. On a drill press with a spade or forstner bit, start with countersunk holes to a depth that will hide the bolt heads.
6. Choosing a bit diameter that matches the bolt size, bore through and center to the countersunk holes to complete the bolt holes.
7. On a band saw, cut out the cleat's profile.
8. Avoid difficult cutting around sharp curves on the band saw. Where possible, bore relief holes as shown for a cleaner and easier cut.
9. Use the band saw to finish cutting out the cleat's profile.
10. Use a router to ease all the edges, except for the four along the bottom.
11. Smooth over with sanding to keep lines from abrading.
12. Finish with a treatment of linseed oil.

it should be about six times the diameter of your line. Galvanized iron cleats, imported in bulk to the supplier, are popular as a low-cost durable option, and are likely what you find on the shelf at a nearby hardware store. They are usually available in various lengths, but sometimes with no installation tips or user guidance for the consumer. If your line is ⅜ inch (1 centimeter) or ½ inch (13 millimeters) in diameter, an 8-inch (20-centimeter) length is ideal. A ⅝-inch (16-millimeter) diameter line will work better with a 10-inch (25-centimeter) length. The finish on iron cleats may be rough and not so friendly to the fibers in your dock line, so be sure to lightly smooth over any unwanted bumps or edges.

Cleat Installation

The cleat you tie to must never leave you with any doubt about its integrity and ability to hold your boat. Too often, the convenient approach is taken, using lag screws that can be easily turned in from the top side. Though often safe under light service, this method gets overly relied on where wave action causes lines to go taut, stressing the lags until failure happens. When a cleat is under strain, its load will be concentrated where it has been installed and will depend on the strength of the material it has been fastened to. Therefore, its ability to hold is only as good as the material it is attached to and the fasteners holding that material. The reinforcement methods described below transfer the strain into the frame where the greatest strength lies. The proven methods described just ahead will require access below the decking surface, an easier feat while building the dock but not to be feared when desired on an existing dock. Gain access under an existing dock by removing the adjacent deck board nearest the ones that the cleat base will be mounted upon. Handle with care to minimize damage to the decking, albeit sometimes inevitable, so be prepared with a replacement board. Try getting away with removing just one board. Remove others if needed for better access.

Reinforcement Block Method

To properly install a reinforced cleat, one way is to make a reinforcement block that is positioned under the deck board(s) while against the stringer. The block is to be through-bolted to the stringer and the cleat is to be through-bolted to the block. Be sure to use bolt sizes that are recommended by the cleat manufacturer. If there are no recommendations, then choose bolts that fit snugly in the cleat's holes. Predetermine the lengths you'll need for each bolt based on the total thickness of material the bolts will go through. Since the cleat's fasteners will be subjected to stress from tugging lines, I recommend using liquid thread lock on the bolt threads to prevent loosening.

1. For a common cleat that requires two aligned bolts through its top, reinforcement blocks can be made with wood, a nominal 4x4 (10 by 10 centimeters), cut to the cleat's length.

2. Bore two ⅜-inch (1-centimeter) diameter holes, centered with the width of the block, 1½ inches (38 millimeters) in from each end.

3. Under the deck board where the cleat is to be installed, position the block with screws as shown. It should be snug against the deck board and the frame. Then, use the block's holes as a drill template and bore until the holes are through the frame.

4. Install two carriage bolts through the frame and block. Secure the two carriage bolts with nuts and washers. Place the cleat centered, over the deck board and block. Position so that the cleat's bolt holes are half the block's thickness (1¾" [45 millimeters]) from the stringer.

5. Using the cleat's holes as your drilling template, bore down through the decking and the block. (Safety tip: Prevent the cleat from spinning around on the drill bit by starting the holes at a slow speed while keeping a firm grip on the cleat. Temporarily move the cleat away while drilling through.) Install two bolts down through the cleat and block.

6. See that all the fasteners are firmly tightened with a socket wrench.

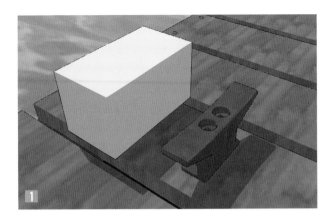

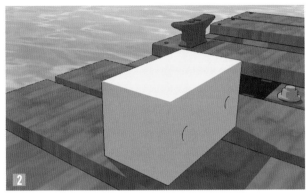

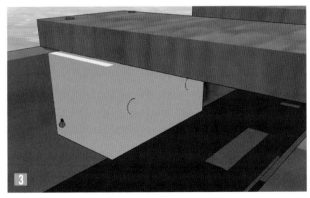

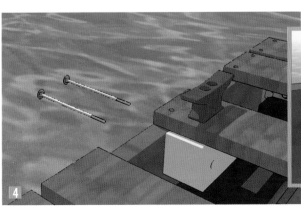

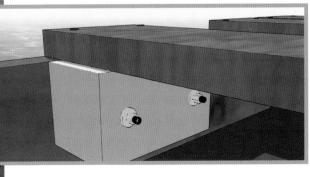

Metal Backer Method

Another cleat reinforcement method that dock builders rely on uses a metal cleat backer or stiffener. The backer is a steel or aluminum angle with holes on both faces. The holes may be slotted so that it can match up to different size cleats. These are available through some dock hardware suppliers or can be homemade from angle iron if you're willing to drill the necessary holes. Sometimes at a hardware store you can find heavy angle (preferably galvanized) that comes perforated and can be cut to an appropriate length. Since the cleat's fasteners will be subjected to stress from tugging lines, I recommend using liquid thread lock on the bolt threads to prevent loosening.

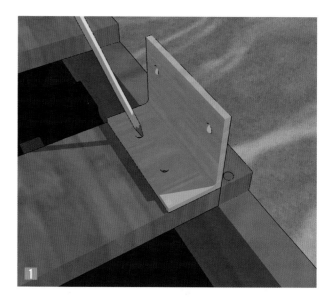

1. As a drilling template for locating bolt holes on the deck, place the top side of the cleat backer down and against the deck where you want to install the cleat. Keep the other face of the cleat backer turned to the outside while lining it up with the back side of the stringer. Trace the holes onto the deck board.

2. Place the cleat with its bolt holes over the traced holes that you made with the template. With the appropriate drill bit, drill out the holes. Sometimes the cleat is held in place and used to guide the drill bit straight down. (Safety tip: Be careful your spinning bit doesn't grab inside the cleat hole, turning the cleat into a propeller. Drill slowly and keep a firm grip on the cleat.)

3. Holding the cleat backer under the deck board with its top face turned up and the other face turned against the stringer, fasten the cleat to the cleat backer with appropriate bolts, nuts, and washers.

4. At the cleat backer's holes that are against the frame, drill through the stringer from the inside. Then install carriage bolts from the outside so that nuts and washers are tightened against the cleat backer.

5. See that all fasteners are firmly tightened with a socket wrench.

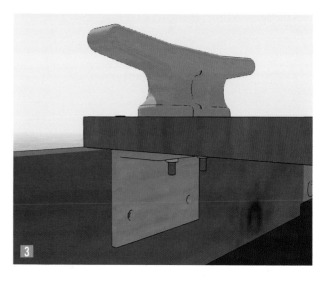

Backer Board Method

Some deck products, such as hollow composites or molded and extruded plastics made up with thin walls and ribs, may not transfer strain well from the cleat to the stringer. Cleats mounted to these surfaces should have a backer board above and below the decking, creating a sandwich that disperses the strain over a larger area. The board under the decking can be long enough to reach across several deck boards while secured to the stringer with corner irons. The board just under the cleat, being exposed to foot traffic, should have a rounded or beveled edge so that it doesn't become a "toe catcher." DIYers have been known to use a thick piece of aluminum plate for this, or a solid composite board with a color that is coordinated with the color of their deck.

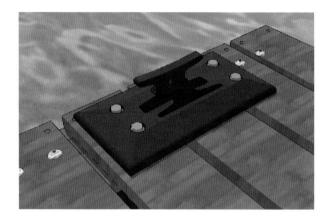

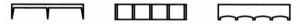

Cross section samples of hollow synthetic decking.

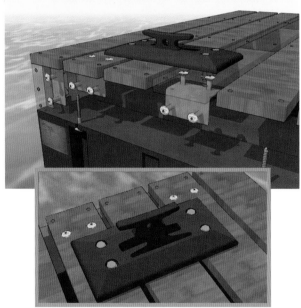

For cleats that have a broad base and hole pattern that may be incompatible with a reinforcement block or cleat backer, use a corner iron or cleat backer under the deck board(s) that the cleat will be mounted to. Fasten the corner irons or cleat backers through the deck board and the stringer with carriage bolts. Then, bolt the cleat to the deck board adjacent to the corner iron or cleat backer.

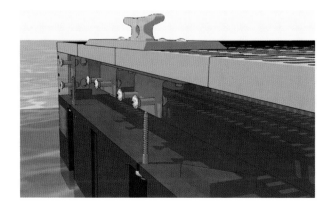

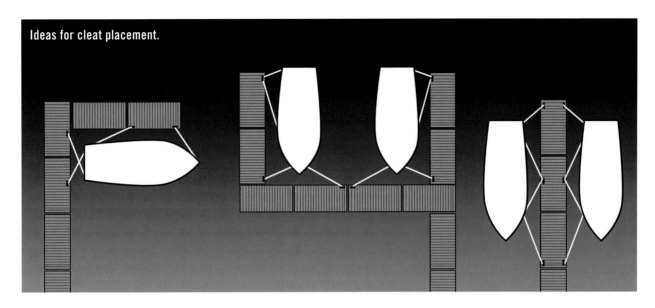

Ideas for cleat placement.

Cleats on Removable Deck Panels

For docks that have removable deck panels, mainly where portability is required, pipe legs or posts often become the tie-up points. However, if cleats on the deck are desired, they should be mounted only to decking that is fixed to the frame. It is not uncommon for a dock section with removable deck panels to have some of the decking fastened permanently for cleats.

Number of Cleats and Positioning

As with electrical wall outlets, I always want a cleat where one is not located, so a couple extra than the minimum required is always appreciated. If the minimum is all you want, install one for the fore end, one for the aft end, and one for the beam. If possible, spread them out past the length of the boat so that your lines can have some length. This will reduce shock on the lines and cleats while the boat is tied and tugging at them. If the boat will be berthed in a slip area, add a cleat where it can help hold the boat away from the dock.

Trip and Fall Prevention

Laugh if you want, but the fear of tripping over a cleat will discourage some from installing any more than necessary. Aside from the cleat that folds down

Contrasting colors help the cleat stand out.

when not in use, you can apply white marine paint to an iron cleat to improve visibility of it, unless of course the deck is white. Another idea that helps is to paint an area around the cleat with a stark contrasting color from the cleat. It's amazing how noticeable the cleat is after this is done.

Tie-up Rail and Bit

Often seen on floating docks, the tie-up rail, made with a simple 2x4 (38 by 92 millimeters) and elevated with 2x4 (38 by 92 millimeters) blocks, provides a continual fixture to lash your line around.

With the blocks spaced apart about an arm's length, the tie-up rail is nailed together, then bolted down through the decking into a cleat backer or stiffener.

When the diameter of your line is too fat for the typical cleat or tie-up rail, consider a bit instead. Bits may have a mounting flange that bolts through the deck. Just as with cleats, make sure your bit is reinforced by the frame. You can make a bit using a short wooden 4x4 (10- by 10-centimeter) post. Simply shape the top end to your liking. Bore a hole for a 1-inch by 6-inch (25- by 140-millimeter) dowel to pass through the side, down from the top, and secure the dowel with a heavy screw. The bit can be through-bolted directly to the frame. Fasten a support block onto the bit to support the deck board.

Tie-up rail.

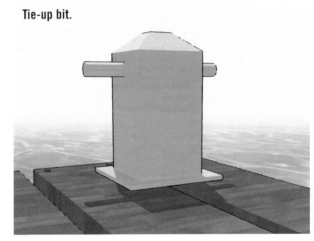

Tie-up bit.

Tie-up bit.

Closure for Cleats

While I've often gone on, talking up docks like they're central to everyone's waterfront life, such as the origin of fun family memories and romance, I get it. The dock for some could just be a place to park the boat and nothing more. For them, it's the cleats that count—the thing that makes tying off doable. For such an important feature, let's make sure our cleats measure up to their importance. On many docks it's common to find at least one or two that are barely secure. Even when properly installed, eventually they may need to undergo some rehab. Given the direct tugging and jarring caused by the boat, we're expecting a great service from these fixtures. Just as you should regularly check the tires on your car, check the tightness and security of your tie-up features. Shouldn't the value of what they are holding deserve our ongoing attention?

CHAPTER 23:
SAFEGUARDING FROM WIND AND WAVES

Any experienced boater knows that wide open spaces on the water can mean trouble for boats tied to nearby docks. Whether generated by driving winds or boat traffic, incessant waves are the scourge of small vessels left at berth. Depending on the severity of your maximum exposure, the level of remedy you choose may only require a simple method to protect your boat. However, an accurate assessment of your specific conditions must be taken seriously to avoid underestimating the level of protection needed.

Fenders—Fatter ones and more of them may be all it takes. Too often I see sizable boats taking a beating because all the protection was left to two or three 5-inch (13-centimeter) diameter fenders, a severe mismatch for the environment. There just isn't enough cushion in them to do the job, especially if one comes loose or flops up onto the dock. Visit Chapter 24, Fender Friends (page 216) to learn about making fenders and bumpers more helpful.

Wind Advantage—A predominant wind can be helpful. Upon docking a boat, approach to the dock's windward side makes it easier to land, of course, but tying up to the leeward side will keep the wind from pushing and banging the boat into the dock. It's

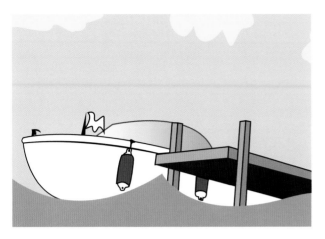

Observe your boat when tied to its dock during the worst conditions. See that the quantity, size, and placement of fenders are providing enough protection.

---

even better if you have a side to the dock that puts the bow into the wind while slightly pushing away from the dock.

Tie-up Methods—Put some length into your lines between the dock and the boat. I agree, you don't want the boat drifting too far off the mark, but you also don't want it reined in so tight that it can't rise and fall with the chop. Leaving too little line between the dock's cleat and the boat's cleat can result in damaging shock as the boat pitches and yaws. Along with shock, a boat's hull with all its lifting capacity can hoist a dock's legs right out of the lake bed or seabed should the perfect wave come along. Extending the bow and stern lines to cleats that are positioned beyond the boat's length with the use of a spring line in between will keep the boat near while giving it just enough freedom to go with the flow.

Shock Absorption—I can't be more emphatic that I am a fanatic about the snubber, a heavy rubber cord that has an eyelet on each end. Run your dock line through one eyelet, then wrap around the snubber three times before feeding through the other eyelet. With that, your dock line has effectively become a bungee cord. Though rope has some elasticity on its own, it isn't enough to prevent the unwanted jar when your boat is lurched by waves,

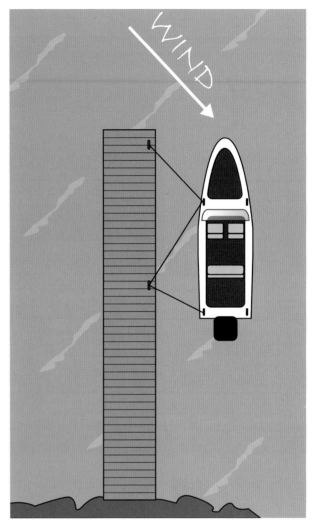

When possible, use the predominant wind to your advantage when tied to the dock.

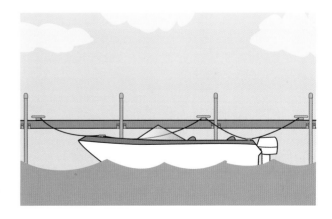

As passing waves lift the boat, there should be enough play in the lines so that the boat doesn't lift the dock.

When dock lines go taut from passing waves, the resulting shock can be damaging to the boat and dock. A snubber adds elasticity to your dock lines, eliminating unwanted shock.

causing the line to go taut. Energy that causes the annoying jolt is responsible for cleat bolts loosening and other fasteners meant to hold your dock together. The snubber disperses that energy caused by the waves and eliminates all kinds of problems. You'll notice the improvement while sitting leisurely out on your dock—the sudden lurch you once felt from tugging lines will dampen to a more fluid and relaxed motion.

Stand-Off Devices—Whips and rocker arms are two product options that pull the boat away from the dock via upward tension on the lines. The amount of tension can be customized to resist forces that push the boat into your dock. Additional lines that extend perpendicular between the dock and boat can be preset to limit the standoff distance at about 5 feet (1.5 meters). These products have had decades to prove themselves very effective, especially to protect from everyday boat chop. I would not rely on them under severe windy weather conditions when the boat would be better moored offshore, on a lift, or hauled out. There are a few notable precautions worth considering before choosing a specific product.

- Consider the amount of space that the product's mounting bracket requires on the dock, especially if your dock is narrow.

- Be sure to follow the product's instructions carefully and remember to attach spring lines.
- See that the top end of the product, such as the end of a whip, as it reaches out and over the boat will not be close to any tall structures, such as the boat's canopy.
- Watch that the lines extending down from above are clear from rubbing on any portion of the boat, such as the exposed upholstery on deck. Add a cleat to the boat, if necessary, in a spot that would prevent line chaffing on parts of the boat.
- If your boat is in a shared slip with another boat, make sure there will be enough room for the added space that the boat will standoff. Holding the boat in close, a distance less than the maximum wave height will defeat the functioning of the device.

Outbound Lines—Tying off to something that will hold the boat away from the dock such as another dock, free-standing pile, or mooring can work amazingly well. I used to park my pontoon boat safe on a lift, but it kept me from learning about affective lower cost options. To this end, I chose to keep my boat broadside to the south wind that delivered white-capped waves daily from a 2-mile (3.2-kilometer) fetch. I parked on the windward side of the dock without a lift,

Mooring whips.

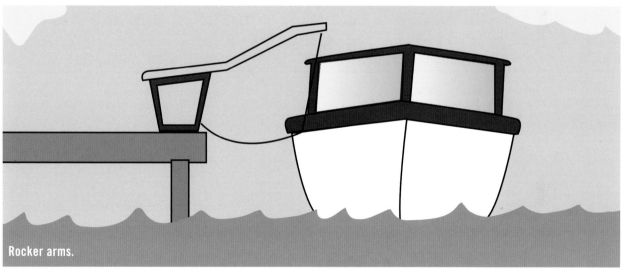

Rocker arms.

intentionally putting myself in an unfavorable situation. Windward of the boat's side, I installed two helical anchors, one to hold off the bow and one to hold off the stern. Each anchor held a ½-inch (13-millimeter) solid braid nylon line to be crisscrossed upon connecting to the boat. Using nylon allows the line to sink, keeping it clear of the boat's prop upon entry to the berth. I used a small buoy to float the line just over the anchor, making it reachable with a boat hook. For shock absorption, I included a snubber with each line.

The results, I must say, exceeded my expectations. For two complete seasons, subjected on my lake to what would be the equivalent of a giant slosh basin, I could not have been more pleased as this method kept my boat completely unscathed.

Mooring Offshore—In an environment that receives conditions too severe for clever tie-offs, snubbers, and fenders, my default advice for anyone has always been to have a reliable mooring installed offshore. It would be available in case harsh conditions come up or when you're not present and

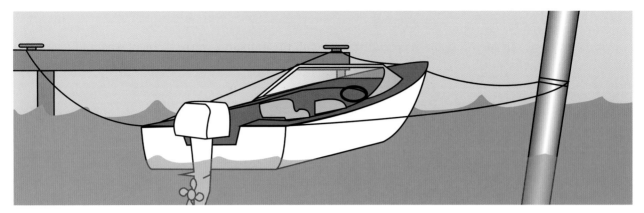

Hold your boat away from the dock using outbound lines to another fixed object.

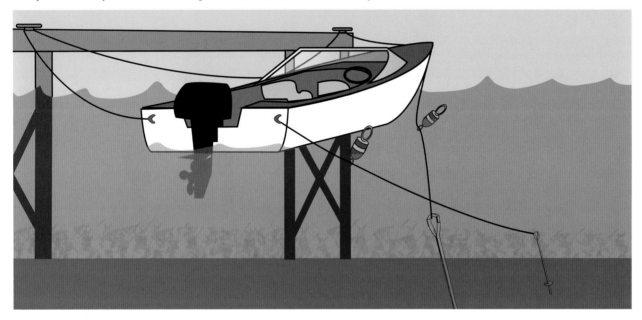

Helical anchors can be turned into the lake bed, riverbed, or seabed, away from the boat, for attachment of outbound lines. A small buoy on each line facilitates retrieval with a boat hook upon tying up.

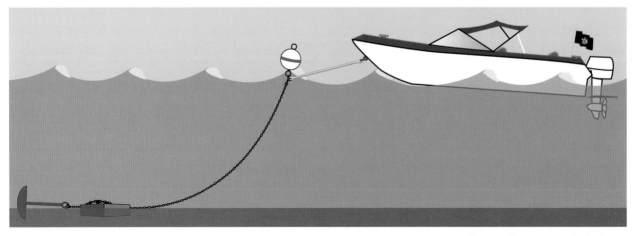

If the exposure is potentially too rough for leaving a boat tied to the dock, a permanent mooring offshore offers peace of mind.

able to keep a watchful eye on things. Offshore, the boat can safely ride out the wind and waves until there is a better time to keep it at the dock. Before attempting to make your own mooring, be sure to follow standard proven methods and only use genuine mooring components.

Boat Lifts—If you'd rather avoid rowing a dinghy from ship to shore, consider upgrading your mooring to a boat lift. On the right body of water, it offers exceptional peace of mind and ease of operation. Once in place, the dock is no longer responsible for holding the boat; it will be all on the lift. Though the idea of a boat lift sounds great, before you jump too quick, determine if your shorefront is right for one and recognize the ongoing expense associated with required service as they are not fully carefree. Portable lifts on lakes that freeze in the winter will require moving twice annually, so decide if you're prepared to manage the mobilization with the help of friends or hired help. If you have that part covered, be aware of your lake's potential water level to suddenly rise or fall. A body of water that can rise suddenly from a profuse rain event may result in floating your boat off the lift before you're aware of what's going on. This happened to me once, and had I not taken precautions, my boat would have gone bye-bye. Some lakes that are controlled by a dam can drop suddenly, leaving too-little water at the lift to launch the boat. If you're not overly familiar with the nature of your body of water, ask neighbors how it behaves. Explore the shore to see what others have for boat lifts. You can learn much more about your lake when you see what everyone else uses.

Vigilance

Finally, no matter how confident you become in the method you've chosen, no remedy is too good for a watchful eye. Likely, no one is going to care about your dock and boat more than you, so periodic checking to make sure everything is functioning properly often heads off bigger problems down the road.

Standing hoists and lifts hold their boats above the waves.

CHAPTER 24:

FENDER FRIENDS

Now that you've made the investment into a sturdy dock to bring your boat into, it's not the time to skimp where the rubber meets the road or, better yet, where the cushion meets the hull. Except for places highly exposed to large waves driven by strong winds, a dock should be a refuge for the boat, putting your mind at ease knowing it is in a good place. Before your boat ends up with an unsightly scar, be prepared with plenty of padding to land against. Some deficiencies are due to inexperience whereby the dock's owner just didn't know how much was needed or didn't know proper methods of fending. In other cases, it's an example of being penny-wise and pound-foolish. Albeit an effort was made, scaling back size, quantity and quality of cushions, resulted in boat repairs that cost more than what was spent on the attempt to prevent them. If your dock is in a well-protected area and you're good at docking, then you may not need much, but in areas exposed to wind, chop, and currents, your method of cushioning deserves careful attention. Old tires repurposed into dock bumpers may not be all that attractive looking, but if you have nothing else, use them. I expect you'd prefer to clean off black marks than pay for a hull repair any day. Before you ante up the cash for real dock bumpers that you'll entrust your hull to, let's consider how your boat will be in contact with the dock.

Fenders, Always

First and foremost, no matter how soft and cushy the bumpers or rub-rails are that you've affixed to the dock, always use your fenders that dangle from a rope as your primary buffer for the hull. When snugged up to a fixed bumper for a length of time, the resulting friction from rubbing can damage the boat's finish. However, the hanging fender is free to rotate and release friction as the boat grinds into it. Choose sizes and quantities that are right for the boat's weight, length, and exposure to waves.

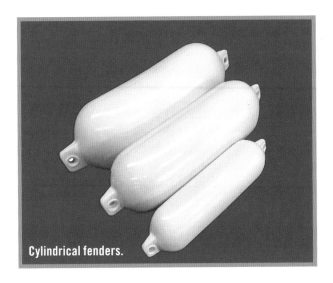

Cylindrical fenders.

Spherical fender.

As a guide, when looking at cylindrical fenders, there should be 1 inch (25 millimeters) of diameter for every 4 feet (122 centimeters) of boat length. For spherical fenders there should be 2 inches (5 centimeters) of diameter for every 4 feet (122 centimeters) of boat length.

When frequently exposed to harsh chop from wind and boats, here again, size matters, so plan on stepping up to a bigger fender. Seriously, too often boaters try to get by with the typical 5-inch (13-centimeter) diameter fenders on bodies of water plagued with incessant chop. It will cost more to make that jump, but the situation demands it and you'll see the difference. Important as size is, so is the quantity. Use one per 10 feet (3 meters) of waterline, minimum three; one at the fore, aft, and at maximum beam. Keep in mind, this is a recommendation for a minimum quantity and that more should be used if possible. For best positioning, hang the fenders as low as possible without them touching the waterline. While under chop, this will help prevent them from flipping up onto the dock and leaving the hull unprotected. This standard should not preclude positioning higher if the point of contact requires it. A small weight, such as a nylon sock filled with sand, tied to the bottom eyelet of a cylindrical fender will help keep it in the proper place as well.

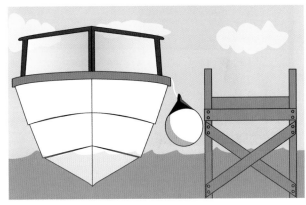

When docking in choppy waters and counting on fenders, bigger is better.

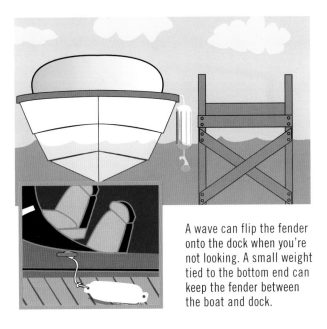

A wave can flip the fender onto the dock when you're not looking. A small weight tied to the bottom end can keep the fender between the boat and dock.

Shape Matters

As for bumpers affixed to the dock, naturally, DIYers will prioritize the installation of padding or a vinyl rub-rail, run horizontally along the dock's edge. It may be flush with or rise slightly over the decking surface, including a cushion that is made specifically for the outside corner. This is one reason I recommend that the decking be flush with the frame and not extend over, as is often done on porches and decks.

Just as an overhanging deck-board is something for a boat's gunwale to catch and cause damage, so too can the rub-rail or padding be damaged if it isn't the ideal shape. Choose horizontal bumpers or rub-rail to affix along the dock's edge that won't be prone to catch a dock line or an edge on the boat's hull. I once tried a new product that was impressive by its size—blocky and girthy, with a generous amount of cushion that dwarfed most other dock bumpers. Measuring about the length of my arm, I bolted several of them horizontally to the outside

While offering cushioning against impact and occasional rubbing, a dock bumper's shape should deflect the boat to minimize contact.

Though a fat profile is expected to offer better protection, its shape must not be prone to snags with lines and the boat's gunwale. Such bumpers may be best mounted in a vertical direction.

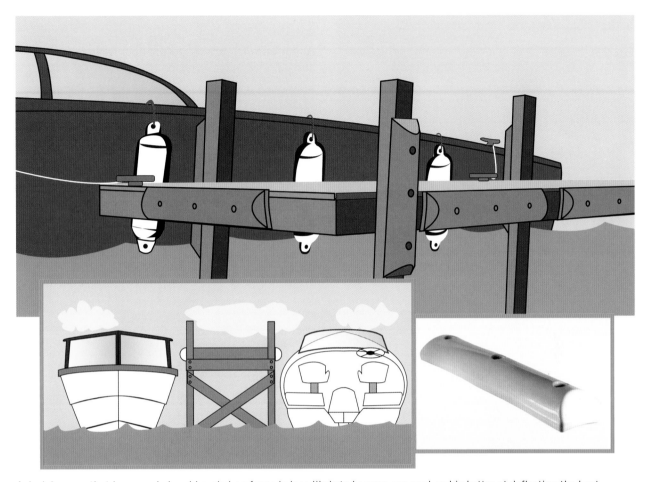

A dock bumper that has rounded and beveled surfaces is less likely to become snagged and is better at deflecting the boat.

face along my dock. I soon realized the blocky shape was not the advantage I expected. By their bold, protruding right-angled edges, they became something for the boat and dock lines to catch on. Be it the hull pitching down onto the bumper's top surface or the stern's gunwale rising and catching them from below, the gargantuan bumpers did not hold up. I had a couple of them tear simply from dock lines going taut in the waves while caught on their squared-off corners.

That whole experience revealed to me that lower profile with rounded or beveled edges is better. Years later, I developed my own bumper, named The Guardian. It mimicked the product I once tried that had failed, only with added curves and beveled ends to deflect a boat and its dock lines.

Horizontal Profiles

Extruded PVC profiles, made specifically to fasten along the dock's edge, have pretty much replaced the old fire hose your grandfather used. Be sure to compare the sizes and weights when shopping—like most things, you get what you pay for. There are two profiles most commonly found on the market; one is clearly intended to fit horizontally along the dock's edge, likened to the letter "P." The other popular one is in the shape of a "C" with fastening flanges that may be a better shape to use on vertical surfaces.

Upon entering the berth, a boat may glance and rub the profile as it moves along. The profile should not protrude without all planes having a bevel so that any vertical motion by the boat will be deflected

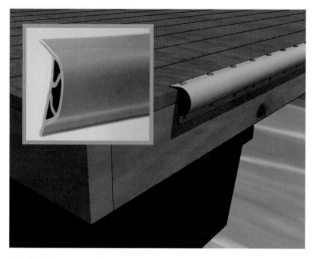

The "P" shape profile is a favorite choice to be used horizontally along the dock's edge.

The "C" shape profile is chosen for either horizontal or vertical surfaces. When applied horizontally, a low-profile "C" is less likely to become snagged, pulled, and torn by a boat.

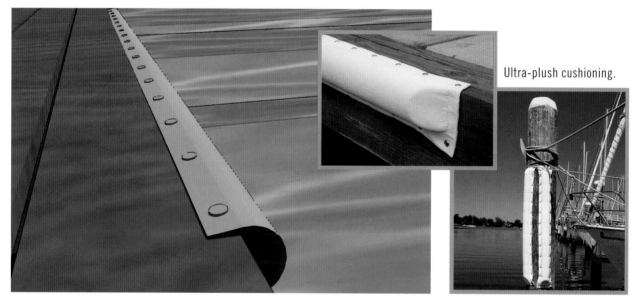

Ultra-plush cushioning.

Use a generous number of fasteners along a profile's flange to prevent tearing away.

upon contact. A profile that resembles a shelf or flange is a place for the boat to catch and tear.

Unless the product specifies a different fastener, you can typically use stainless screws or ring-shanked stainless roofing nails, spaced every 6 to 8 inches (15 to 20 centimeters) to secure along the flanges. Under the sun, many resin-based bumper products soften, becoming less slippery, and may seemingly smear by a hull's grip. To prevent the

profile from tearing under these circumstances, see to it that a generous number of fasteners are in place to hold when under fire.

For an ultra-plush cushion, there is a polyethylene foam sheathed by a nylon weave that resembles the outer layer of fire hose. Though usually more expensive than extruded or molded bumpers per surface area, it is perhaps one of the most hull-friendly choices that I have used.

Bumpers for Removable Decking

If you have removable decking made in panels, use bumpers that fasten only to the dock's side. Consider molded bumpers that don't require top surface fastening, keeping in mind the importance of beveled and rounded edges that deflect contact with the boat.

Vertical Bumpers

Though there may seem an urgency to mount horizontal bumpers along a dock's edge, your posts, pipe legs, or pilings set off from the decking, are the first places I would take advantage of. Padding along these vertical surfaces will protect small and large boats that make contact, glancing off at various heights. As a boat pitches next to the dock in passing waves, its rub-rail, gunwale, or hull are often protected more by the vertical bumper than a horizontal one. Alongside boats up to 25 feet (7.6 meters), there should be a minimum of two vertical bumpers for the boat to bear up against, one near the stern and one just forward of the beam.

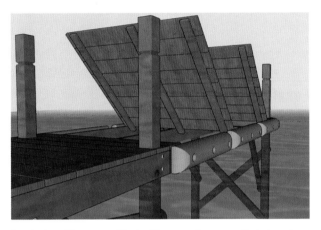

For docks with removable decking, use bumpers that do not require fastening along the top or deck surface.

Adding vertical dock bumpers at the right spacing will guard a small boat from drifting under the dock.

While tossed in waves and subjected to water level changes, a boat's point of contact with the dock has a vertical range that calls for vertical dock bumpers.

While tied alongside the fixed dock, small boats with low gunwales tend to drift under the dock, resulting in damage caused by passing waves.

Pilings or posts alongside the dock are to your advantage for making vertical dock bumpers.

Make sure all vertical surfaces that the boat may brush against have a bumper. If the distance between the posts, pipe legs, or pilings is too far so that there isn't a vertical surface where you need one, don't hesitate to add another leg to the dock just for the bumper. Otherwise, make a vertical bumper that attaches to the frame at the desired spot.

Owners of short-length boats, such as personal watercrafts, will often learn the hard truth upon returning that one end of their boat drifted under the dock. This is never good for either the boat or dock. Stringing up more fenders and line may help temporarily, but there is nothing like the ease and safety of having at least two solid vertical bumpers at the right spacing.

Fanatical for Vertical

Vertical bumpers are not just for docks on posts, pipe legs, or pilings, but should be used on concrete docks, seawalls, and even floating docks if necessary. I even put them on my daughter's backyard swing set supports. Where there is a risk that waves could pick a boat up and let it back down onto the dock's deck, vertical bumpers set high enough will deflect

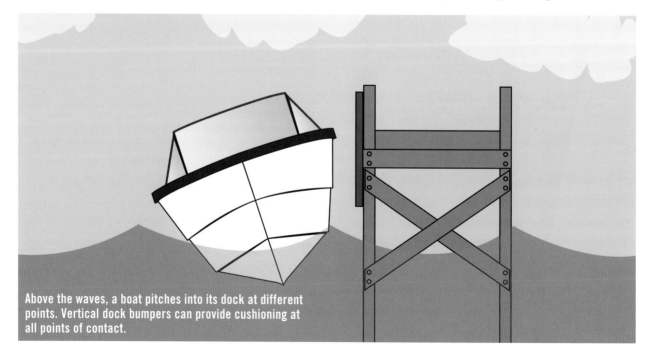

Above the waves, a boat pitches into its dock at different points. Vertical dock bumpers can provide cushioning at all points of contact.

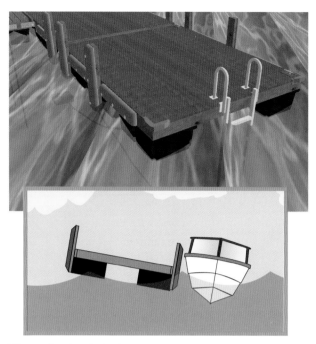

When a floating dock dips into a wave, vertical dock bumpers can prevent the juxtaposed boat from riding over the dock's edge.

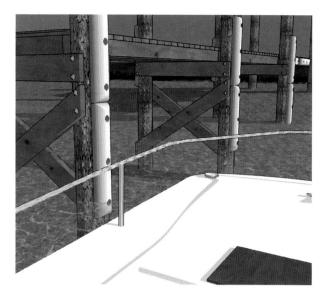

Vertical dock bumpers may be extended on the posts and pilings of fixed docks subject to extreme water level changes.

the hull, quickly justifying the forethought and effort. Boats tied to floating docks while exposed to large chop are especially prone to this since the dock dips into the wave's trough while the adjacent boat is on the wave's crest. This is preventable with the addition of two or more vertical bumpers that extend well above the dock's deck.

Cushion Your Confidence

Dock bumpers are one of the features worth dedicating a generous amount of thought and investment toward, for the safety of a boat. The main thing is to think about the nature in which your boat will make its contact with the dock, factoring the boat's pitch in the waves and what it will take to deflect it without damage to either the boat, dock, or bumpers. These considerations before buying the bumpers and installing them will prevent a futile investment. Given the cost of boat repairs, you don't need to hear it from me that the payoffs for your extra attention to this detail are warranted.

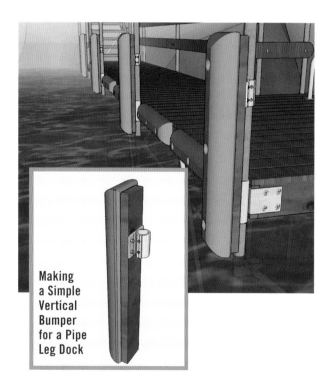

Making a Simple Vertical Bumper for a Pipe Leg Dock

Vertical dock bumpers make their way onto docks with pipe legs. The idea simply uses a wooden plank, with the bumper fastened to one side and a bracket on the other side that locks to a pipe leg. The finished bumper fits down over the top of a pipe leg, with the bumper facing out. Its height on the pipe leg can be set by tightening the bracket's setscrews.

CHAPTER 25:
ACCESSORIZING

Whether planned from the beginning or an afterthought, accessories can be a small investment that multiplies the value of your dock. This is where your creativity can run wild generating unique ideas that could fill a book on the subject. For this chapter, there are several I felt are worth noting. Some are commonly thought of like butter on baked potato while others may enlighten you.

Ladders and Stairs

On your short list should be a way to climb in or out of the water at the dock. This makes good sense when, after all, the dock is about access to the water and a ladder or stair completes that objective. Beginning with ladders alone, there are so many ready-made on the market with useful features that it would be impractical to mimic by fabricating your own. If you don't have the convenience of a marine store that stocks what you're looking for, I would encourage anyone to shop for them online since most can be shipped to your door. As with anything, expect prices to vary based on the factors, such as the size or amount of material it was made with, amount of assembly left to the customer, and unique features that add value not found in the lower priced

ladders. There are some features worth looking for during your search that should be considered. They may be to your advantage or not depending on where and how you'll use it.

Ladders

- The alloy matters when left in the water for weeks and weeks on end. Make sure the alloy, be it aluminum, coated steel, or stainless steel is compatible with your type of water.
- Choose a length that will reach below the waterline from your dock. You should have at least two steps under the surface. Where it is shallow, make sure that your ladder choice has clearance above the bottom. This is especially important on floating docks that pitch in the waves, putting feet in danger that end up between the ground and the bottom step.
- For comfort, a 20-degree slant, like a stepladder, is much easier to climb on than a vertical ladder. Swimmers who suffer with less upper body strength or bad knees will appreciate them.
- If the ladder must install near the path of a boat, the vertical option may be best to minimize interference. Otherwise, find a spot where the slanted ladder won't be in the way such as the narrow end of a dock that is often useless for boat parking.
- Stepping on a narrow ladder tread with bare feet can hurt. The wider a tread, the more surface area is supported under your feet. I found that a a 4-inch (10cm) wide tread on a slanted ladder was enough. Dock ladders, especially slanted ones with extra-wide non-perforated treads, take more of a pounding from waves that slap the underside, causing unwanted vibration.
- Ladders with a raise-up feature are handy for keeping the lower portion free of corrosion, algae, and other marine growth when not in use. This is also helpful where docks on tidal waters ground out at low tide and when removing seasonal docks and rafts to keep the ladder from dragging.

Arguably, every dock should have a ladder, for safety's sake alone.

An attachable stair takes the idea of a ladder accessory to a new level.

When building a wooden stair into the water, an anti-skid tread surface should be in your plans. A perforated tread reduces pounding and lifting from waves that pass under the stairs.

Stairs

Choices for ready-made stairs aren't as abundant as with ladders, but you may find an option that will do just what you want. Where a fixed dock passes over bare turf or shallow water near shore, a short stair to get you safely onto the ground is handy for all ages. Once in place, a stair that goes into the water becomes a convenient bench for sitting while bathing your feet. Should you decide to build wooden stairs that will extend into the water, I recommend using only stainless fasteners. Since wood floats, you'll want to fashion a way to hold the stair down, either with pipe legs driven near the base or hang weights, such as cinder blocks from underneath. Wooden treads immersed in water will get slippery in no time so you should apply an anti-skid surface to them, such as outdoor carpet. Ideally, instead of wood treads, a perforated synthetic panel should be used that has an anti-skid finish and allows wave pressure to break through. A hand rail, one for adults and another midway for small children, is a nice way to finish the job.

Boarding Step

On a fixed dock that may be set too high for access in and out of the boat, consider a boarding step to get you closer to the water. Sometimes they are made to fit between two posts and can be height-adjusted much easier than changing the height of the entire dock. Since they are often cantilevered, boarding steps are not safe to use on docks where legs are not driven into the bottom. In waters protected from wind chop and headway speed zones, solid decking on boarding steps is fine. Otherwise,

A boarding step mounts along the side of a dock, at a lower level, to aid in access when the dock is too high off the water. It also makes a great swimmer's bench.

The cantilevering bench frees up space on the dock.

only perforated decking should be used. Imagine how much easier it will be to board kayaks, rowing shells, and other small crafts once this is in place.

Dock Bench

You're right. What could I possibly say more than you already know about how great they are? Allow me, though, to leave you with a few pointers about dock benches. On a fixed dock in a spot where it won't interfere with other activities, they can be made to extend over the edge to minimize space consumption on the dock. This should only be done when the dock's legs are firmly driven into the bottom. Otherwise, loads on the bench can cause a narrow dock to flip like a picnic table that lacks counterweight. An option to consider, provided the bench supports reach the bottom, would be to extend outriggers off the base of the legs heading away from the dock. If that doesn't sound good, then just keep the bench squarely over the dock, but as close to the edge as you can.

Benches on the side of a floating dock often do not work well. Unless the float section is wide enough so that there is adequate counterweight opposite the bench, the dock will list. If this is a "must have" situation and the floating dock isn't all that wide, then you can mount up the flotation

A bench upon the edge of a floating dock will require extra flotation to prevent listing.

Though seemingly more for decoration than its original purpose, you won't regret having a life ring on the dock for the swimmer who is in trouble.

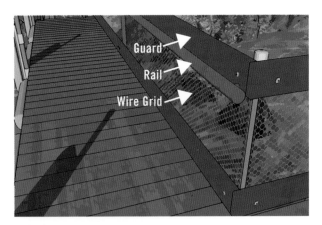

Guard
Rail
Wire Grid

When it is required to close in the space below the guard, consider using a heavy-gauge, dark-colored wire grid. Check to see if this method is code-compliant. You may find it less obstructive to water views than plain balusters.

where the bench will set or box out an area alongside the main dock that is just for the bench with its own flotation.

Throwable Device

Surprisingly, a most essential appurtenance that should be present often gets forgotten. Hopefully, you'll never need a throwable rescue device, but the outbound end of a dock sure seems like the right place for one, especially if swimming is a regular thing where the dock is.

Railings and Guards

If you're a building contractor, you're likely familiar with the distinction between rails and guards. Rails are for holding on when climbing, and guards, positioned higher than the rail, prevent falls from heights.

These two features are found described in most building codes. Docks may not be exempt from these codes, so it would be best to find out what your legal obligation is concerning them. Conceivably, these features could prohibit access between the dock and boat without special provisions. I suppose that would explain why you often don't see them on docks unless it is along a ramp or stair appurtenance. Though they may not be required by code, I recommend adding them in places where common sense speaks to you—for peace of mind if for no other reason. Portions of fixed dock near the bank may bridge above areas of terrain before extending over water. When elevated above 30 inches (76 centimeters) high or when over dangerous rocks, stumps, and other objects, the addition of railing and guards to keep people and pets from spilling off will prevent somebody from having a bad day. Balusters close in the area beneath the guard, a must for keeping small children and pets from falling. Often, these are given even less priority if the code doesn't require them due to the added cost and encumbrance to the view they may cause. An alternative to balusters would be a

Unless local building codes specify requirements for fall prevention, your discretion and common sense should determine the level of protection for your specific needs.

heavy wire–coated mesh with squares at 4 inches (10 centimeters) or less, covering below the guard. A dark color choice of green or black gives off less glare so that you can see through it. Some DIYers go for the decorative rope look that is swaged between posts. This may serve as your rail while dressing

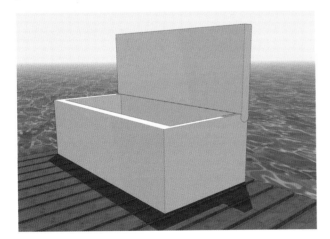

For all the things you frequently use at the dock, such as folding chairs, fishing gear, and binoculars, nothing could be handier than a storage box for it all, right on the dock.

things up, but it is not nearly as effective as rigid and structural material.

Storage Box

You certainly could build your own storage box and it will probably fit the look better with everything else you've made. Nevertheless, some of the premanufactured options are well made and have some nice features. My only comment on them is that I have no trouble finding things to put in them.

Small Boat Storage Arms

Not many families have just one kayak. Have you ever been on a dock where kayaks took over, leaving no room to step around them? Arms that extend over the side of a dock made for holding small boats such as kayaks, canoes, and rowing shells make all the difference. Some people with small boats who secure them high and dry on shore find they don't use their boats enough because of the work in hauling up and down, over the shore. For them,

You might use the canoe or kayak more if the carry to the water isn't far and cumbersome.

the small boat storage arms can be a life-changing experience . . . in a good way.

Solar Lights

I'm not a regular night boater, but for the few times in a summer when I'll return after dark, I couldn't be more grateful for the solar lights on my dock. While elegant, they mark out where my dock is to help find my way in. I even have one on my swim raft, turning it into a landmark while helping other boaters avoid collision.

Talking to DIYers about solar lights on their dock, disappointment is rare, especially when you weigh the low cost against the benefits. Plenty of people have them now, so that suggests a positive level of satisfaction can be expected. The question I get all the time though is, "Why have my lights stopped working?" It's simple; a marine environment has lots of moisture that can cause corrosion on the terminals. Don't give up on them. The better-quality lights are made to come apart so you can access

spots where cleaning with an eraser or small wire brush can make all the difference. Also, batteries and bulbs do have a life. Batteries may last a year or two, and I would expect twice that from the LED bulbs. All these parts are replaceable to keep your lights going.

Though your local home and hardware centers carry solar lights, look online for ones that are dock specific to enlighten your way. The dock can be a busy place with the coming and going of people, carrying their water toys, movement of nearby boats, and the tossing and crossing of dock lines. You can expect solar lights frequently end up in the drink. Unless you're after a specific look, I recommend fixtures that are round and cylindrical or that don't have right-angled edges (places to catch or snag that lead to the fixtures' demise). Lights that are streamlined are more apt to deflect lines or anything for that matter. You can find lights made specific for a dock's post, pipe, or pilings. They will cost a bit more than many of the options found at a nearby home center, but they are made more suitable for a marine environment and less apt to quit in the middle of summer.

A Means to an End

There is not a better platform for accessorizing than at the dock. The ones I've highlighted here only scratch the surface for possibilities but are some of the most popular talked about with DIYers. There are a few others—such as bumpers and whips—that deserve special attention in the form of their own chapters. The final touches on the dock, for some, are where the rubber meets the road. True, a safe and dependable dock must come first, but for many, a good dock is the means to the end, the end being all the benefits that can be delivered by accessories.

Whether you're on foot or on a boat, solar lights improve navigation for everyone.

CHAPTER 26:
UNDERSTANDING ICE-OVER AND WINTER STORAGE

Remove or Refuse

If your waterfront is on a part of the planet that is severely affected by climate changes just after the winter solstice, then this chapter was written for you. By late January, ice on my lake will get close to 2 feet (60 centimeters) thick. Not much further north and it gets even thicker by about 30 percent. Experienced people know they shouldn't leave their dock to the mercy of these elements unless they want to see it self-destruct. Crib and concrete docks that were hoped to be invincible remain on many lakes today, either in ruins or kept up with to some degree. But with modern environmental laws, getting a permit for a new permanent dock is unlikely in many regions. Therefore, I'll present two choices: either build a dock that is meant to take apart and remove before winter or run a circulator pump under your dock that pulls warmer water from below to the surface, preventing a freeze over. The latter

While ice forms on a lake's surface, it expands and causes pressure ridges like the one shown here. Docks that are left frozen in a lake of this size are subject to the same forces that cause a pressure ridge.

Thanks to a circulator pump that pulls warmer water up from the bottom, the area around these pilings is free of ice. At winter's end, when the ice begins to break apart, a circulator pump will not stop large masses of ice from drifting into its area.

Bent pipe legs and split stringers are a common occurrence for docks left in a body of water that freezes.

of these options is very effective with its choice of settings, that when turned up, can clear out an acre or more of ice. That's more than enough for most docks and would seem like a no-brainer if you're immune to a power outage. What it won't prevent is drifting ice pushed by wind during the spring melt that can slam into your dock. That potential, along with the risk of the circulator quitting for some reason, could explain why so many still choose to pull their dock out. Where I live, the law states that the dock must come out of the water if it is classified as a temporary dock.

Broad bodies of water that freeze over are so certain to destroy a dock in the first winter that it seems the word is out and most take the right precautions. It's the docks on smaller bodies of water such as inlets and capillaries to the broad bodies that are often ignored, left to be frozen into the lake. These docks seem to come out of it unscathed due to the short distance between shores and, therefore, less ice to have its way with a dock. What these dock owners may be unaware of is that damage is happening. It just takes more years to realize the effects under reduced exposure.

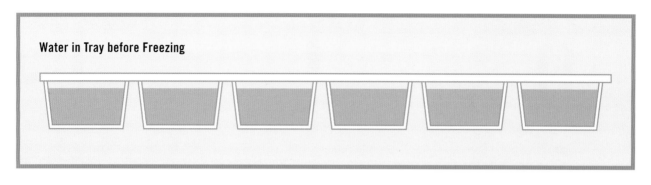

Water in Tray before Freezing

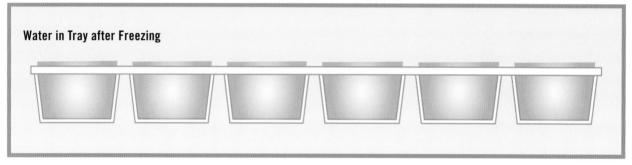

Water in Tray after Freezing

As water freezes in an ice cube tray, you can observe its expansion. The same kind of expansion happens on a body of water, but on a much greater scale.

Explaining Expansion

To understand what the ice does that causes damage, whether a little or a lot, it helps to visualize an ice cube tray with its tapered molds. When water freezes in the molds, it expands outward and upward simultaneously. Thanks to the taper in the mold, the expansion has a place to go. Without the taper, the expanding ice could break the mold.

In a lake that is freezing over, its tapered shores are like the tapered wall of an ice cube tray. As water freezes on the lake's surface, expansion of the ice creeps up the shore like a slow-moving bulldozer, either gliding over some objects while plowing others toward the shore. If it comes against a vertical surface in its path, such as a driven post or seawall, the ice can push until the post gives way or the seawall cracks. Have you ever noticed a shoreline that is raised up like a berm? This is a result of ice

pushing into the bank down low, causing the top of the bank to rise.

Now that we have a good picture in our minds of expanding ice, we can bet that all docks that remain left in the water experience damage to some degree. With legs or posts set into the lake bed, the dock cannot give as the expanding ice, locked to it, pushes toward the shore. On a small water body, it may be only a little bit each year, but with every winter, a little bit of strain on the materials each year adds up. After five or so years of that, we can expect the dock to feel rickety and due for replacement.

I'll leave you with one final word of caution as it relates to ice expansion. Some lakes that are regulated by a dam are drawn low, leaving docks high and dry before winter. Naturally, this condition will lure people to not bother with dock removal. While everything looks safe, and the water's edge is clearly beyond the dock's legs, don't be fooled. As the lake freezes and ice thickens, it will grow its way back toward the dock. It may reach just one leg on the dock, but with all the legs, framing, and decking as one structure, the damage will likely spread far beyond that one leg.

Lake Water Level Drawn Down in Autumn

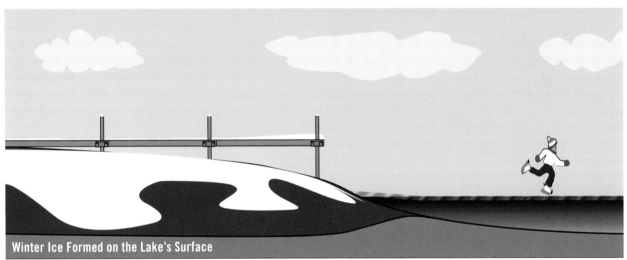

Winter Ice Formed on the Lake's Surface

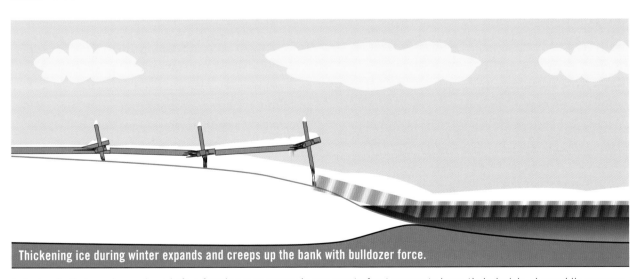

Thickening ice during winter expands and creeps up the bank with bulldozer force.

Lake levels that are drawn down before freezing may persuade some waterfront owners to leave their dock in place while unaware of the threat from expanding ice.

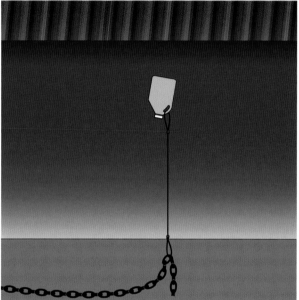

Winter Storage

During the summer, while all the family and friends are enjoying your waterfront, choose your team members who'll return after summer for dock removal. Don't miss the chance to get their commitment while they are having such a great time at your expense. Set the date and lock them in. I recommend late September, taking advantage of the warmer autumn weather so it will be a positive experience for all. When removing a dock from the water to avoid winter's ice grip, any part of the dock that ice could lock itself to or push against should be included. Here are some pointers for putting your dock to bed.

1. Moorings that hold floating docks are usually well below the surface where it doesn't freeze. They are typically left in place unless the law requires that they get removed too. Should you leave the anchors, I recommend tying a nylon line to the top of each chain that can extend toward the shallow area of your shorefront. At a depth that won't freeze, but shallow enough to reach with a boat hook in the spring, leave the nylon line on the bottom tied to a white rag, such as a T-shirt. The white rag gives you more to snag and more to see upon retrieval. Otherwise, a buoy may be tied to the chain, small enough so that the chain's weight will hold it below the ice. Come spring, the buoy just under the surface will be easier to find than the chain that may sink into the bottom.

2. As you remove sections of a fixed dock, put a permanent mark on each pipe leg or post to reference where it belongs on the dock in the spring.

3. All dock components should be brought to shore above the maximum high-water level. If not feasible due to an extensive flood plain, chain large pieces that could float away to a sufficient anchor such as a tree. Dock sections can be stacked and elevated with blocking, enough so that sufficient airflow can ventilate underneath. Wood components should not be left in direct contact with the ground.

4. Support all four corners of your dock stack evenly to prevent warping. Should you choose to tarp over your dock stack, see to it that the ground under the stack has good drainage. Otherwise, excessive moisture in the ground under a tarp becomes trapped and may prove better to leave un-tarped.

5. Inspect for any repairs that may be needed. Repairs to decking, framing, or any other component will go better right after removal when it is all fresh on your mind. Doing the repairs just before re-installation in spring can present unnecessary pressure, especially if your team of helpers is waiting around for a part or repair before they can do their job.

Before winter ice sets in, a dock's sections are removed from the lake and stacked neatly above the maximum high-water level.

6. This is a time of year many choose to refinish the surface of wood decking. Since you shouldn't apply cleaning solutions and preservatives on decking over the water, waiting until docks come out is best. In the spring, with all that you have going on, that box will already be checked.

7. All setscrews on pipe dock hardware should get removed, dipped into outboard grease, and reinserted. This will keep them from seizing up and provide years of trouble-free service. Keep all fasteners and small parts bagged together in a safe place where you can find them in the spring. Re-sealable freezer bags are handy for this.

8. Finally, pay it forward to a neighbor. Lend a hand with their dock and guide them with your wisdom. There is nothing like good neighbors who have each other's back.

In the spring, here are a few pointers for reinstalling your dock.

1. Wait until the ice is completely gone from the lake's surface before reinstalling your dock. Though your shore is all clear, remaining ice on the lake can shift with the wind's direction and come crashing into your dock.

2. I can't blame you for wanting the dock installed asap after ice-out. Beware, a heavy snow melt combined with heavy spring rains can result in flooding for some lakes, wreaking havoc on fixed docks. I've also known refreezing to occur after everyone thought the ice was gone. Talk about a nightmare. If your lake is prone to any of this, it's not a bad idea to wait until the coast is clear.

3. For fixed docks on lakes with water levels that start out high, DIYers are tempted to install the dock low to the water with anticipation that it will be at the right height with some time. Beware, if your exposure to chop from high winds can be severe, let's hope it holds off before the water level drops. I recommend setting the dock high enough that wind chop will clear underneath. Later, when the water drops enough, lower the dock at that time.

4. Finally, before the day arrives when the help will show up to reinstall, inspect all your dock components. Make sure that everything is where you left it and in working order. Remember to get out the fasteners that were safely stowed away. Being prepared will prevent lost time and opportunity with your zealous crew.

CHAPTER 27:
PRESERVATIVES ON WOOD DOCKS

After decades, operating an evolving dock business that has advanced into modern materials, the sight of a freshly built traditional wood dock today continues to strike me with a sensation of delight and admiration. So that your wooden dock may keep its charm for as long as reasonably possible, let me provide some perspective from a veteran "Dock Pro."

Treating Pressure-Treated Wood

In my corner of the world, pressure-treated yellow pine and Douglas fir have been the "go to" materials preferred by dock building DIYers. Its relatively low cost for the years that it lasts are perceived to be a good value. Consumers are familiar with it while availability at local lumberyards is reliable. Popular as it continues to be, you don't have to go far before finding a pressure-treated structure that is weathered, cracked, and splintered. Climate and/or lack of care for the material has usually everything to do with the deterioration you see. A deck surface, being horizontal, catches damaging sun rays and collects moisture, more so than a vertical surface. On top of the natural elements, a deck surface bears all the abrasion from foot traffic and accoutrements upon it. When you stop and think about it, expectations of an outdoor deck surface to resist the elements, keeping its good looks while remaining safe under bare feet, is a tall order.

From comments I have heard made by consumers over the years regarding deck maintenance, I have surmised that euphoria over the manufacturer's generous warranty against rot could explain a settled

way of thinking that results in neglect. Long before it would ever rot, the degree of warping, twisting, and checking preventable with regular treatment become its demise. To prevent this from happening, a commitment is required to applying preservative, formulated for pressure-treated wood, such as a sealer or semi-solid stain on an "as needed" basis. This might be once a year or every two years. When

Pressure-treated decking.

Though weathered and neglected for several years, the life of this dock could be extended significantly if routine care is not put off much longer.

pressure-treated wood is new, it may be damp or sopping wet, leaving DIYers to assume that preservatives shouldn't be applied for at least a year. But it really doesn't take all that long to dry once exposed to air and it should be done as soon as the wood is ready. The preservative will penetrate at the time when water will no longer bead up on its surface. Make sure the instructions provided by the preservative manufacturer are followed.

Worn and Weathered Wood

If the pressure-treated wood is badly weathered but the grain is still holding together, I would attempt recovery before replacement. Planks that have severe grain separation, dangerous and beyond hope, should be replaced with ones that are acceptable. A belt sander with a course grit can knock down and smooth over some trouble spots. Remove any loose material and clean with a deck wash or bleach solution. It will take a wash to remove before the preservative will take to the wood. After the wash, allow a couple of good drying days before applying a preservative. I prefer a semi-solid pigmented stain applied in more than one coat for added durability against wear. As always, follow the instructions provided by the manufacturer.

Natural Resistance

Cedar and redwood deck planks are stable, not known for cupping and warping the way pressure-treated planks do. They have a natural resistance to rot that some DIYers trust in, letting go of maintenance and appreciating the natural gray weathered look. Though natural resistance to rot sounds nice, putting your cedar or redwood decking on a routine treatment of a semi-transparent, wood deck preservative will buy more years of life. I recommend a light-colored stain preservative for the added UV protection that is in pigment. If your wood surfaces are older and haven't been cared for, so long as they are still in pretty good shape, I would begin an annual routine of applying a preservative.

A semi-transparent stain is vigorously applied to a new cedar deck board.

Expected to weather quickly, a newly built dock has no wood preservative on its red cedar decking. For some, the look is preferable over extending the life of the wood.

Guard Your Environment

Remember to take proper environmental precautions on or around the water. Do not use a preservative over the water without drop cloths suspended below to catch the drippings. An environmental permit conditional on following specific precautions when doing this work over water would not be all that unusual. If on a body of water that lowers its level away from the dock, take advantage of that time to apply it. Docks with removable deck panels afford ease of moving material over dry land to be treated while the dock remains installed over water. Removable docks that are brought to shore before winter should be treated in the autumn or spring while over dry land.

Application Tips

Don't sweat it. Applying deck stain once a year or as needed can go quick with the right tool. For standard-size deck boards, I've always used rectangular, bristled foam pads that are just a bit wider than the board made to thread onto a broom handle. This will allow you to apply while standing and get both hands onto the handle for more pressure against the wood. I use a paint pan to hold my preservative for dipping my pad into.

With new cedar or redwood boards that are clean and dry, wiping the surface with a damp cloth just before brushing on the preservative will slightly raise the grain and improve penetration. A vigorous needling action with the bristles or scrubbing with the pad to work the preservative in may also help before completing with a clean final stroke.

For wood that is weathered or needs retreating, preparation with a thorough deck wash followed with ample drying time is key for the preservative to bleed into and bond with the wood fibers. After skipping this step in haste, you might ask, "Why is there never enough time to do it right, but always enough time to do it over?"

A bristled foam pad like this, which can fit onto a broom or mop handle, applies preservative to decking surfaces with ease.

Sometimes, a quick assessment of a dock's condition is biased toward the condition of its decking regardless of how good or bad all other features may be holding up. It's no wonder, given the deck has the largest square foot (square meter) surface of any part of the dock and it is likely what we notice first. For a wood deck to keep the dock looking good, we can expect that a treatment of preservative isn't a one-time hit that will be permanent, but will need repeating, possibly every year. If you'd rather not be bothered with that, a wood alternative, such as composites and various like petroleum-based products, may be your out. Although, merited with reduced upkeep, many of them introduce their own set of challenges that must be weighed in and are the reason wood remains a viable choice. It is important to recognize that when routine wood maintenance begins at the beginning of a dock's life, it is relatively easy to keep up with, considering all that we're asking of it and all that it does a great job at delivering.

On new decking, preservative will penetrate wood surfaces better when the grain is raised beforehand. This can be done, simply, by wiping down with a clean, damp cloth.

CHAPTER 28:
WOOD DOCK REPAIRS

No matter what material your dock is made of—be it wood, aluminum, molded plastic, or concrete—probability is that repairs will be needed at some point in its life. One significant advantage to a wood dock over others is that it's easy to repair. The material is readily on hand at your local lumberyard, and the skillset is easy to come by. In this chapter, we'll look at the two most common repairs done on wooden docks: deck board replacement and stringer replacement.

Decking

For whatever reason a deck board goes bad, replacement is usually very simple. Removing the bad board may be the most challenging part. First, remove any accessories that may interfere with your work. If the board was fastened down with screws,

A dock left in a frozen lake has a few bent pipe legs and cracked stringers. It is not a total loss if the repairs are simple.

When backing out old screws to remove a deck board, a gripping tool is handy to twist out the ones that are stripped.

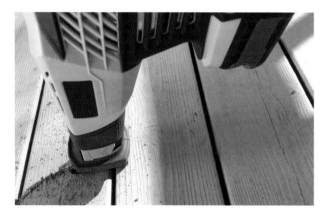

Rather than backing out screws or pulling up nails, consider cutting across the bad deck board on each side of the middle stringer(s) using a cordless reciprocating saw as shown.

After the cuts are made, push down on one of the cut ends and pull up on the other. Alternate between the two, working each one up and down until both pieces break free. Either remove remaining broken nails or screws stuck in the stringers, or use the same saw to cut off flush with a metal cutting blade.

slowly back the screws out using an appropriate bit with a variable speed cordless screw gun. Should any of the heads strip out or break off while attempting this, chip the material with a wood chisel away from the screw until you can clamp it with a set of vise-grips. Use the vise-grips to turn the screw until it releases.

When the board has been nailed down, cut through and across the board between the stringers using a cordless jigsaw or reciprocating saw.

Wearing gloves, push one cut end down and pull the opposite cut end up. Alternate this action with each of the cut pieces while using them as leverage on the nails until they pry up. Finally, with the exposed stringers free of fastener remnants and wood blisters, place the new cut-to-length deck board into position (preferably with the crown side up) and fasten. Often, there is one side to a board that looks better than the other. The better side is the one I'd face up, regardless of the crown.

Cut to length and install the replacement deck board.

Framing

Having a stringer break should be a rare event. In climates where docks are removed and reinstalled to avoid winter ice, extra handling can put stringers at risk. Should it happen to you, here is how I'd go about replacing it. First, remove anything attached to the stringer such as posts, brackets, timber hangers, and accessories. If the decking and framing are screwed, back out all the screws that fasten into the broken stringer. For nails or screws that won't back out, it's relatively easy to cut through them. Using a cordless reciprocating saw with a metal cutting blade, begin at one end and work the blade into the seam between the decking and broken stringer. Using the seam as a guide for the blade, move the saw along toward the opposite end, cutting through every nail or screw.

You can repeat this procedure where the stringer fastens to the header at each end. Remove and dispose of all nail and screw parts along the ends of the deck boards. Clamp the new stringer into position while you apply new fasteners. Begin with securing them to the headers at each end, then go on to the decking. Repairing the dock may not be how you want to spend your time, but it beats putting a splice on or completely building a new section. Now that you know how to do it, the job is really not that bad.

If a dock section becomes racked or skewed after taking a sever impact on its corner, DIYers may attempt to square it back up again with varying results. Easier when the dock section is removed from the water and placed upside down, a ratchet strap hooked into opposite corners may draw the structure back to its original shape. Before the ratchet strap is released, a wooden diagonal brace should be lagged on across the bottom of the stringers that runs parallel to the strap to hold the section square.

With a metal cutting blade on a reciprocating saw, work the blade along, under the decking, to cut through all the nails. Either remove or cut through the nails that hold the stringer to the headers.

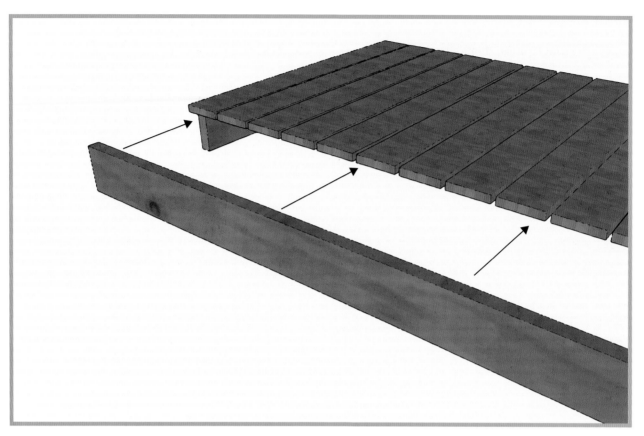

Position the replacement stringer and nail or screw it to the headers at each end of the dock section. Remove what remains of the nails in each of the deck boards so that their holes can be re-used to fasten into the new stringer.

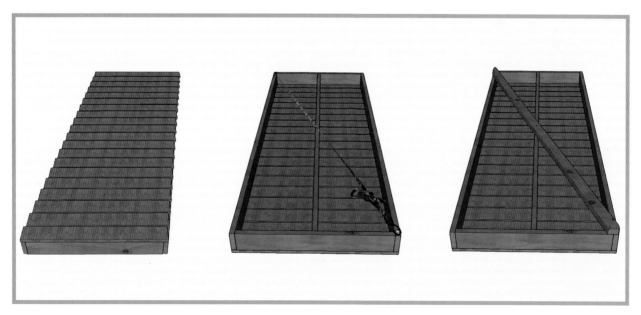

Squaring up a dock section that has been racked can be done with a ratchet strap and a wooden brace. Turning the section over, use the ratchet strap as shown to draw the section back to square. Fasten a wooden brace diagonally across the bottom before taking the ratchet strap away.

GLOSSARY OF TERMS

As a young adult, I began featuring my docks at trade shows to get the company name out and make some contacts beyond my community. Proud of my presentation, a portfolio on steroids, and confident in my knowledge of docks, I took pleasure in hearing accolades and assumed confirmation by my audience. One time, at a crowded show, an aged and mysterious man was waiting his turn to speak with me. Without introduction or small talk, he boldly stepped forward, lowered his brow, and began to speak in a mighty, corrective tone.

"You are not a dock company!" He said.

"Excuse me," I replied.

"Docks are not the business you are in, and the word 'dock' should not be in your company name! A dock is the space that a vessel occupies when it is next to a pier. Therefore, your company builds piers, not docks, and you should change your business name."

Without pause or signal to debate, while I stammered for a good comeback, he turned swiftly and disappeared into the crowd. For a moment, it felt like my chair was kicked out from under me, and for the next several days his words replayed in my head, over and over. Though he didn't move me to make a name change from "docks" to "piers," his conviction on the issue got me to consider that he might have been right, if not at the present time and place, a time and place I was not familiar with.

Recognizing that a given language evolves in time and words vary in meaning from place to place reveals a source of confusion. Soft drinks are called "soda" in New England and are called "Coke" in Georgia. In the same way, when talking docks, terms and phrases change over time and vary from place to place. Therefore, I've provided this glossary of terms to aid my readers who are not familiar with any "dock language" at all or for readers whose "dock language" doesn't quite match up with mine.

Articulate: *verb* – Joints between sections of dock that allow movement.

Backer Board: *noun* – A board installed under the decking to reinforce a cleat that has a broad base.

Back Water: *noun* – A branch of a river that has less current and offers more protection than the main river.

Beam: *noun* – The widest part of a boat's hull, usually centered along its length.

Bed: *noun* – The floor or bottom of a lake, river, or sea.

Berm: (1) *verb* – To elevate. (2) *noun* – An elevated area of turf above the typical grade that can appear along a shore, formed by winter's expanding ice on the water's surface.

Berth: (1) *verb* – To park a boat. (2) *noun* – The space that a parked boat occupies at a dock.

Blocking: (1) *verb* – To insert short pieces of framing, called blocks or blocking, fitted between stringers. (2) *noun* – Used to store docks upon, above ground for improved air flow and drying.

Boarding Step: *noun* – A long narrow step attached to the side of a dock and sets lower to the water than the main dock for aiding access to and from a boat.

Bottom: *noun* – The floor or bed of a lake, river, or sea.

Box Nail: *noun* – Like a common nail but with a smaller wire size to reduce splitting when nailing a wood joint together. They come in plain, spiraled, or ring shanked.

Butt Joint: *noun* – A most basic assembly joint, held by fasteners where one board abuts another.

Cap Board: *noun* – A board or timber fastened horizontally between adjacent vertical posts or pilings to form an "H." It supports the dock's framing at the end of each span.

Cleat: *noun* – (1) A tie-off point that is shaped for hitching a line; (2) a raised edge made of a rigid material, often repeated in a series along a sloped ramp for traction.

Crib: *noun* – A timber framework, usually heavy, that is filled with rocks and may be used as the foundation for docks.

Corner Iron: *noun* – A short angle iron or formed steel plate at 90 degrees, having bolt holes and used to reinforce a butt joint.

Countersink/-sunk: *verb or adj.* – A fastener hole that is broadened to a limited depth for the purpose of recessing the head or the nut on a bolt.

Coupler: *noun* – A standard trailer hitch that fits over a ball, used to make a swaying stand-off arm.

Crown: *adj.* – The surface of a board that has a natural convex curve on one side.

Cupping: *adj.* – The surface of a board that has a natural concave curve or curl on one side.

Dead Loads: *noun* – The weight of a structure and its fixtures that are static.

Decking: *noun* – The floor, surface material, such as wood or plastic plank, upon a dock's frame.

Deck Wash: *noun* – A formulated detergent for removing dirt from a wooden deck surface.

DIY/DIYer: *adj./noun* – Acronym for do-it-yourself/do-it-yourselfer, as opposed to hiring someone in the trade.

Dock: (1) *verb* – To dock a boat or bring the boat to dock. (2) *noun* – A structure, by which its purpose is primarily for access to and from a boat. (3) *adj.* – a docked boat is moored to a dock.

Dock Bumper: *noun* – A cushion, padding, or rub-rail, attached to a dock to protect the dock and boat.

Driving Cap: *noun* – A protective steel cap, used for hitting the top of a pipe or post with a sledge hammer.

Extrusion: *noun* – A manufacturing process for forming vinyl dock bumpers, whereby resin is heated and forced through a die.

Fender: *noun* – A cylindrical or ball-like cushion that hangs on a rope on the side of a boat.

Fetch: *noun* – The distance between opposite shores for wind and waves to travel.

Float Drum: *noun* – Usually a manufactured plastic flotation enclosure, often filled with foam, to support a floating dock.

Foam Billet: *noun* – A long, rectangular, solid piece of foam used to support a floating dock.

Frame/Framing: *noun* – The assembly of stringers to support a deck surface.

Gall: *verb* – Seizing at the threads between a nut and bolt upon tightening, caused by pressure and excessive friction, a typical trait of stainless fasteners.

Guard: *noun* – Often referred to as railing, a horizontal barrier set at height to prevent falling off the side of a dock, ramp, or stair.

Header: *noun* – The stringer at the end of a frame or section that other stringers perpendicularly butt and fasten to.

Heart Wood: *noun* – The inner rings or core region of a round piling.

Hinge Plate: *noun* – Connecting hardware made of steel plate that allows joints between sections of floating dock to articulate.

Horned Cleat: *noun* – A hardware component that typically fastens to the deck on a boat or dock for hitching lines to. Its shape may resemble symmetrical horns on livestock.

Hot Wire: *noun* – A wire that is heated with a mild electrical current for cutting through synthetic foam.

Inbound: *adj.* – The direction heading toward the shore.

Intermediate Stringer: *noun* – Internal framing members in a dock section.

J-Bracket: *noun* – A hardware component, shaped like the letter "J," used to connect sections of fixed dock together.

Lateral: *adj.* – At or from the side.

Ledger Block: *noun* – A structural piece of lumber that serves as a resting point for an adjoining section of dock.

Leeward: *adj.* – Downwind, or the side that is sheltered from the wind.

Leveling Winch: *noun* – A tool that uses a winch to lift sections of dock and hold level during dock installation.

Line: *adj.* – Rope or cordage.

Liquid Thread Lock: *noun* – Also known as thread-locking fluid, is an adhesive applied to fastener threads for preventing loosening under vibration.

Live Loads: *adj.* – The weight of all moving loads, animate or inanimate, upon a structure.

Longitude/Longitudinal: *adj.* – Running lengthwise.

Long-link: *adj.* – Links in a chain that are more oblong than usual to facilitate connecting with other chains and/or hardware.

Medial: *adj.* – A position that is centered and aligned.

Metal Backer: *noun* – A hardware component, usually steel or aluminum, shaped like an angle with bolt holes, for the purpose of reinforcing one board to another.

Mooring: (1) *noun* – An assembly of line and or chain to an anchor for holding a boat or a dock against the wind and current. (2) *verb* – To moor or to tie off a boat at the dock or a mooring.

O.D.: *adj.* – Acronym for outside diameter.

Outbound: *adj.* – The direction heading away from the shore.

Outbound Lines: *noun* – Tie-up lines that assist in securing a boat at a dock tied to fixed points that are away from the dock.

Outrigger: *noun* – (1) An extension off to the side of a floating dock that increases and disperses flotation over a broader area for improved stability.

Pad-eye: *noun* – The portion of a hinge plate resembling an ear or a tab that protrudes forward from the main plate.

Permanent: *adj.* – Referring to a dock that is intended to be installed indefinitely or permanent, not removable or portable.

Pile/Piling: *noun* – A round wooden timber or log used as a column or post for support of a fixed dock or as an anchor point to hold and guide a floating dock.

Pitch: *adj.* – Lengthwise, the up and down movement or tilt at either end of a dock section or a boat.

Portable: *adj.* – Docks that are made for moving, usually on a seasonal basis, away from the water before winter ice causes damage.

Pre-drill: *verb* – Drilling a hole near the end of a board to drive a nail or screw into so that the board doesn't split.

Pre-panelized Decking: *noun* – A section of decking that is pre-manufactured, molded, or assembled with low-maintenance materials and for the purpose of saving time during construction.

Pressure Treated: (1) *noun* – Lumber that has been impregnated under pressure with preservative. (2) *verb* – a process of treating lumber with preservative.

P.T.: *adj.* – Acronym for pressure treated.

Rack/Racking: *verb* – Referring to a section of dock that has been skewed by lateral forces.

Rail: *noun* – A rigid and slender cylinder for hands to grasp while climbing, whether on a ramp, stairway, or ladder.

Reach: *adj.* – A continuous extent of water stretched between two points of land.

Refusal: *adj.* – The point at which a post or piling can no longer be driven into a lake bed, riverbed, or seabed.

Relief Hole: *noun* – A hole that is bored at tight curves to aid in the cutting of curved shape from a wooden plank.

Removable Decking: *noun* – Decking that is made in portable panels and can be separated from the dock's frame for a lighter carry.

RTV silicone: *noun* – Room-temperature vulcanizing silicone, a substitute for liquid thread lock.

Sap Wood: *noun* – The outer rings of a round piling that surround the heartwood.

Semi-solid/Semi-transparent: *adj.* – Wood preservative or stain that has some pigment for color and UV protection while visually revealing the wood's grain.

Shore Anchor: *noun* – That which anchors the end of a floating dock at the shore or inbound end.

Shore End: *adj.* – The end of a dock that is at or toward the shore.

Shore Scape: *noun* – A landscape, often natural, along the shore.

Snubber: *noun* – A heavy, solid, rubber cord with an eyelet on each end, used with dock lines to add elasticity and prevent shock.

Spring Line: *noun* – a tie-up line that is secured to a boat's bow or stern cleat and extended diagonally to the dock or a fixed point, restricting the boat's movement in a longitudinal direction.

Stand-off: *adj.* – To hold a floating dock at a fixed distance from its shore anchor or off a fixed dock.

Stick Built/Stick Build: *adj.* – To build a structure in place, piece by piece, versus pre-building to completion before installing in place.

Stringer: *noun* – A longitudinal structural member in a frame to support a decking surface and expected loads.

Structural Screw: *noun* – A screw made with a heavy wire that can be driven by a cordless impact wrench for fastening framework together.

Support Block: *noun* – A block of wood fastened into the dock's frame to support the end of a deck board that is not supported by a stringer.

Temporary: *adj.* – Referring to a dock that is portable, removed before winter and reinstalled in the spring.

Through-bolt: *adj.* – Referring to a threaded bolt that passes all the way through the material and is secured with a nut.

Toe catcher: *adj.* – A tripping hazard.

Torsional: *adj.* – Referring to the twisting of a material or structure. Torsional strength refers to an object's resistance to a twisting force.

Transverse: *adj.* – Across the width, side to side, as appose to the length.

UHMW: *noun* – Acronym for Ultra High Molecular Weight resins, used on ramp rollers, or rub points to reduce friction.

Wear Block: *noun* – A sacrificial short piece of lumber, sometimes of thick plastic, fastened between two surfaces that rub.

Windward: *adj.* – Into the wind or on the side facing the wind.

Yaw: *verb* – Side to side, the up and down movement or tilt on either side of a dock section or a boat

MATERIAL SOURCES

The following source directory lists some of the manufacturers and/or retailers of products described in this book. Some manufacturers sell direct, while others will provide names of retailers who carry their products. The companies listed here are just a sampling to help initiate your online searching, where you can expect to find others.

Chapter 3 (Docks in Sections)

Pre-panelized synthetic decking is first referenced in Chapter 3, then later in Chapter 7, and may not be available at local retail stores. Listed here are a few brands or suppliers of the products described. They will either sell direct or refer you to their dealers.

- Dock.shop
- Sunwalk Superior Surfaces (Canada): sunwalkdocks.com
- Perspective Products (US): perspectiveproducts (US).com
- Titan Deck (US): titandeck.net
- Thru-flow Premium Decking Solutions (Canada): thruflow.com

Chapter 7 (Permanent Post Dock)

Steel points and ground screws that fit onto a square post for setting into the lake bed, riverbed, or seabed are mentioned in Chapter 7.

- Milspec Anchors (US): milspecanchors.com
- Ozco Building Products (US): ozcobp.com

Chapter 8 (Post and Bracket Dock)

The following list includes manufacturers and or suppliers of special brackets designed to support a fixed dock on wooden posts. If a manufacturer does not sell direct, it should refer you to its dealers.

- Dock.shop
- Great Northern Docks (US): greatnortherndocks.com
- Hebert Foundry and Machine (US): castings@hebertfoundry.com
- RDS Dock Hardware (US): rdsdockhardware.com

Chapter 9 (The Pipe Leg Dock)

The following list includes manufacturers and/or suppliers of special brackets designed to support a fixed dock on pipe. If a manufacturer does not sell direct, it should refer you to its dealers.

- American Muscle Docks and Fabrication (US): americanmuscledocks.com
- Dock.shop
- Great Northern Docks (US): greatnortherndocks.com

- Hebert Foundry and Machine (US): castings@hebertfoundry.com
- RDS Dock Hardware (US): rdsdockhardware.com

Chapter 10 (Stabilizing a Fixed Dock)

For pipe leg docks, a self-locking brace is described in Chapter 10 that clamps to the leg from above the water's surface.

- Great Northern Docks (US): greatnortherndocks.com

Chapter 12 (Roll'n Docks)

Hollow plastic tires designed to support a portable dock while rolling to and from the water can be found at these companies.

- Dock Edge (Canada): dockedge.com
- Great Northern Docks (US): greatnortherndocks.com
- Playstar Inc. (US): playstarinc.com
- Wave Armor (US): wavearmor.com

Chapter 16 (Connections of Sections) through Chapter 25 (Accessorizing)

Products described in this book, including hardware for floating docks, flotation, bumpers, fenders, and accessories are manufactured or retailed through these companies.

- American Muscle Docks and Fabrication (US): americanmuscledocks.com
- Dock Hardware (US): dockhardware.com
- Dock.shop (US): dock.shop
- Great Northern Docks (US): greatnortherndocks.com
- Merco Marine Boat Docks (US): mercoboatdocks.com
- Technidock (US): technidock.com

ACKNOWLEDGMENTS

We all understand that water is one of the most fundamental needs of every living creature on the planet. Whether for drinking, bathing or boating, safe and convenient access to it is a must that has constituted my lifelong career in docks. Therefore, the topic of docks is a worthy subject to write about. It pleases me to know that the experience and knowledge I've acquired over the years will not end with me but will be shared with you.

Believing in the significance of this book was perhaps my greatest motivator for answering the call to write *Building Your Own Dock*. However, it came as no surprise that my own motivation would not be enough to see it through. As expected, I would come to rely on the support of others closest to me and guidance from experts in a variety of sub-topics covered in the book. To them, they have my most heartfelt gratitude.

During the process of building the book, chapter by chapter, the displacement of time from my family was always my biggest concern. My responsibilities as husband and father continued regardless of how important the task seemed. Inevitably, the project would have to insert its way into nights and weekends with them. Though it was a compromise to all of us, I must say, I couldn't have asked for a more positive support group at home. Thanks to my wife, Dawn, and her unfailing encouragement, often bearing my share while cheering me on; I recognize her as the cornerstone that engaged the whole family with the project. I am fortunate to be her guy. For necessary diversions and lifting my head up from long periods of writing, I must thank my three children: Gabriel, Elaina, and Charlotte. They kept me whole and human.

When I'm not at home, I'm usually with my team at work. They, too, have my gratitude for their enthusiasm during the book's process while perpetuating a positive and winning environment. Best to all of them.

Other contributors I must recognize:

Carpentry consulting
- Walt Klinger

Dock set-up
- Allied Dock Service
- Lakeside Dock Service

Engineering consulting
- Darren Fickett
- Stephen Merriam

Fender/bumper consultants
- Taylor Made Products

Land owners
- Dianne Geiser
- Larry Merrifield

Photography
- Heather Anderson
- Josh Foley
- Hadley Merriam
- Charlotte Merriam
- Dawn Merriam
- Elaina Merriam
- Romotech – Rotational Molding

Post and pile setting
- Mil-spec Earth Anchors

Wood treatment consulting
- The Maine Wood Treaters Inc.

INDEX

ABOUT THE AUTHOR

Sam Merriam, who as a child was drawn to the outdoors and the waters of southern Maine, first dreamed of becoming a firefighter but later aspired to become a reporter. After achieving his college degree in Communications, the first in his family to do so, he shifted gears and began working in sales with his father, Fremont, owner of Great Northern Docks (GND) (but as the child of a business owner, he of course began working at the ripe age of 12 staining docks and painting hardware). Gifted in drawing and writing, and with boundless creativity paired with ceaseless energy, he was able to weave his talents into the business, helping it to grow and develop into a company trusted by customers to provide excellent products with superior service.

When Fremont decided he wanted to retire in 1999, Sam took the reins, the only child of seven who at the time wished to live in Maine and work within the company. Both Sam and the company have been immeasurably changed since. However, Sam would say that the successes of GND are due to the hard work, smarts, and dedication of his professional team.

A problem solver, creative thinker, impromptu piano player, storyteller, businessman, husband, and father, Sam now lends himself to aid the waterfront owner in creating the perfect dock to provide the spot where the grandest of memories may be made.

ABOUT THE ARTIST

Seth Merriam is the author's brother and the youngest of seven siblings. His artistic talent and interest in leading-edge graphic technology led him into his arts career on the west coast at a young age. Upon returning to Maine, Seth took over the management of media content for Great Northern Docks, Inc.

Seth is a water sports athlete and avid boater who is no stranger to the dock business. He has a hands-on approach and a knack for trouble shooting structural and mechanical challenges. His combination of talents and knowledge of docks was a significant time saver during this book's photography and illustration process.